Antiquaries & Archaists

the Past in the Past
the Past in the Present

Antiquaries & Archaists

the Past in the Past
the Past in the Present

Edited by
Megan Aldrich and Robert J. Wallis

Spire Books Ltd
PO Box 2336, Reading RG4 5WJ
www.spirebooks.com

Spire Books Ltd
PO Box 2336
Reading RG4 5WJ
www.spirebooks.com

The editors and Spire Books Ltd are deeply grateful to Sotheby's Institute
of Art, London, for financial assistance towards this publication.

CIP data:
A catalogue record for this book is available
from the British Library
ISBN 978-1-904965-23-7

Designed and produced by John Elliott
Text set in Bembo

Cover pictures
Front: Aerial view of Avebury, Wiltshire. [*English Heritage Photographic Archive*]
Back: Druids process ritually around the Neolithic monument of Avebury
Henge. [*Robert J. Wallis*]

Contents

Preface

Megan Aldrich and Robert J. Wallis

The idea for producing this book arose out of a conversation in a pub – or, to be precise, out of a series of conversations held in several pubs during the summer of 2006. The editors, an architectural and design historian, and an archaeologist, respectively, were introduced to each other by Alex Seago, a sociologist (see the Afterword) and began to explore commonalities between their respective academic fields. Very quickly these conversations began to throw up interesting synergies and were broadened to include the work of other colleagues in a range of disciplines. A joint 'field trip' to the Uffington White Horse, Uffington Castle and Wayland's Smithy long barrow in Oxfordshire, and Avebury stone circles and West Kennet long barrow in Wiltshire, resulted in these sites being considered from a variety of perspectives: ancient, antiquarian and contemporary. The past, clearly, far from being a settled and defined phenomenon, is a shape-shifter, continually assuming new guises as the context for it has evolved. A chance conversation with a colleague, Anne Farrer, a specialist in Chinese art, broadened the conversation to include the way in which Asian art has continuously drawn upon its distant past in order to create images and objects up to the present day. The editors wish to acknowledge a particular debt to her for moving the discussion beyond the well-trodden territory of the British Isles, and for suggesting that the term 'archaist' would be more appropriate than 'antiquarian' in this context. Anne was a moving force in our organising a conference at the Society of Antiquaries of London, entitled 'Antiquaries and Archaists: Explorations of Cultural Memory', held in October 2007 in the lecture room of the Society in Burlington House. The Society was celebrating its tercentenary with a series of events including the exhibition 'Making History: Antiquaries in Britain, 1707–2007' next door at the Royal Academy of Arts. The timing of our conference was therefore appropriate.

The editors thank both of our home institutions – Sotheby's Institute of Art London and Richmond the American International University in London – which generously contributed to the costs of the conference. We are also grateful to the delegates at the conference for a memorable day which raised stimulating and important discussion, reflected in the papers in the volume, especially regarding the nature of antiquarianism within a global perspective. In particular, we thank Simon Jervis and Rosemary Hill, Fellows of the Society of Antiquaries, for their engaging contributions to the discussion. We also wish to thank Neil Mortimer, former editor of *3rd Stone: The Magazine for the New Antiquarian* and now co-editor of *Time & Mind: The Journal of Archaeology, Consciousness and Culture*, for his support. We are grateful to students of the MA in Art History class of 2006-07 at Richmond University for their assistance with audio-visual technology, ushering and refreshments.

The editors wish to warmly thank all the authors who generously gave their time in order to produce the chapters contained here. Alex Seago and Anne Farrer supported the idea of *Antiquaries and Archaists* from the start, and their belief in the project has helped it to become a reality. All of the seven contributors to the volume besides ourselves bore the brunt of ongoing editorial requests from us, often at times of significant workload, and we thank them for their co-operation and commitment to the project. We are also indebted to Geoff Brandwood and the team at Spire Books for enthusiastically embracing the idea of publishing this book, despite the inevitable hiccups and delays involved in such a multi-author volume produced within a fairly short time-frame; we are most grateful to Geoff for advising and supporting this antiquarian venture with expertise, diligence and aplomb. Equally, thanks are due to Michael McCarthy and Sam Smiles, and especially to Jos Hackforth-Jones, formerly President at Richmond the American University in London and now Director of Sotheby's Institute of Art London, for supporting this project from the outset.

Introduction: Enchantment, Disenchantment, Re-enchantment

Megan Aldrich and Robert J. Wallis

In 2007 the Society of Antiquaries of London celebrated their tercentenary. This, Britain's oldest learned society, is housed at Burlington Gardens in Piccadilly, and it was next door at the Royal Academy of Arts that David Starkey guest-curated the exhibition 'Making History: Antiquaries in Britain, 1707-2007' as part of these celebrations.[1] In October 2007, while 'Making History' was showing, the editors held a day conference in the lecture room of the society entitled, 'Antiquaries and Archaists: Explorations of Cultural Memory', which brought together nine scholars from across the disciplines of archaeology, art history, architectural history, history and folkloristics, as well as independent scholars and curators. While the 'Making History' exhibition focused on Britain and the ways in which antiquaries contributed to our understanding of the past, and how this knowledge changed over four hundred years, our interest was in antiquaries and archaists from an international perspective, through time and across disciplines. We examined the ways in which the past is mediated across and between cultures, and we considered the role of cultural memory in constructing and negotiating multiple pasts, through antiquities, art, monuments and architecture. The scope of the conference ranged chronologically from prehistory to the present day and adopted a broad geographical scope, with papers on China, Japan and Africa, alongside the more familiar territory of Britain.

The authors represented in this book were all conference participants, although Sarah Semple was unable to present on the day. Thomas Dowson, an independent archaeologist, widened our geographical remit by presenting a very welcome paper entitled, 'Are £s and $s Mightier than Artefacts? Rock Art, Benin Art, and the Construction of "African Art"'. In particular, Dowson examined the British reception of the court art of Benin after the punitive raid in 1897, tracing through archival research the dispersal of Benin ivories, bronzes and other art into public and private collections, arguing that this was a key moment in how the West came to define 'African art'. Regrettably, he was unable to contribute a chapter to this volume. Therefore the book you now hold in your hands contains eight chapters, plus an Afterword. The eight essays consider a broad range of visual and material culture, from Japanese antiquities and cultural identity to the British antiquary

William Stukeley, and from the changing perceptions of ancient British monuments to the use of archaisms in contemporary Chinese prints.

A volume engaging with antiquaries and archaists must define these terms and consider a significant scholarship. Stuart Piggott's work, *Ancient Britons and the Antiquarian Imagination*, set the benchmark, arguing that the antiquaries were more than grave-robbers whose achievements and failures were shaped by the prevailing worldviews of their time.[2] William Stukeley, for one, saw value in recording sites in his engravings. While these are often inventive, they also have been key sources for archaeologists when considering features at sites which may once have existed but have since been destroyed. The Beckhampton avenue at Avebury, for instance, once thought to be an invention of Stukeley's to complete his 'serpent', which also encompassed the West Kennet Avenue, is now known through excavation to have existed.[3] Nonetheless, Piggott marked out archaeologists as the true inheritors and rehabilitators of the antiquarian tradition, and arguably it is university-based archaeologists who are now held as the experts. Following Piggott, however, the earth mystic John Michell examined the variety of interpretations of the megaliths of Britain and Brittany proposed by the antiquaries and their inheritors; Michell's work is a celebration of *Megalithomania*, encouraging this phenomenon in others.[4] This, along with other scholarly work outside the conventional academic community, led to a significant number of stones enthusiasts, marked in the 1990s by the periodicals *3rd Stone: The Magazine for the New Antiquarian* and *At the Edge: Exploring New Interpretations of Past and Place in Archaeology, Folklore and Mythology*.

Returning to academe, the early chapters of Bruce Trigger's magisterial work, *A History of Archaeological Thought*, offered a sustained analysis of the development of antiquarianism from medieval thought, looking towards the 'scientific antiquarianism' of Stukeley and others, hindered though it was by romanticism and reliance on the presumed veracity of written documents.[5] More focussed studies expanding this scholarship into a burgeoning sub-discipline of the history of antiquarianism include Philippa Levine's *The Amateur and the Professional: Antiquarians, Historians and Archaeologists in Victorian England, 1838-1886*; Graham Parry's *The Trophies of Time: English Antiquarians of the Seventeenth Century*; Rosemary Sweet's *Antiquaries: The Discovery of the Past in Eighteenth-Century Britain*; Susan Pearce's *Visions of Antiquity: The Society of Antiquaries of London, 1707-2007*; and Joan Rockley's *Antiquarians and Archaeology in Nineteenth-Century Cork*.[6] Significantly, in the context of the present volume, the art historian Sam Smiles has expanded the study of antiquaries into the visual field in *The Image of Antiquity: Ancient Britain and the Romantic Imagination*.[7] While the early antiquaries saw visual representation – Stukeley's engravings mark an example – as equally important to their studies of antiquities, only in the latter part of the twentieth century has the significance of art to archaeology come to be appreciated.[8] Smiles examines how British artists of the eighteenth and nineteenth centuries portrayed the archaic past, arguing that these representations are inseparable from socio-political concerns and the formation of national identities. More recently, the edited volume, *Tracing Architecture: The Aesthetics of Antiquarianism*, extends the study and influence of the antiquaries into architectural history.[9] The papers in this volume take up a number of themes raised by this previous scholarship.

Clearly, what makes an antiquary in one place may not make an antiquary elsewhere. Based on her interests in Chinese printmaking, Anne Farrer proposed to us that the term 'archaist' would be more appropriate in certain contexts than 'antiquary'. What we mean by antiquary, then, is an interest in the material remains ('antiquities' or 'antiques') of the past, from texts and paintings to artefacts – without necessarily a specific disciplinary remit. Antiquarian interests, as indicated by the diversity of the eight chapters in this book, are broadly cast. Archaists, on the other hand, tend to reify the past in the present, sometimes in problematic ways which romanticise the past and impose the present onto past, sometimes with a critical eye on both the past and the present.

In preparing this book, the topics of enchantment, disenchantment and re-enchantment became broad linking themes. While they often worked systematically and founded some of the earliest archaeological methods, the early antiquaries were nonetheless enchanted by a prehistoric past which, in some instances, was the province of Druids and other anachronistic groups. Modern archaeology, for its part, having deconstructed previous thought and mystical speculation on the past and developed scientific techniques of excavation and analysis, has for some interest groups disenchanted the past. More recently, a variety of earth mystics, alternative archaeologists, contemporary Druids and other pagans have found ways of re-enchanting the past. Enchantment, disenchantment and re-enchantment across this spectrum are all critically engaged with by the contributors in this volume.

We took the view, as editors, that the multiplicity of voices, perspectives, and writing styles of the contributing authors should, as far as possible, be respected in order to showcase the depth, range and variety of ongoing work regarding the impact of the past on the past, and the past on the present. In addition, the attempt here has not been to produce an academic textbook, although academics are contributors. It is hoped that *Antiquaries and Archaists* will be accessible and useful to individuals operating in a number of spheres, from archaeologists, art historians, folklorists and anthropologists, to undergraduate and postgraduate students, and those who read it out of no other purpose than interest in the subject matter.

We begin with the chapter by Jeremy Harte, a museum curator and specialist in folklore. Harte explores themes of medieval 'enchantment' of the historic landscape, particularly prehistoric barrows. Elves, dragons, giants and others, it was perceived, inhabited these sites, and they were held to contain various treasures. Harte analyses myths, place names and folklore in the British Isles in order to approach this association between barrows and their guardians, with a particular focus on the Anglo-Saxon heroic poem *Beowulf*. Medieval people were not quite so naïve about these matters as one might be tempted to think. Following this chapter, Sarah Semple, an archaeologist, explores ways in which the Anglo-Saxons responded to the historic landscape in which they lived, particularly with respect to funerary practice, offering a detailed discussion of the evidence from across England. This work draws on recent trends in archaeology which consider memory, and the agency of the past in the past.[10] It is clear from these two chapters that medieval communities were keenly aware of ancient sites and often treated them with great respect.

No volume which touches upon antiquarianism in the British Isles can escape mention of William Stukeley. David Haycock, a historian writing in chapter 3, continues a key idea raised by Harte and Semple – that is, the interrelationship between the past and the historic landscape. While there has already been substantial work done on this key antiquarian figure,[11] Haycock ties in Stukeley's antiquarianism to the broader eighteenth-century context of the growing fascination for the landscape garden, arguing that Stukeley's approach to the historic and prehistoric landscape was informed significantly by his horticultural interests. In chapter 4, which closes the first part of this book ('The Past in the Past'), Megan Aldrich examines the self-taught Quaker architect Thomas Rickman, who, by 1817, had developed the first accurate history of medieval architecture through drawing upon taxonomic methods of ordering knowledge of the natural world. Rickman's book is well-known in architectural circles even today, but what is less appreciated is the extent to which he drew upon Linnean method and contemporary scientific developments. This section of *Antiquaries and Archaists*, therefore, begins with Harte's essay on the enchantment of the past, and closes with Aldrich's examination of the 'disenchantment' of the past – although it is unlikely that Thomas Rickman would have seen it that way.

Part Two of *Antiquaries and Archaists* ('The Past in the Present') begins with chapter 5 by Simon Kaner, a historian of archaeology specialising in Japan. Kaner details the coming together in the nineteenth and early twentieth centuries of established antiquarian activity in Japan with scientifically-based archaeological practice imported from the West, and from Britain, in particular. Kaner's postcolonial analysis, focusing on the antiquary William Gowland, argues for a creative dialectic between local, regional and national forces that had, and continues to exert, a major influence on the ways in which the 'archaeology of Japan' is constituted and understood. The creative conflict between local, regional and national Japanese identities emerges. This study is followed by chapter 6, written by Simon Watney, an art historian and established expert in contemporary photography and critical theory. Here he shows a very different side to his professional activity. As a case recorder engaged in fieldwork, Watney explores the founding of the Church Monuments Society and related societies in the twentieth century which actively seek to preserve monuments from the past now under threat. Watney's chapter locates the preservation of church monuments as a much-overlooked but key area of antiquarian activity in need of urgent attention. Robert Wallis picks up the theme of re-enchantment in chapter 7, chronicling how a variety of earth mystics, stones enthusiasts, Druids and other contemporary 'pagans' engage with the past, focusing on pagan use of ancient sites for religious and commemorative purposes. The issues surrounding calls for the reburial of prehistoric human remains, in particular, are timely and far-reaching. To conclude the volume, in chapter 8, Anne Farrer, an academic with a background in curatorship, articulates the way in which some contemporary Chinese artists use motifs drawn from the past as references and symbols in their work. Contemporary Chinese art as currently celebrated by the art market often resonates with conceptual art in the West, work that wears its challenge and intelligence upfront. Chinese contemporary art is more diverse than this. Farrer discusses the woodblock prints of Wang Chao which revive traditional techniques and motifs but skilfully regenerate these in a contemporary setting and demand sustained looking in order to open up their complexity, subtlety and irony. Wallis and Farrer suggest that both contemporary British pagans and contemporary Chinese printmakers may in some instances be usefully approached as 'archaists' in terms of their deliberate re-use of the past in the present.

We thus come full cycle from enchantment to disenchantment to re-enchantment of the past by antiquaries and archaists. Antiquarian interests in the past, as reflected by the Society of Antiquaries, extend for over four hundred years; in the first decade of the twenty-first century, the papers in this volume demonstrate that the importance of the past in the past and the past in the present extends not only through time but also across cultures.

1

Dragons, Elves and Giants: Some Pre-archaeological Occupants of British Barrows

Jeremy Harte

History is usually written by winners, and the historiography of archaeological studies is no exception to this rule. Though a great deal was said and thought about ancient sites during the thousand years before the foundation of the Society of Antiquaries, very little of this was concerned with the objective interpretation of facts, so it has been dismissed from the self-image of archaeology. 'The Saxon Conquerors (being no searchers into matters of Antiquity)', John Aubrey tells us, 'ascribed Works great, and strange, to the Devil, or some Giant... and handed downe to us only Fables'.[1]

It is true that when the Anglo-Saxons set out to describe an ancient monument, they would attribute it to giants. In *Beowulf* (lines 2715-7) 'the prince walked across/ to the side of the barrow, considering deeply;/ he sat down on a ledge, looked at the giant-work'.[2] It is doubtful whether imagery of this kind should be ascribed to popular tradition. *Beowulf* is not the work of an ordinary hand. The poet is at ease in the company of white-haired kings, battle-tried warriors, gracious queens, and brave retainers, pitched in action against giants, sea-serpents, fiend-like monsters and a dragon. The only commoner in the poem is anonymous, a 'nameless slave... on the run from a flogging... a sin-tormented soul' (2223-6). He is, as one might expect, an archaeologist, if that is the right word for someone who opens barrows to see what might be inside them. There the slave finds 'heaps of hoard-things in the hall underground/ which once in gone days gleamed and rang/ the treasure of a race rusting derelict' (2230-3), out of which he takes a single cup. Thus he awakes the wrath of the dragon, and sets in motion the events which will end in the death of Beowulf and the fall of the Geatish nation.

The dragon, like the earth, hoards gold and makes no use of it. He is 'keeper of treasures' (2779), an epithet also applied to kings; but whereas kings put the heroic cycle into action by distributing gold to their followers and receiving it back in the form of booty, the dragon, like the grave, represents the ultimate futility to which this cycle must descend. Greed for gold brings disaster, both at the level of the slave – the only character for whom the hoard is straight bullion, to be robbed for its cash value – and for the more heroic characters, who covet treasure as the material embodiment of their honour.

1.1: Sutton Hoo is the location of two Anglo-Saxon cemeteries dated to the sixth and early seventh centuries. For many years *Beowulf* + Sutton Hoo acted as a kind of composite text in Anglo-Saxon studies. 'Mound 2', shown here, is the only one of the barrows which has been reconstructed to what is thought to have been its original height. The ship burial yielded rich burial goods, a not uncommon association between barrow and treasure that hints at the dragon's hoard. In the literature there is one dragon, Fafnir, who was a man, or at all events a giant, before he changed shape and set guard over his hoard: dragon with hoard in hill = dead man with grave goods in barrow. [*Robert J. Wallis*]

Barrows, dragons and gold: from *Beowulf* to *Drakehull*

Beowulf, then, is about a dragon and a barrow, in much the same sense that *Moby Dick* is about a whale and the sea; there is much more going on in the poem than might appear from the plot. Being so early an epic, it has to stand in for its own sources; we don't know where the poet got his ideas from, and are irresistibly tempted to try and deduce them from the work itself. Thus the images of the poem are susceptible not just to a literary interpretation of their meaning in the text but to a cultural derivation of their roots in folk tradition.

That has led to a naturalistic theory for the origin of the three linked factors of barrow, dragon, and gold.[3] We can begin with the fact that the pagan Saxons, like other Germanic tribes, sometimes buried their dead in barrows. A handful of these burials were accompanied by treasure. The example of Sutton Hoo comes to mind, and, indeed, for many years *Beowulf* + Sutton Hoo acted as a kind of composite text in Anglo-Saxon studies **[Fig. 1.1]**. The dead man guards his treasures, in some stories; there are others where dead men become snakes; and there is at least one dragon, Fafnir, who was a man, or at all events a giant, before he changed shape and set guard over his hoard. If we follow this line of thinking – dragon with hoard in hill = dead man with grave goods in barrow – then it will enable us to explain much about the folklore of ancient sites as a reflection of real facts. We need no longer be distracted in our analysis of tales by such suspiciously literary concepts as motive or meaning. That is the attraction of this mode of thought, and of course its weakness, too. It is also very hard to square the naturalistic model with the evidence of tradition itself.

Most archaeologists have reconciled themselves to the fact that ancient sites do not contain treasure. The Rillaton cup, Mold cape, and Bush Barrow plaque notwithstanding, you could spend a long time opening grave mounds without coming across anything of value, and several frustrated seekers in the Middle Ages did just that.[4] They would not have tried, though, without some hope of success, and this suggests that they still shared, more literally than we do, in the thought-world of Anglo-Saxon epic, even though this was not based on fact.

Consider whether an episode which took place in 1344 is anything to go by:

> A Muslim came to the earl of Warenne with a request. He was a doctor, and he wanted permission to capture a serpent which, he said, was to be found at a place called Brunsfeld, part of the earl's lands in the Welsh Marches. He captured the serpent through his incantations, and then reported that a great hoard of treasure was to be found in a place near the cave in which it had lived. News got out about this, and some men from Hereford, led by a money-lender called Piers Pykard, started to dig there. They found that everything was true which the Muslim had foretold. They had come together for several nights to work at this, until the Earl's servants heard about it, and then they were caught and put in prison. The Earl is supposed to have been considerably enriched by this business.[5]

1.2: *Drakehull* (1318) near Guildford. This steep hill has been crowned since the fourteenth century by a chapel of St Catherine. The *Drake* in the title denotes that this is the hill of a dragon. [*Author*]

It was generally accepted that that hidden wealth would come under the protection of a fiend in animal or human shape, so treasure-hunters usually drafted in a magician of some kind.[6] This placed them at a double risk since conjuring was, if anything, even less legal than appropriating the royal prerogative of treasure trove. It is tempting to suppose that at Brunsfeld the Muslim doctor took this chance because he was acting as a front man for a second syndicate of gold-seekers, who knew that the Hereford men were on their trail, and wanted the Earl of Warenne as a protector even at the cost of sharing the wealth with him. In that case, the dragon would have provided an excuse for opening the subject, as well as supplying a discreet answer to the question of how they came to know of the treasure in the first place.

Dragons, however exotic their origins, had already made themselves at home in the English landscape. Numerous medieval place-names witness their presence, including the village of Drakelow in Derbyshire, which appears as *dracanhlawen* in a charter of 942. *Draca* is also found compounded with *hlāw* at two sites in Northamptonshire (*c.*1199 and *c.*1500), Wolverley in Worcestershire (1240), and Lower Bebington in Cheshire (1357). *Beorh*, the other word commonly used in *Beowulf* for the dragon's lair, makes a single appearance in *Drakebergh* at Merstham in Surrey (1384). There are also several forms with the Old Norse word *haugr*, the semantic equivalent of *hlāw*. *Drakehov* appears at Kirk Smeaton in the West Riding (*c.*1220), and other forms are recorded at Whatton in Nottinghamshire (late thirteenth century), Flitcham in Norfolk (1328), Owmby by Spital (*c.*1330) in Lincolnshire and at Maltby, again in the West Riding (1335). A single North Riding form, *Drechowe* (1336), comes from the Old Norse *dreki* and not the Old English *draca*; it must therefore belong to the period when Old Norse was predominant, say, between 900 and 1100.[7]

These three generics — *beorh*, *hlāw* and *haugr* — are all found with the sense of 'burial mound'. Does this preserve an ancient folk belief that dead men survived as treasure-guarding dragons? Given the learned origins of much dragon lore, this seems unlikely, and it is by no means certain that these places were, in fact, barrows in the archaeological sense. *Beorh* very often has the sense of rounded hill, and the other two words are also used to describe marker mounds and natural knolls.[8] The *Drakehull* (1318) near Guildford is an isolated hill overlooking the river Wey, crowned since the fourteenth century by a chapel of St. Catherine **[Fig. 1.2]**.[9] A climb up the steep riverside bank will leave your clothes stained bright yellow, since the hill is an outcrop of loose golden sand **[Fig. 1.3]**. This is no doubt the dragon's treasure, and it suggests a more playful attitude to tradition than one had expected. Like the Brunsfeld escapade, these names are not reflecting a literal belief in dragons. Instead, they are making creative use of ideas about them.

1.3: A climb up the steep riverside bank at *Drakehull* stains clothes bright yellow, since the hill is an outcrop of loose golden sand – this is no doubt the dragon's treasure, and perhaps we see here also a dragon's nest. The link between dragon and golden 'treasure' in this instance suggests a more playful attitude to tradition than one might expect. [*Author*]

Indeed, the barrow in *Beowulf* is itself a more inventive piece of fantasy architecture than might at first appear. Entered by a stone doorway, 'the age-old earth-hall contained/ stone arches anchored on pillars' (2718-9). It had also accommodated a fifty-foot long dragon, and had a roof high enough to support a golden banner overhead. Eight men needed torchlight to see their way before they were able to penetrate its interior to carry out the hoard (3042, 3125). This is no ordinary Anglo-Saxon barrow. It is a magical building, the final work of that mysterious race of whom the last survivor is the only representative. He himself is introduced only to make his '*ubi sunt?*' speech, and then to die.

'The Work of Giants': from the *Ruin* to *Des Grantz Geanz*

Old English poetry loves to dwell on transience. 'They have had their hall-days', concludes the last survivor, just as the author of the *Ruin* writes 'Wondrous is this masonry:/ shattered by fate, the fortifications have given way,/ the buildings raised by giants are crumbling'.[10] The giant-wrought buildings are described in both poems by the same phrase, *eald enta geweorc*, one of the formulaic half-lines which the poetic tradition had inherited from its oral predecessors. The phrase must have been in use during the Migration period, since its equivalent form *wrisilic gewerc*, 'the work of giants', survived on the Continent in Old Saxon poetry. The phrase was still being used in the late thirteenth century, when Sir Tristrem, in the Middle English version of the romance, escapes from the court to live in an 'erthe house' which 'etenes bi old dayse had wrought'.[11] A poetic formula which lasts for almost a thousand years must have touched a nerve.

But who were the giants? A naturalistic explanation springs to mind, just as it did with dragons. If a people should enter into a strange land, as the Anglo-Saxons certainly did, and should encounter monuments of stupendous size, then popular tradition will attribute them to a lost race of heroic stature. However, as with the dragons, this explanation tells us nothing about the meanings or motives which were brought into play when giants were evoked in representations of past glories. Facts alone are not enough to explain such a recurrent poetic trope, and, in any case, the facts were not in much doubt. The *Ruin* is a learned poem, the work of an author who knew his Venantius Fortunatus.[12] Stepping through the crumbling precincts of Bath, he was perfectly well aware that this had been a classical city. The epigraphy of the jumbled tombstones and votive altars that built up the city wall was not for him, as it is for the host of today's tourists, a lost language. If he described Roman masonry as *eald enta geweorc*, he must have had a reason for doing so.

The same mismatch between epic stature and literal height confronts us at one of the best-known works of giants, Stonehenge. The illustration to the British Library MS Egerton 3028 shows a huge Merlin, twice the size of those around him, shunting a trilithon into place.[13] The French text, however, is derived from Geoffrey of Monmouth, who describes how Merlin dismantled the stone circle at its original location with special machinery, and reassembled it in the same way, 'thus proving that his artistry was worth more than any brute strength'. Merlin is a man amongst other men, but he is also a magician, and his magical skills have put him, as far as the artist is concerned, onto a quite different plane. He is one with the giants who originally brought the great stones from the confines of Africa and set them up in Ireland 'at a time when they inhabited that country'.[14]

This would presumably be at the time when Britain, too, 'was uninhabited except for a few giants', of whom the last was Goemagot, slain in an epic wrestling match in the confines of Cornwall by Corineus. Geoffrey does not explain how the giants came to be there in the first place, but this was added in a supplementary work of the thirteenth century, the Anglo-French *Des Grantz Geanz*. This tells us how the fifty daughters of the King of Greece, having proposed to murder their husbands on their wedding night, were found out and exiled by their indignant father. Landing in Britain, they lived in isolation until certain lustful demons took advantage of them and fathered a race of giants who afterwards populated the island through incest with their mothers. 'Cele gent de faerie', says the poet, 'this brood of enchantment/ multiplied in vast numbers./ They filled the land/ and made caves in the earth./ They raised great walls around them/ and surrounded them with ditches./ They settled on the mountains/ where they felt most secure/ and in many places can still be seen/ the great walls that they raised,/ though many have been thrown down/ by storms and the work of time.[15]

Romans, demons and other giants

This mixture of lubricious fantasy and sober fieldwork sets a very bad precedent for subsequent generations, which is why the author of *Des Grantz Geanz* has not received his due as the founder of British prehistory. In any case, deduction from material evidence was already standard practice in Roman studies. At Cratendune near Ely, 'one frequently finds implements of ironwork and the coinage of past kings, and the fact that it was for a long time a place inhabited by men is clear from various pieces of evidence'.[16] Similarly in the twelfth-century Colchester Oath Book, the Roman origin of the town 'is conjectured from those things which people digging have excavated from the earth: iron, precious stones, and minted coins, and buildings found beneath the earth'.[17]

Having set the scene in this way, the chronicler of Ely gets onto the main point, which is to celebrate the miraculous powers and interventions of his patron saint. It disorients a modern reader, this easy passage from the antiquarian to the supernatural. People knew the difference between Romans and giants, apparently, but they didn't really care that there was one. The two races occupied much the same imaginative space. When Ranulph Higden came to speculate on the origins of his home town of Chester, he wrote 'the founder of this citee is vnknowe, for who that seeth the foundementis of the grete stones wolde rather wene that it were Romayns werke, other werke of geauntes, than work i-made by swettynge of Bretouns'.[18]

Another ancient town in the Welsh borderland features in

the hallucinatory opening sequence to the romance of Fulk Fitz-Warin. William I is venturing somewhere west of Ludlow when he camps below 'a very large town, formerly enclosed, which was entirely burnt and pillaged'. That is because a devil has taken over, long ago, the body of the dead giant who fought with Corineus – Geomagog, in this version – and the fiend-giant now fights with all who enter. The bold Sir Payne Peverel overcomes this adversary, who confesses that he has been guarding the great treasure which the giant heaped up in life, 'and placed in a house which he made underground in this town', a treasure which included a golden bull which told the future and which he and his fellow giants would worship in their idolatry.[19] This romance inverts the sequence which we met in the *Grantz Geanz*. This time the giants come first and the demons after, but to mention one is to suggest the possibility of the other. Perversion, sorcery, monstrosity and lust swirl around in a cauldron of linked ideas, and the word 'giant' was never an innocent reference to great size or powers but always came loaded with these meanings.

This sheds a new and rather unexpected light on the barrow in *Beowulf*. It was new in the time of the last survivor and must, therefore, have been built by that last race, whoever they were. The fact that it is *enta geweorc* suggests that they were giants. Certainly the impressionistic detail, with its stone arches and pillars, sounds Roman. In the romance-hagiography *Andreas*, which is influenced by *Beowulf* (or vice versa), St Andrew is incarcerated in the prison-larder of the cannibal Mermedonians, a double of the dragon's lair, where he sees 'wonderfully wrought,/ great pillars round his prison:/ columns that had crumbled under the storm,/ old giant-work'.[20]

The imaginative model is one of a splendid but ruined hall, set on a hill inside some kind of wall and precinct. This can, at a pinch, be mapped onto a barrow, with its outer surface representing the wall, once we have remembered that heroic and enchanted barrows are much larger on the inside than they appear to outward view. Like the giants/ dwarfs, their dimensions vary according to the needs of the story, and, indeed, a giant's barrow, *entan hlǽw*, is recorded in the Test valley on the border between Quidhampton and Polhampton in a boundary charter of 940.[21]

The earthworks of the *Grantz Geantz* sound more like hillforts. True, they are supposed to have had caves inside them, but these may have been visible only to the eye of faith. Again, there are two entrenchments associated with giants in the place-name record, both again from Hampshire. Andyke in Barton Stacey was *auntediche* in the thirteenth century, which is the same as the *ænta dic* (for *enta dic*) recorded, a little way to the south in the boundary charter for Kings Worthy in 1026.[22]

Giants in decline

Giants represented both the envied powers and the pagan horrors of remote antiquity, but with the passage of time, these feelings were beginning to wane. In his journey of 1480, William Worcestre was shown Maesbury Castle, two miles east of Wells. It was 'built on a high hill by a giant called Merk. It was thrown down, but more than a hundred thousand cartloads of stones are heaped there'.[23] Not far away, at Clifton Camp on the outskirts of Bristol, he knew of another entrenchment 'not a quarter of a mile distant from Gyston Cliff, as it is called by the common people… founded there before the time of William the Conqueror by the Saracens or Jews, by a certain Ghyst, a giant portrayed on the ground'. Again, it was the amount of work needed to construct the hillfort which came foremost to his thoughts. 'It remains to this day as a large circle of great stones piled up, and small ones lying thus, in an orderly ring and great circle, whereby a very strong castle is seen to have been there, which hundreds of years ago has been destroyed and thrown to the ground'. Worcestre concludes, with a touch of local patriotism, that so great a fortification was 'a credit and an honour to the district of Bristol'.[24] Late medieval England no longer stood in awe of the past, and giants had became the subjects of civic pride. Even the fearsome Goemagot was fondly remembered at Plymouth, where they cut another hill figure to represent him on the Hoe, and had it regularly maintained by the Corporation.[25]

In the 1530s, John Twyne still took it much for granted that British giants were responsible for 'mounds, fortifications, caves, monuments of stone, giants' dances, and tombs'.[26] Although

1.4: Wayland's Smithy long barrow, a Neolithic monument on the Ridgeway in Oxfordshire. The name may hint that "Weland" the master-smith of Northern myth was a barrow-dweller; he was also known as 'leader of elves', or 'wise one of the elves'. [*Robert J. Wallis*]

he cites all the appropriate Biblical authorities, his conclusions have already exchanged the lively involvement of legend for the distant curiosity of scholarship. In his travels as King's Antiquary, Leland covered much of the same ground as Worcestre, and was given similar information, but he brushed it aside as no longer relevant to his purpose. At Corbridge 'hath beene a forteres or castelle. The people there say that ther dwelled in it one Yoton, whom they fable to have beene a gygant'.[27] His failure even to recognise the word *eoten* is symptomatic of a wider disengagement from popular culture. Camden did little better; although he recognised that eatons was the word 'in the North parts' for giants, he thought it a corruption of 'heathens'. Ancient buildings 'were so very stately', he adds in the measured tones of one reporting a common error, that 'the common people will have these Roman fabricks to be the works of the Gyants'.[28]

The work of disenchantment was complete. Far away in Anglesey, Sion Dafydd Rhys was compiling his indignant treatise on *Cewri Cymru*, 'The Giants of Wales', listing hill after hill which could still be seen crowned by the fortifications of giants.[29] Many of these were of irrefutable historical authority, for had they not been overcome by Arthur himself? Thus the case for the reality of giants was left to those who wrote in defence of the British history itself, and they were a diminishing band. The debate moved insensibly from the realms of myth and religion to minute examination of various skeletal remains, all of prodigious size, and some of more or less human shape.[30]

These scavenged fossils are a poor substitute for the heroic crafts which had provided visible tokens of the giant race in earlier lore. In the underwater dwelling of Grendel's mother, Beowulf had looked up and seen, 'among the armour there, the sword to bring him victory,/ a giant-sword from former days: formidable were its edges,/ a warrior's admiration' (1557-9). The sword is so huge that only a hero can lift it, but Beowulf grasps it and strikes off the head of the she-monster, only to see the blade melt in her venomous blood. Blades and armour of giant workmanship recur through the poem, as the Scandinavian literature features those forged by dwarfs. The effect is the same in both contexts – things that are wonderful and intricate, but too often deadly in their use, can only come from the old races inimical to man.

'The Art of the Heathen': barrows and elves

The master-smith Weland, who wrought sword and mail-shirt for the ancestors in *Beowulf*, seems to have been a barrow-dweller, for the mound of Wayland's Smithy on the Ridgeway has carried his name since 955 **[Fig. 1.4]**.[31] In an alternative tradition, he was based in the haunted precincts of an old Roman city. Geoffrey of Monmouth, in his *Vita Merlini*, has the mad seer being tempted back from the woodland by the offer of 'cups which Weland fashioned in the city of Sigenis', better known as Segontium, the Roman fort at Caernarvon.[32]

Weland was not a giant; he belonged to the *ælf* people, the elves of Old English mythology. In the Norse *Völundarkviða* he appears twice as *vísi álfar*, an adaptation of an Old English phrase meaning 'leader of elves', or 'wise one of the elves'.[33] His artistry is not the heavy work of the blacksmith, but the subtle fabrication of things too intricate to be worked by human hand. Just as Roman architecture was so stupendous that it called out for identification with giants, so Roman repoussé goldwork was best admired by attributing it to the elves. It is interesting that, of all the different kinds of antiquity disinterred in an ancient city, Geoffrey chose cups as the ones that could best be assigned to Weland. A goblet was also the treasure chosen by the slave in *Beowulf* for his loot from the barrow, with unfortunate consequences. Cups are magical things. That is why an Old English missal contains a form of prayer 'over vessels found in some ancient place, that were made by the art of the heathen', in order that 'cleansed of every offence' they may be used without harm by the faithful.[34]

Sometimes Dutch courage could fortify men to deeds which neither exorcism nor heroism were able to achieve. In mid-twelfth-century Yorkshire, the young William of Newburgh was told how a man was riding back from a drunken party past a mound – almost certainly the barrow which still stands today at Willy Howe. From this mound:

> he heard the voices of people singing… He was curious and decided to take a closer look. That was when he saw a door standing open in the side of the mound, and as he got nearer and looked inside, he saw a capacious house, brightly lit, and full of people. They were sitting down, men and women together, as if they were at a magnificent feast. One of the servants, seeing him standing there at the entrance, offered him a cup. He took it, but after a moment's thought he decided not to drink from it; instead he poured out what was in it and clutching onto the vessel, fled as fast as he could. The feasters were in an uproar when they saw their cup had been taken, and poured out after him, but he was on a swift horse and he got away.[35]

We are not told what these people in the mound were called, but they were almost certainly elves. In place-names, *ælf* is regularly compounded with words for 'hill'. It appears with *dun* at Elvendon Farm near Goring in Oxfordshire (*c.*1260) and Eldon Hole near Castleton in Derbyshire (1285). It is found with *hyll* at Edgefield in Norfolk (*c.*1300), at Carlisle (1359) and at Aspatria in Cumberland (1578). In the North of England, it appears several times with *haugr*, which is also the generic of Willy Howe itself; Ailey Hill in the North Riding was *Elveshowe* (1228), and there is a more modern Elf Howe at Folkton. Elva

Hill at Hutton-in-the-Forest, again in Cumberland, is *Elfhow* in 1488, and the same county has an *Elvinhowe* in 1577 at Gosforth and a modern Elva Hill in Setmurthy. Ailcy Hill near Ripon, was *Elueshowe* in 1288, and the West Riding has another *Alfhov* from the thirteenth century and an *Elfe-knolle* recorded in 1310.[36]

In short, the toponymic pattern for *ælf* is very similar to that for *draca* – except that, while a dragon is always called a dragon, elves blend imperceptibly in Middle and Modern English place-names with pucks, bugs, hobs, kows, boggarts, goblins and fairies, and that's just the names. Grinsell, in his great survey of the folklore of prehistoric sites, lists over twenty sites where tradition associated barrows with fairy beings of one kind of another. For the medieval peasant, it seems, a *hlāw* or *haugr* was not an ancient monument but a green mound with spirits inside it.

Can this be accounted for? It should come by now as no surprise that there is a naturalistic explanation for fairies, just as there was for other occupants of barrows. In Northern Europe people who were buried in mounds were sometimes venerated. Fairies, too, received something that looks very like worship, since they were invoked for good luck and various magical purposes, while there are many sources in which fairies are said to be among, or resembling, or numbered with dead people. Is this not a sufficient explanation of the unusual events at Willy Howe? Can we translate the 'spacious building, well lit, filled with people' into an earth-house of the powerful heathen dead? The Yorkshire story is certainly very similar to Scandinavian accounts of the dead feasting within hills. Thus when Thorsteinn Thorskabít of Iceland died in a fishing expedition, a shepherd on the hills told how he had looked over to Helgafell, the holy mountain venerated by Thorsteinn and his father, and saw the hill stand open, with sounds of merriment and feasting coming from inside as the company welcomed the young master and his crew.[37] The northern links of the tradition at Willy Howe are strengthened when we recall the Viking settlement of the East Riding. Indeed, the story of the cup stolen from the fairies is a typically Viking one, frequent in Scandinavia, known also on the Isle of Man, but rare in England apart from this Danelaw account.

Fairy hills and elf arrows

The fairies are an elusive people, and cannot be pinned down to archaeological facts in this way. Elsewhere in the British Isles, over the very extensive areas of Irish and Gaelic speech, we find a fully developed mythology of fairy hills – the *sí* or *brú*, the *sithean* – in which live the otherworldly people. Already in Irish literature of the twelfth century this fantasy landscape is fully worked out, with its chieftains, retinues, conflicts and alliances. Much of this is literary embellishment, the deliberate creation of a vernacular mythology to stand against that of Greece and

Rome, but the earliest commentators were convinced that, like classical myth, it took its inspiration from actual religious practice. Before Patrick came, says his biographer, Fiacc, 'on Erin's land lay darkness; the tribes worshipped the *sí*'.[38]

Sí and *ælf* are kindred spirits, a proud people of great beauty, sometimes at war with the heroes of old, and sometimes in league with them, with many marriages and alliances across the boundary between this world and the other. Both *ælf* and *sí* can be found in hills, but here any archaeological explanation for the origins of legend must break down completely, for, while the elf traditions circulated in an area which had only recently given up barrow burial, in Ireland this practice had been extinct for thousands of years. There was nothing in popular memory or actual experience that would lead an Irish storyteller to associate mounds with dead people. When we look more closely at the *brú* or *sithean*, we find that, more often than not, it is a natural hill. Newgrange, the chambered tomb and home of Aengus Óg, is the exception [Fig. 1.5]. Much more typical is the Fairy Hill at Aberfoyle, a natural hillock into which the Reverend Kirk disappeared after making too probing an enquiry into the nature and habits of the secret people.[39]

This suggests that the physical barrow, with its dead man within, is not the origin of the legendary hollow hill. It is the legend which exists first, and which is more or less universal. The power of storytelling derives from the fusion of this received knowledge with lived experience; if we find that story has made a transmutation of fact, that may be the living contribution of the storyteller, and not some perpetuated detail of old knowledge.

1.5: Newgrange, the Neolithic passage grave in Brú na Bóinne, County Meath, Ireland. This huge monument, entirely human-made, marks an exception in being a mound linked to the *sí* or fairies which is not a natural hill or hillock. [*Robert J. Wallis*]

The fairy hill was a symbol which could serve many turns. It was on 'ane hillock called the Elphillok', said Andro Man, that the Queen of Elfame made his cattle die. He protested at the injustice of the thing, and she capriciously promised to do him good after evil, and became his lover. She had a grip of all the craft; she made any follower king as she pleased, and lay with whom she liked.[40] There may have been a 'genuine' tradition at the hillock, but it is just as likely that Man imagined it as a background for the things that mattered to him – his passage from failed cattle farmer to magically privileged insider of the Seeley Court. A story must carry conviction to overcome the challenges of unbelief. Where does the magician get his power? From the arts taught by fairies, some might say, or from the ability to conjure a compelling story out of the hard facts of life. The two formulations are not so very different.

Andro Man was not alone. Katherine Ross 'would gang in Hillis to speik the elf folk'. Isobel Haldane of Perth was carried out of her bed by the fairies and borne into a hill where she stayed for three days and acquired magical knowledge. 'The hill oppynit, and scho enterit in'.[41] The fairy hill was the place from which they took their power. These hills, in the by now familiar manner of imaginary places, are much larger on the inside than the outside. There was one between Edinburgh and Leith where a boy met every Thursday night with a multitude of fairies, for whom he played on his drum. 'There was a great pair of gates that opened to them, though they were invisible to others: and … within there were brave large rooms, as well accommodated as most of Scotland'.[42] Isobel Gowdie told her interrogators that, 'we went in to the Downie hillis; the hill opened, and we cam to an fair and large braw rowme in the day tym'. It was in these hills that Gowdie saw the fairies at work on one of their mysterious crafts. 'As for Elf-arrow heidis, the Divell shapes them with his awin hand, and syne deliveris thame to Elf-boyes, who whyttis and dightis them with a sharp thing lyke a paking needle; bot whan I was in Elfland I saw them whytting and dighting them'.[43]

Elf arrows were familiar enough. These thin pointed stones could be picked up wherever fairies, or the witches who rode with them on the wind, had flicked them to kill people or cattle. Many cunning-folk kept one amongst their magical cures, boiling the stone in water and using the water to heal an elf-shot beast or patient.[44] Sometimes they were set in silver, as a relic or a healing charm might be. From the examples that have survived in this way, we know that elf arrows were in fact barbed and tanged flint arrowheads, but for a long time they had remained anomalous. To Robert Kirk, writing his learned treatise on the nature and customs of the secret people, they were a complete mystery. It was obvious that they had been made in some way, and this looked very much as if this had been whittling away by a knife, though clearly they 'could not be cut so small and neat, of so brittle a Substance, by all the Airt of Man'.[45]

For a brief period in the late seventeenth century, then, elf-arrows served the world of scholarship as an example of what Fort called 'damned data' – things that ought not to have existed, but were patently there. Like the dragon skins hung up in churches, or the giants' bones put on display by enterprising showmen, they used the new-found language of natural science to preserve stories which would otherwise have been dismissed as popular credulity. Robert Sibbald included a number of these arrows in his *Prodromus Historiae Naturalis*, with details of their provenance; they had been picked up from fields and by the roadside, wherever they had been shot by the elves and witches. Edward Lhuyd was shown round Sibbald's collection in 1699, and made some polite remarks, as befitted a guest and scholar. When he got back to his office at the Ashmolean, he wrote up the experience in an amused note to a friend. Elf arrows? Why, 'they are just the same chip'd flints the natives of New England head their arrows with to this day.'[46]

Conclusion

The study of folklore was just beginning to emerge in the days of Lhuyd and Aubrey at the same time as archaeological scholarship, and for the same reasons. Once the world had become disenchanted, it was possible to study antiquities as things in themselves, and not as signs of supernatural presence in the landscape. This meant that legends were cut away from their task of telling truth through material embodiments. Instead, belief became an object of study in its own right. No longer a revelation of an unseen world, it was reclassified as a curious mental habit of the common people, and so we have 'folklore'.

Stories are not fossils of belief, passed down from some ancestral pagan to his peasant lineage. Stories have a life of their own, and this comes not from ancient facts, but from inward meanings. When people first picked up courage to trench the old mounds, they found no giants, elves or dragons lurking within. It looked as if old William of Newburgh's Yorkshire peasant was mistaken, but that may not be as conclusive as it seems. Those who cut open barrows in the light of day are not always best suited to slip through the twilight doorways that stand open into the human mind.

2

Recycling the Past: Ancient Monuments and Changing Meanings in Early Medieval Britain

Sarah Semple

Early medieval reuse of prehistoric and Roman remains has been examined by numerous scholars from various disciplines.[1] They have all observed that ancient structures, among them Roman villas and towns, long barrows, round barrows, chambered tombs, hill forts, henges, dolmens and linear dykes, were reused, named and incorporated into oral and written stories, poetry and legends. As we have seen in the previous chapter by Jeremy Harte, this use of the ancient within the landscape is only one element of an apparently insatiable curiosity inherent in early medieval communities which led them to revere, recycle and even, by the ninth and tenth centuries AD, fear the physical remains of the ancient past.[2]

The landscape is just one strand within this complex re-negotiation of the ancient; Roman and prehistoric artefacts were used and imbued with significance, as well. Stone axes were recycled as talismans, Roman sarcophagi reused for saintly burial, and Roman gemstones and Iron-age beads reworked and reset into pendants and jewels. In broader terms, scholars have argued for the importance of *romanitas* to emerging authorities in the early medieval era, in terms of costume, burial rites, symbols of office and new forms of architecture in the secular and ecclesiastical spheres.[3] Prehistoric objects and monuments were emulated, as well, from the large, earthen, purpose-built mounds used for assemblies, to the fashioning of strap-ends in imitation of flint arrowheads.[4] The sheer diversity of 'reuse' or 'recycling' across the period from AD 400-1100 is evidence neither of the ubiquity of ancient features and artefacts, nor of an unselective approach towards their use. The practices reviewed above encompass the wider array of 'reused' objects and monuments, but also the diversity of motivations and contexts in which the past was selectively brought into use within the present, directly and indirectly, in material, landscape, and even textual and artistic terms.[5]

'Reuse' and 'recycling' of the past is not confined to the medieval period; the literature and research on prehistoric reuse is exceptionally large, with widespread European evidence for the readoption and manipulation of monumental remains from the Neolithic through to the Roman Iron Age.[6] Individual monuments, as well as groups of remains and whole landscapes,

2.1 (*above*) and 2.2: Avebury and Silbury Hill, Wiltshire, aerial views. The landscape is dominated by the prehistoric remains, which even today dwarf the village and church. These include, shown here, the henge and stone circles. [*English Heritage Photographic Archive, date unknown*]

could be reworked, absorbed and changed in subsequent periods. The selective and strategic adaptation of the past as a meaningful and nuanced process is, however, a theme that archaeologists have been more adept at exploring within recent centuries, up to the present day.[7] The early medieval period in Britain is particularly rich in evidence for the recycling of the prehistoric and Roman pasts — in particular, the processes apparent within the English landscape, between AD 400-1100. The discussion presented here is not restricted to an examination of reuse within the funerary or settlement arenas, areas which have already received much attention in the published literature.[8] Instead, this chapter draws on a variety of emergent themes suggestive of varied and changing uses of the ancient within the landscape in order to examine the use of ancient landscapes as frames, or theatres, for activities.[9] It seeks to establish how the landscape was used and viewed differently both over time and by different and competing groups at regional and localised levels.

Numerous commentaries in the last two decades have variously interpreted the appropriation of the past as evidence of continuity of place, processes of legitimation, displays of land ownership and power, representations of active political discourse or demonstrations of identity.[10] Many interpretations assume a degree of understanding or recognition by the individual, the community, or the ruling elite, of the ancient properties of the monuments or artefacts involved. What is less well understood is the possibility of regional, and even local, diversity in choice and use — if using the past is about identity creation, we might at least expect differences in the ways in which the past was manipulated by competing groups or hierarchies within society, perhaps at local and individual levels. Archaeologists have become increasingly aware in recent years of a need for more regionally situated case-studies.[11] Regional studies at nested scales are relevant and necessary here if we are to try and understand the intention and design leading to reuse, and to critically appraise it in terms of selection and choice by populations, and the meanings of such actions.

A variety of practices were situated within, and sited in reference to, enceintes of ancient remains — namely, community cemeteries, assemblies, royal palaces, burials, monastic foundations and execution cemeteries. The focus here is the changing dynamics of reuse within England in the period AD 400-1100. It is hoped that new perspectives offered here are relevant to those working on similar themes in Britain and abroad, and to those working outside the chronological perimeters of this study. The ways in which different landscapes provided templates for the enactment of power are explored, alongside how the reception of the ancient changed over time, and how diversity in perception and use of the landscape can be recognised at regional and local levels.

Funerary reuse: regional and sub-regional diversity

It has become increasingly clear that mapping of funerary practices at more regional or localised scales suggests that monument reuse was highly varied from region to region.[12] However, to date the exploration in detail of this local and regional variability – that is, the scales closer to those by which early medieval individuals and communities engaged with and experienced their environment – have received relatively limited attention.[13] In particular, looking at local areas in detail, and then taking a comparative approach by isolating the shared themes and differences between them, provides the basis for an enriched appreciation of early medieval perceptions and engagements with ancient monuments. If we examine the early medieval funerary evidence from three areas chosen because of their rich archaeological data but differing topographies and early medieval historical backgrounds, distinctive contrasts are apparent in the ways in which ancient remains were used for burial. The three regions in question are: 1) North Wiltshire (part of the West Saxon kingdom); 2) West Sussex (part of the kingdom of the South Saxons later annexed by Wessex); and 3) East Yorkshire (a core region of Deira, the southern kingdom of Northumbria).

The rolling chalk hills of the Marlborough Downs, North Wiltshire, are marked by numerous small villages and towns. It is a landscape that even today is dominated by prehistoric remains **[Figs 2.1, 2.2]**. Chambered tombs, henges, standing stones and stone circles, as well as numerous Bronze-age barrow cemeteries, are all visually apparent within the modern environs of the great Neolithic henge at Avebury, itself. Between AD 400-800, the funerary use of prehistoric remains in this region was common-place, with ancient barrows frequently adopted as funerary locales.[14] On Roundway Down overlooking the clays of the Vale of Chippenham, four burials of possible Anglo-Saxon date, including the well-known, rich, seventh-century female grave, were excavated by antiquarians, and three of these were revealed as secondary within Bronze-age barrows.[15] Traces of cremation and inhumation burials of the fifth and sixth centuries were discovered at Overton, to the east of Avebury, intrusive and inserted into Roman round barrows, and a seventh-century grave was discovered, again a secondary interment, within a large prehistoric round barrow at Yatesbury to the west.[16] Although secondary burials using prehistoric remains occurred as early as the fifth and sixth centuries (Overton Down) and as late as the ninth century (Ogbourne St Andrew), the record is dominated by a glut of rich, isolated graves, inserted into prehistoric barrows broadly within the seventh century. The evidence suggests the power play between elite groups in a region known from documentary sources as a contested and fought over territory, disputed between the predatory kingdoms of Mercia and Wessex.[17] Despite this seventh-century surge in the use of the ancient prehistoric palimpsest across the period AD 400-800, the frequent evidence of funerary reuse suggests that the prehistoric, particularly the more distant Neolithic and Bronze-age pasts, represented the landscape with which the early medieval population in this region found most affinity. They commonly buried their dead in relation to ancient monuments, particularly barrows, with such traditions persisting as late as the ninth century. On the whole, however, these were isolated acts, individual burials perhaps deployed to define territorial claims.

Contrasting modes of recycling the landscape can be found in the South Saxon kingdom. The chalk downland of Sussex, scored through by the major river valleys of the Arun, Adur, Ouse and Cuckmere, has been shown to have been well-populated in the early and middle Anglo-Saxon period, with settlements often situated within the valleys, and cemeteries evident on the downland slopes and the chalk uplands.[18] Recent discoveries of burials just above the coastal plain at Westhampnett imply there is more funerary activity yet to be found on the lower downland slopes and lowlands, but a general patterning of burials and cemeteries on the downs and settlements situated within the river valleys is accepted.[19] The landscape now and, of course, then was marked by numerous surviving monuments and remains from the prehistoric and Roman past: barrows, settlement and stock enclosures, flint mines, hill forts and villas. Here, too, between AD 400 to 800 prehistoric remains were frequently reused as places of burial, but, in contrast to other regions, a diverse array of monuments were reused. At Blackpatch, the spoil heaps from prehistoric flint mines, and perhaps the open mine shafts too, attracted a series of primary barrow burials and secondary interments using the discarded mine-workings.[20]

Close by at Clapham (New Barn Down), the house platforms of a Neolithic settlement provided a focus for a small grouping of primary barrow burials, clustered around the distinctive, surviving earthworks. The modes of reuse were also distinctly different again to those seen in Wiltshire, and elsewhere. The dead were often buried in cemeteries composed of numerous small, primary barrow burials. These barrow cemeteries, on the whole, clustered around individual prehistoric monuments and groups of monuments with the more ancient remains, larger and more visually dominant than the surrounding, smaller, grave markers. Such associative rather than intrusive practices (also apparent at Bishopstone, West Sussex and Bowcombe Down, Isle of Wight), point to a need in communities to bury their dead in close proximity to the ancient and, perhaps, ancestral past, but without replacing the past by partially destroying or recycling the monument.[21] In a period of flux and change, the populations inhabiting the West Sussex landscape defined themselves and the land they inhabited by reforging ancestral ties with the landscape, thereby creating new visual and physical links with perceived ancestors by using a variety of ancient monuments close in visual and physical terms to their settlements. The kind of territorial definition and defiance apparent in the use of rich, isolated, secondary barrow burials in North Wiltshire is virtually absent in this landscape, attesting perhaps to the slow emergence of a single unifying royal and administrative political force within the kingdom in the period AD400–800.[22]

Once again a differing pattern of landscape use can be seen on the Wolds of East Yorkshire. The chalk upland, intersected by numerous dales or dry valleys, has seen successive human use over thousands of years [Fig. 2.3]. Linear dykes mark the modern landscape, alongside Bronze-age round barrows and Iron-age square barrows with earthwork enclosures and settlement remains of varying date, occasionally visible as upstanding earthworks.[23] In the period between AD 400 to 800, this was a region in which early medieval populations used prehistoric remains as funerary locations. Lucy's study of East Yorkshire examined the full variety of funerary practices in the region in the early medieval period, and, although not focusing wholly on monument reuse, he recognised the common use of round barrows and the less frequent, but nevertheless notable, reuse of square barrow cemeteries and linear earthworks.[24] A more detailed examination of funerary practices in the region reaching from Market Weighton north to Rudston confirms that communities seem to have made use of what was visually available: round barrows, square barrows and linear earthworks, and in one instance an earthwork enclosure.[25] Linear earthworks were, in fact, used in four separate instances for burial, making this type of appropriation very distinctive to this region.

The ways in which the East Yorkshire population used these

2.3: The Adur Valley, West Sussex, landscape showing the downland slopes and the chalk uplands that surround the Rivers Arun and Adur. The area was well-populated in the early and middle Anglo-Saxon period. [*Andy Horton, 2007*]

monuments is also distinctive. The dead were buried intrusively in prehistoric barrows and linear earthworks in East Yorkshire, but were situated within relatively large communal cemeteries. The Uncleby cemetery is particularly illustrative, as is Garton Slack I.[26] On the whole, rich, individual, ostentatious burials in prehistoric monuments were not a feature of this region, and neither were the types of small associative cemeteries apparent in West Sussex. Relatively large community cemeteries, with burials inserted into the prehistoric barrow or earthwork, were more the norm. In fact, the reuse of prehistoric remains as locations for community cemeteries persisted in use into the seventh and eighth centuries and may even have increased in frequency within the Conversion Period.[27]

Material Identities

Increasingly, mortuary archaeology is moving away from discussions of ethnic affinities, and funerary evidence is frequently viewed as an arena within which 'syncretic processes' took place – that is, a theatre within which mourners combined differing strands of influence into regionally distinctive and material identities.[28] This can be envisaged in material terms, particularly with regard to grave assemblages, dress fittings, modes and styles of burial and interment, but the landscape setting – the geography – of burial can be said to be equally distinctive and diverse in terms of natural settings and the adoption of ancient palimpsests of monumental remains. Whilst processes of legitimating ownership, land claims or power are without question at play in this era, we have underestimated just how complex and individualised the messages created by framing and shaping funerary rituals within selected theatres of prehistoric and Roman remains actually were, and the extent to which they complemented and were emphasised by related modes of recycling and reuse across the period. At one level, in the fifth through eighth centuries, the evidence points to an increasing interest in the monuments of the past, and an upsurge in recycling these monuments as locales for burial, particularly within the seventh century. Within a regional framework, however, the types of monuments and the ways in which they were used vary dramatically, pointing to highly regionalised conceptions of landscape, and thus of origins, identity, the past, and land ownership.

Communities seem to have selected and made use of the ancient monuments most common within their landscape and most familiar to them, but with clear preferences for differing types of remains. Similarly, the modes of use are also different, implying that the ways people chose to use these sites as funerary arenas reflects regionalised, if not localised, preferences, tastes, and definitions of identity. Contrasting patterns can be discerned across England and remain to be fully uncovered. For example, a close relationship with Roman remains, particularly forts, has long been recognised between cemeteries and burials from the fifth to the eighth centuries along the Tyne Valley, Northumberland.[29] This could imply that the communities of the North East, particularly those within the frontier region, may have had more affinity with the physical remains of a Roman and Romano-British past than with the earlier Bronze-age or even Neolithic landscape. At Binchester, for example, graves of the sixth, eighth and nineth centuries are believed to attest to the use of the fort as a Royal settlement or palace.[30] Some would argue for the continuity of a power centre, but perhaps we should think, too, in terms of enduring connections between communities and their past, real or mythic, articulated and expressed in physical terms through the medium of the landscape.[31]

Royal and elite funerary fashions

By the late sixth and seventh centuries, an increasing conformity can be detected in the ways in which the landscape was used for funerary purposes. An upsurge in monument reuse seems to occur in the seventh century, which, as discussed below, was not entirely confined to mortuary practices.[32] The use of prehistoric remains for burial, however, certainly became more frequent, and although an increasing number of elite graves, such as those discussed above within Wessex, were being cut into prehistoric monuments, the increase in practice was not the preserve of the emerging aristocratic classes.[33]

The elite graves of the late sixth to seventh centuries provide an interesting window on an emerging conformity in aristocratic funerary practices which seems to have been shared by elite groups irrespective of emerging kingdoms, boundaries and invented ethnicities. These rich, individualised burials, both male and female, exemplified at Sutton Hoo (Suffolk) and Prittlewell (Essex), display elements of experimentation – that is, explorations by elite groups of eclectic funerary rites that recycled Continental artefacts and materials, old and contemporary, and enmeshed them within visual displays within the arena of the grave.[34] However, on the basis of the grave forms and burial locations, an increasingly restrictive pattern can be argued. Barrow burial became normative, with the *tumuli* (reused or contemporary) positioned in places that were highly visible, overlooking or next to thoroughfares and routeways.[35] These attributes are suggestive of an intention by those designing and directing these funerary events to make prominent and visual statements, in particular within view of those moving through the landscape on major waterways and thoroughfares. This is underpinned by the extraordinary wealth of some assemblages, the interment of which, in itself, would have become a source of memory, myth and legend.[36]

In contrast to the variability of preferences apparent at a regional and sub-regional level in the fifth to seventh centuries with regard to ancient remains, and, indeed, the diversity of funerary traditions that emerge in the seventh century, a more conformist approach can be discerned in the ways in which elite burials are sited and ancient monuments are used as locales for burial. The types of monuments chosen narrow considerably, and the ways in which they are used seems extremely limited, confined by the mid-late seventh century to a rite involving centrally placed, isolated, secondary burials. The spread of this type of reuse is also surprising, stretching out far beyond any single kingdom or region. The prehistoric past, and in particular the prehistoric burial mounds within the landscape, seem, therefore, to have become increasingly the preserve of aristocratic and elite communities, a resource used by competing families in their attempts to extend their power and influence over increasingly larger tracts of land and contesting frontiers with other kingdoms. The burial mounds and ancient remains of the long distant past were no longer just locales of ancestral reverence and spiritual importance for communities in their need to define themselves and their place in the world. They were emerging as theatres for the elite, within which a whole range of activities could be sited to signal authority, ownership, legitimate descent, spiritual continuity and, ultimately, to display the power of a new, emergent generation of hereditary kings.

An explosion of recycling

In contrast to the relatively limited modes of using ancient monuments within elite funerary ritual, and, indeed, the apparently predominant funerary reuse of the ancient in the early Anglo-Saxon period, the recycling of the ancient within the landscape underwent an extraordinary diversification in the seventh and eighth centuries. Settlements and palaces continued to be, and perhaps were increasingly, located in the enceintes of ancient monuments, both prehistoric and Roman; churches were founded in, beside, and on prehistoric remains, as well as Roman monuments and ruins. Written documents begin to record assemblies at outdoor locations, sited within and on arenas of monuments, and even the first evidence for judicial execution are the graves and cemeteries of the executed felons located at prehistoric barrows.

Settlements and prehistoric remains

Despite the difficulties of establishing archaeological relationships with prehistoric remains, in several clear-cut instances settlements were sited within enceintes of ancient monuments with direct intention and design. The most well known and evocative example is Yeavering, Northumberland, where an early medieval settlement developed in the sixth and

2.4: Willy Howe, East Yorkshire Wolds. The chalk upland, intersected by numerous dales, or dry valleys, has seen successive human use over thousands of years. [*Author, 1999*].

seventh centuries in a landscape resonant with visual reminders of the past. At its height, the settlement at Yeavering emerged as a full-blown palace complex, documented as a place of assembly in the seventh century, and as a place of conversion.[37]

Such direct relationships between settlement and monument are often less certain. At New Wintles, Eynsham and Cowdery's Down, Hampshire, for instance, excavation has shown that the pre-existing remains had been entirely ploughed away by the Iron-age or Roman periods, whilst the pre-existing prehistoric and Roman field ditches and enclosures at Mucking seem to have structured the setting out of *grubenhäuser*, or 'grave houses'.[38] A clear-cut instance of prehistoric and Roman features influencing the morphology of an early Anglo-Saxon settlement would be Heslerton, Yorkshire, where a Romano-British sacred or ritual site, centred on natural springs, served to demarcate areas of early medieval settlement, and prehistoric monuments acted as arenas of burial. At Barrow Hills, Radley, a fifth- and sixth-century settlement seems to have been sited within a circuit of seven barrows with a *grübenhaus* positioned centrally to one prehistoric monument.

It is within the kingdom of Northumbria, and particularly in the area of the Tweed Valley, that settlements and palaces seem to have been topographically situated with the intention of using the prehistoric landscape, as well as the dramatic natural topography, as frames for seats of royal power. Yeavering and Milfield are documented palaces expressly situated in relation to the wide array of prehistoric remains surviving around them.[39] These northern royal sites may form part of a Northern tradition within which royal centres made use of ancient remains.[40] Whilst there are, without doubt, definite shared traditions and influences at play, the locations of royal palace and assembly sites in southern England have been underestimated. An assembly was held at the royal palace at Amesbury, Wiltshire, in AD 858, framed by a landscape full of mementoes of the prehistoric past. Not only was the site overlooked by the large Iron Age hill fort now known as Vespasian's Camp, but the roads and routes into the settlement were flanked by ancient prehistoric barrows and monuments [Fig. 2.4].

Ryan Lavelle has similarly drawn attention to the topographic position of the royal palace documented as a place of assembly at Grateley, Hampshire, arguing that the visual and physical prominence of the hill fort to those approaching the palace site along Roman routes would have served to impress on any royal assembly the antique pre-eminence of the power and presence of lordship.[41] One might even take such 'intentions' a step further: it is possible that palaces used as sites of royal assembly may have been chosen precisely for their history and prehistory, the surroundings intentionally chosen to enhance and emphasise the pre-eminence of the events taking place.

Churches and monuments

In the Conversion Period, the newly established monuments of the Christian church were often juxtaposed with the ancient remains of the past.[42] The recycling of Roman structures and the situating of churches within Roman ruins was relatively commonplace, and the use of Roman stone, ceramic and brick can be found in Northumbria, Kent, the South East, and elsewhere.[43] Such reuse has been explored in ideological terms as Anglo-Saxons rebuilding the ruins of Roman occupation. The Christian church was, itself, rebuilding Roman power and influence, in particular the power and influence of the Roman church. In many senses there was also a functional motivation, for ready-cut architectural stone fragments, transportable by river, would have presumably provided an invaluable resource to the masons constructing Monkwearmouth or Jarrow. What is interesting, however, is that alongside this use of the Roman past within the fabric of the Christian resurgence, prehistoric monuments were appropriated, too.

Churches juxtaposed with prehistoric monuments are a scarce but persistent feature of the English landscape, with the well-known examples of Avebury (Wiltshire), Knowlton (Dorset), and Stanton Drew (Somerset) exemplifying the use of large-scale prehistoric remains as frames for Christian activity. Neolithic, Bronze-age, and Iron-age earthwork enclosures, Bronze-age round barrows, standing stones and stone circles were all brought into use. Scholars have suggested these arrangements might reflect the Christianisation of pagan sacred sites.[44] The presence of a church within the henge at Knowlton (Dorset), and a similar arrangement at Paddock Hill, Thwing (East Yorkshire), raises the possibility that such monuments retained, or acquired, special meaning in the pre-Christian period, leading to the establishment of churches after the conversion. The relationship between megaliths and medieval churches at Awliscombe (Devon), Stanton Drew (Somerset), and Rudston (Yorkshire) could suggest that these monuments were also singled out because they were venerated in a pre-Christian era.[45]

The adoption of ancient enclosures, however, is almost certainly more common than the appropriation of megaliths, although less frequent than the use of Roman sites. Mid-Saxon minsters set within Iron-age hill forts are known at Hanbury (Worcestershire), Tetbury (Gloucestershire), Breedon-on-the-Hill (Leicestershire), and Aylesbury (Buckinghamshire). Such appropriations have been interpreted as actions representing a need for political or ritual emphasis to a new religious foundation.[46] Whereas, ancient barrows and megaliths were absorbed within the fabric and theatre of the church in a process of ritual continuity, the monument having accrued significance as a pagan religious focus, which in turn attracted Christian attention.[47] Morris argues that pre-Christian cult sites may have been regenerative – that is, ancient monuments which re-emerged as religious *foci* in the pre-Christian to early medieval period.[48] Perhaps the most convincing case study to have emerged through excavated evidence is the close association between an early foundation and Bronze Age barrows at Bampton (Oxfordshire). The Deanery, an early Norman two-storey chapel, overlies a Bronze-age ring-ditch, and the church, with a possible early Norman or Late Anglo-Saxon core, overlies a second smaller ring-ditch, whilst a third barrow is suggested on the south side of the church, within the churchyard. Three fragmentary, *in situ* burials overlay the inner lip of the smaller ring-ditch, with the earliest dated to *c*.AD 700.[49] Burial was thus taking place in relation to the ring-ditches before the first documented reference to the Christian community there in the 950s. In addition to the barrows, the twelfth-century chapel of St Andrew further to the east replaced some kind of pre-conquest post or obelisk, presumably referenced in the name Bampton, which contains the Old English element beam, 'post/ obelisk'.[50] To the west of the Deanery is a fourth potential cult-focus, the Lady Well, a medieval holy-well.

Not only were prehistoric remains brought into use as arenas for the new Christian monumentality and ceremony, but it is clear that very different motivations could prompt such appropriations. Minsters in hill forts and ancient enclosures might represent intentional ideological statements suggesting continuity and legitimation.[51] Whereas, the reuse of stone circles, standing stones and barrows may point to the active role of these types of ancient remains within the rites and rituals of a pre-Christian society. At the very least, the adoption of barrows, prehistoric or Anglo-Saxon, by the church is strongly suggestive of a need to appropriate and convert at least some perceived ancestral sites.

Assembly sites and prehistoric arenas

Within the documents of the post-Conversion era, the moot or assembly, is recorded from the seventh and eighth centuries as a locale of decision-making, administration and governance. In England, as well as other parts of Britain and Europe, the natural landscape, fording points and river crossings, islands, hills and spurs, and open land were all selected as locations for meetings – visible, natural features that provided obvious landmarks for assembly.[52] The reuse of ancient remains for assembly – that is, the surviving monumental remains of the pre-Medieval era – is an acknowledged theme in England and throughout northern Europe.[53] There is a need to make a clear distinction, however, between two different aspects of reuse. Individual monuments, especially mounds and sometimes megalithic remains as in Scutchmer Knob (Berkshire) or Enstone (Oxfordshire), were reused as places of assembly; however, on occasion assemblies were also situated within heartlands of ancient remains spanning a multitude of periods (e.g. Stanborough Hundred, Devon).

Prehistoric mounds were certainly used in England as the *foci* for moots. Meaney postulates they presented a platform for speakers.[54] The potential relationship between the presence of the ancient dead in the burial mound and the use of such features as places for discussion and decision-making links the English predilection for mounds with the Irish and Icelandic written evidence for a need to meet at places where the dead, the spirits, or the ancestors can also assemble.[55] Some meeting mounds are, however, disputed as ancient or even contemporary funerary markers. Adkins and Petchey have argued for Anglo-Saxon, man-made, non-sepulchral structures, based on an absence of evidence for burials, prehistoric or otherwise, in excavated assembly mounds.[56] It is certain that in other areas of Europe, notably Scandinavia and Ireland, new, purpose-built mounds were constructed as locations for assembly. However, these are often set or constructed within extensive landscapes of ancient remains to frame the location and performance of assembly.[57] Rather than a single reused feature, at these locations a complex of ancient remains could form a backdrop to the assembly, and in Ireland different monuments may have even provided differing *foci* for a range of administrative, ritual and royal activities in the Iron Age.[58]

The acquisition of power and authority by the reuse of ancient remains or, indeed, by the emulation or recreation of ancient rites, rituals and objects, is a long-held and acknowledged tradition not exclusive to the British Isles and certainly not confined to the early medieval period. A newly established place of assembly may well have been sited to take advantage of one or more ancient monuments in order to draw on the power of the past and the ancestors.[59] In these terms, the adoption of such monuments could be seen as exploitative, an intentional use to enhance the credibility of a new authority or power structure. Such choices may be evident at the palace sites of Yeavering, Northumberland, and Amesbury, Wiltshire, both considered to be places of assembly in the seventh and eighth centuries. On approaching the palace site, the hill fort of Yeavering Bell, as well as numerous barrows and several standing stones, would have appeared in view, framing both the visual experience and the approach of those arriving for a great assembly.[60] At Amesbury, too, those arriving for a great meeting would have travelled through a landscape full of prehistoric remains and gathered in the shadow of the Iron-age hill fort overlooking the Saxon palace.[61] These two examples depart from the established pattern, for the majority of assembly sites recorded seem to be in locations associated with natural features. When place-name evidence, or, more rarely, the location, itself, indicates or attests to an association between the assembly and a possible prehistoric monument, these features seem to be isolated, as in individual barrows, stones or enclosures.

It is striking that the royal assemblies of the seventh and eighth centuries took place on occasion in precisely the kind of archaic and ancient landscapes that seem to have functioned as similar frames for meetings in Ireland, Scotland and Sweden between the fourth to eleventh centuries. It is possible that, in order to manage a growing kingdom effectively, seats of power set intentionally within the ancient remains of the past offered an impressive means of governing, particularly when a king needed to move from place to place. By the late Anglo-Saxon period, royal power may still have been itinerant to an extent in that the king might over-winter or celebrate Easter at different venues, but the mode of governance had changed, with layers of administrators, or reeves, now taking account of the king's interests.[62] The modes of settling disputes were acted out at more local levels. Thus great ceremonial centres, or theatres of power, were not necessary for every assembly and moot. Perhaps palaces such as Yeavering acted as centres where all aspects of kingship were played out: administration, debate, justice, gift-giving, feasting, and the like. By the late Anglo-Saxon period, it has been argued that such functions had become dispersed within the administrative units of kingdoms.[63] It is possible, therefore, that more extensive 'landscapes of power' existed by the later period within which these dispersed functions of kingship, such as assembly sites, residences, and execution sites, were situated more in terms of communications, visibility and boundaries, and thus in terms of controlling and maintaining power in the landscape, rather than in proximity to and drawing upon the power of the ancient past.[64]

Theatres for judicial killing

Although early Anglo-Saxon communities rarely seem to have chosen megalithic sites as locales for burial, one of the most famous standing stone circles in England - Stonehenge - was used in the eighth century as a place of execution and deviant burial **[Fig. 2.5]**.[65] The grave was positioned in the south-east part of the henge, close to the south barrow. Radiocarbon analysis places the burial late in the eighth century. Although the burial was initially assumed to be a murder victim, it is now considered one of the earliest dated examples of an Anglo-Saxon execution burial. It is also possible that the secondary burial was not isolated – an extended inhumation was recovered in 1922 from the ring-ditch and discarded by the excavator who considered it modern, and a third more or less complete skeleton was discovered within the stone circle, on the central axis in 1926, again undated and now lost.[66]

During the eighth to eleventh centuries, just overlapping with the period when prehistoric monuments were used for unusually rich or prestigious isolated burials, a separate rite emerged involving the burial of bodies which showed signs of trauma and disrespectful treatment in proximity to prehistoric remains.[67] This form of funerary rite, epitomised by the Stonehenge

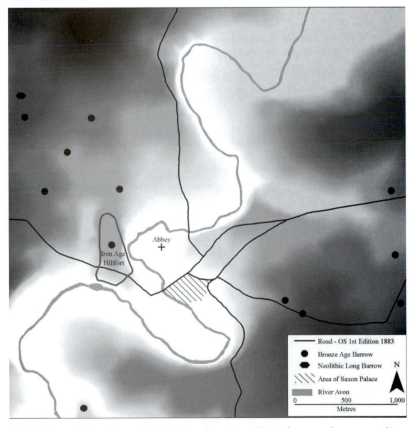

2.5: Map of Amesbury, Wiltshire, showing the palace and surrounding prehistoric remains, and the nearby location of Stonehenge. An assembly was held at the palace in AD 858, framed, as demonstrated here, by a landscape full of mementoes of the prehistoric past. [*A. Turner, 2009*].

burial, represents the initiation of a separate rite for the disposal of the bodies of criminals or social outcasts. Prior to research by Andrew Reynolds, the study of the Anglo-Saxon judicial system had largely been the preserve of constitutional historians.[68] Reynolds has examined the archaeological evidence for deviant burial in Anglo-Saxon England, demonstrating that in the early Anglo-Saxon period bodies treated in an unusual manner were nonetheless included within communal cemeteries, suggesting that, although the treatment of the corpse could indicate that the individual had contravened social norms, his or her body was not excluded from the community burial ground. In the late seventh and eighth centuries, separate cemeteries were established for the disposal of executed criminals and probably for other undesirables such as suicides and the unbaptised (for example, at Bran Ditch, Cambridgeshire, Sutton Hoo, Suffolk and Walkington Wold, Yorkshire). The pathology and body position of the burials in many cases implies the victims may have been brought alive to the site and were then hanged or decapitated before burial, showing that these locations were places of execution as well as locations for the interment of the executed.[69]

This archaeological evidence, in combination with poetic and prose texts and manuscript illuminations, points to a late Anglo-Saxon conception of landscape and particularly of the prehistoric monuments within it as places to be feared, that might be haunted or inhabited by monsters or demons. I have argued that this change in attitude took place within the Conversion Period, perhaps even in part stimulated by a need for the Church to encourage people to distance themselves from past beliefs and modes of burial.[70] These sites were, however, only components in what can be viewed as a more wholesale absorption and subtle re-working of the ancient landscape for elite and perhaps ecclesiastical purposes. As people arrived in the landscape around Amesbury, Wiltshire, for the royal assembly documented in AD 858, they would have approached a royal palace set at the great bend of a river, framed by the natural chalk land and overshadowed by the ancient hill fort of Vespasian's Camp, or Amesbyrig. Along the routes into Amesbury they would have passed the long and round barrows still visible today, and if approaching from the west across the chalk downs, they would have passed the remarkable monuments and remains of the Stonehenge environs. Within the proceedings of the royal court, felons may have been judged, tried, and found guilty. It is also possible that, in the days during the assembly, felons may have been taken from the court and palace, across the river, and along the route to Stonehenge, framed by the myriad of ancient standing stones and barrows of Salisbury plain, to the boundary of the hundred, where by the barrow next to the standing circle of stones from the heathen past, they were killed and buried for their crimes. The use of the ancient past to emphasize the 'heathen' crimes and damnation of the felon was possibly one aspect of a more wide-scale re-working of the landscape, where the ancient was drawn upon in a variety of ways to create theatres and arenas within which power was articulated, enacted, and legitimated in performances framed by the monuments of the past.

A final overview

This chapter offers a broad statement that reuse of ancient monuments in England in the early medieval period was more complex than generally assumed. The scholarly focus on the funerary use of prehistoric remains has, to an extent, obscured a fascinating array of evidence for the re-working of the ancient within differing arenas of secular and ecclesiastical power. Within the fifth to seventh centuries, the ways in which communities used prehistoric and, perhaps, Roman remains can be shown to vary from region to region, and possibly even from locality to locality. Communities manipulated the landscape to forge themselves new identities, drawing in the relics of the past to create physical narratives about their origins. A surge in recycling the past with an increasing intensity and diversity in practices can be seen within the seventh and eighth centuries, precisely the era we associate with kingdom formation and the rise of competing elite groups and lineages. The past, it seems, became less relevant to individual and community narratives linking people to place, and highly relevant in the re-working of elite identities as a means of demonstrating power, lineage, ownership and rights to their people and their competitors. Sites that had once represented, and perhaps continued to represent, places of spiritual importance, locales for the rites and rituals of burial, places of ancestral significance and power, were absorbed into the wider narratives being woven by newly emerging elite families. In middle and later Anglo-Saxon England, the ancient became a commodity used by church and state to signify legitimate authority, in some instances to create the appearance of continuity, in others to create a visual frame of ancestral acceptance, and, conversely, to remove connections with the pre-Christian past in order to show how those outside both law and church, the unrighteous and felons, could be condemned to an eternity of misery, trapped in the burial places of their damned and heathen ancestors.

3

'A Small Journey into the Country': William Stukeley and the Formal Landscapes of Avebury and Stonehenge

David Boyd Haycock

Dr William Stukeley needs little introduction to the historian of antiquarianism in early modern Britain. Born in Lincolnshire in 1687 and educated in medicine at Cambridge University, he moved to London in 1717, where he became a Fellow of the Royal Society, the first Secretary of the re-established Society of Antiquaries, and a scholarly gentleman with broad interests in Newtonian natural philosophy, botany, and theology. However, it was through his diligent and prolonged studies of the prehistoric Wiltshire antiquities of Stonehenge and Avebury during the summer months between 1717 and 1724 that Stukeley made his name and ensured his lasting importance as an early modern archaeologist.[1]

This chapter examines the cultural context behind Stukeley's antiquarian studies at these two sites in order to show how his gentlemanly interest in contemporary gardening and man-made landscapes helped to mould the way in which he perceived, planned and illustrated these prehistoric environments. This can be detected in the text of his two major publications, *Stonehenge* (1740) and *Abury* (1743), which reflect the express influence of contemporary, 'polite' fashions in early eighteenth-century landscape design. It is this interest that also, perhaps, explains why Stukeley was the first visitor to really incorporate the entire landscape that surrounds both Avebury and Stonehenge into his interpretations of the sites. It seems clear that his novel perception and complex interpretation of these environments was clearly influenced by conceptions of the large landscaped garden in the early eighteenth-century. This landscape was a place to be explored and experienced; it was a place in which any physical construction existed only as part of a broader conceptual frame. Stukeley's Stonehenge and Avebury are both clearly interpreted as man-made, and visually complex, landscapes, modelled with the explicit intention of acting upon and being interpreted by the knowledgeable spectator who – most importantly – interacted with the site and participated with its message, and who was thus more than a simple observer of it.

This influence can be further observed in the layout and design of the respective volumes' illustrations, and in Stukeley's interpretation of these ancient sites in terms of 'tours' and 'pictures'. Thus it would appear that Stukeley's novel recognition of the broader landscapes of 'Celtic' temples took its inspiration directly from contemporary tastes in English landscaping – that is, from the vogue for gardens such as Stowe, Stourhead and Studley Royal. Their long vistas and distant views of classical and Gothic temples would have been perambulated at leisure and were intended to stimulate philosophical, political or religious thoughts in the visitor's mind, actively participating in their self-conscious 'theatre'. The eighteenth-century landscape garden was all about participation and interpretation, being a landscape for human interaction, both physical and mental. It provided a space to be physically explored and discovered, while at the same time its meaning was being 'read'.

It must be emphasised, however, that Stukeley never explicitly expresses this relationship between the 'Celtic' religious landscape and the eighteenth-century landscaped garden. Nonetheless, it would appear that this way of seeing the landscape was so sufficiently entrenched within his world view as to have existed without his having been wholly conscious of it, as will be shown below.

'So that the country looks all like a garden': a passion for fashionable garden design

The late 1710s and the 1720s formed the period in which the classical architectural style of Palladianism arrived in Britain and began to become popular. It was during these years that Sir John Vanbrugh and William Kent planned and implemented their designs for the new houses at Castle Howard, Blenheim Palace and Stowe, with their ornamental gardens incorporating temples, rotundas, pyramids, obelisks and mausolea. Although his monographs on the sites did not appear until the 1740s, it was also during this period that Stukeley was making his tours of England and writing his extensive field notes at the 'Celtic' stone circles of Avebury and Stonehenge.

Stukeley was a keen gardener who travelled extensively around England, viewing and recording his comments on the natural and man-made landscapes he encountered. He also regularly employed garden analogies and metaphors in his natural history and antiquarian writings. In his manuscript notes for a journey made to Cambridgeshire in 1754, for example, Roman Britain became, 'a choice spot … well-planted with citys, stations, castles, colonys, municipia, like delicate shrubs, & plants, & flowers of plesure … but the Scots & Picts … never omitted an opportunity to ravage this garden; and serve themselves of the fruits of the labours of the Roman Britains.'[2] By assessing his interpretations of Avebury and Stonehenge in relation to this visual conceit it is possible to draw broader conclusions regarding both his theoretical interpretation of these antiquities (as historical objects rather than just as images), as well as of more current ideas of landscape design. The idea of viewing antiquities as an integral part of their landscapes has been explored in recent phenomenological interpretations of the prehistoric environment. Modern theoretical archaeologists such as Christopher Tilley have highlighted the way in which prehistoric peoples structured their monuments within the landscape, drawing upon various natural features in doing so.[3] A recent archaeological discussion of Stonehenge also notes the 'complex web of intervisibility' of the prehistoric landscape, and suggests that 'one of the major questions about the location and siting of the monument is whether it was sited to be seen from the surrounding landscape or as a point from which to view features and sites around it'.[4] As we see here, Stukeley was aware of such a relationship between the prehistoric archaeological site and its setting in the landscape at least as early as the 1720s. Thus, as he suggested in 1743, 'The whole temple of Abury may be consider'd as a picture, and it really is so. Therefore the authors wisely contriv'd, that a spectator should have an advantageous prospect of it, as he approach'd within view.'[5]

Stukeley was familiar with and interested in the latest fashions in garden design. He recorded with some pride that his late father, who had run a law firm at Holbeach, Lincolnshire, 'was instrumental in promoting more buildings all over the Town, & in planting Trees & quick sett hedges, so that the Country looks all like a Garden'.[6] He enjoyed visiting stately homes such as Chatsworth and Marlborough, and wrote about and illustrated them in his 1723 book, the *Itinerarium Curiosum: or, an Account of the Antiquitys and Remarkable Curiositys in Nature or Art, Observ'd in Travels thro' Great Brittan*. He also appreciated gardens such as that of the seventeenth-century poet Abraham Cowley, and his friend William Warburton was on close terms with Alexander Pope, another famous poet-gardener. Additionally, Stukeley created his own gardens, even building a hermitage in the garden at his home in Stamford, where he spent years landscaping. In the early 1740s he also advised his friend and patron the Duke of Montagu on the landscaping of his extensive country park at Boughton, Northamptonshire. Stukeley suggested the design of serpentine walks through the Duke's woods; he also produced plans for an ornamental gothic bridge and a mausoleum, though neither of these was ever built.[7]

Images of these houses and gardens appeared as prints in books, and as paintings. The most famous were those by the Dutch artists Johannes Kip and Leonard Knyff, who published a series of prints after their paintings in *Nouveau Théâtre de la Grande Bretagne* (1707). It was not just large-scale gardening, however, that was going on during the first decades of the eighteenth century. Contemporary publications such as John Lawrence's *The Clergy-Man's Recreation, shewing the Pleasure and Profit of the Art of Gardening* (1714), Stephen Switzer's *Iconographica Rustica*

(1718), and Joseph Addison's articles in the *Tatler* and *Spectator*, all illustrate and underline the developing popular interest in gardens and landscapes amongst the middling, professional classes as well as the aristocracy. As one newspaper reported in 1739, 'you hardly meet with any Body, who, after the first Compliments, does not inform you, that he is *in Mortar* and *moving of Earth*; the modest terms for Building and Gardening.'[8]

'Walking upon this delightful plain': promoting domestic tourism

Another important developing fashion of the day was domestic tourism. Better roads, maps and coach services had helped to improve land travel around England in the later seventeenth century, and tour guides of Britain were published in increasing numbers from 1700. These books, of which Daniel Defoe's regularly updated *A Tour through the whole Island of Great Britain* was one of the most popular, often included descriptions of stately homes and their gardens. This is a distinct feature of Stukeley's *Itinerarium Curiosum*, which included accounts of Boughton, Blenheim and Chatsworth. Since the seventeenth century, visitors of the right social standing had been accepted into the great houses of the local aristocracy where, if they did not actually meet the owner, a servant would escort them on a tour around the house and its garden. These properties hence served as visible signs of their owner's wealth, taste and status, and this 'conspicuous consumption' was part of the motivation and success behind Kip and Knyff's popular paintings and prints. As Stephen Daniels has observed, their *Nouveau Théâtre de la Grande Bretagne* also 'showed how extensively houses had been rebuilt and grounds extended and newly fashioned, and it acted as a pattern book for further improvements'.[9]

Stukeley was particularly impressed by the new gardens at Blenheim Palace, and the designer's use of a ha-ha. He wrote:

> The garden is a large plot of ground taken out of the park and may still be said to be part of it. [It is] well contriv'd by sinking the outer-wall into a foss, to give one a view quite round and take off the odious appearance of confinement and imitation to the eye, and which quite spoils the pleasur and intention of a garden. [W]ithin, it's well adorn'd with walks, greens, espaliers and visto's to divers remarkable objects that offer themselves in the circumjacent country.[10]

Stukeley had suggested that the prints in his *Itinerarium Curiosum*, 'besides their use in illustrating the discourses, are rang'd in such a manner as to become an index of enquirys for those that travel, or for a British antiquary … The whole is to invite gentlemen and others in the country, to make researches of this nature, and to acquaint the world with them.'[11] Part of the purpose of the *Itinerarium* was to highlight the antiquities

3.1: William Stukeley, 'A Prospect from Abury Steeple', showing part of the village with Windmill Hill and Silbury Hill in the distance; from *Abury* (1743). Stukeley was always keen to find high positions that would give him a clear view of the remains of the prehistoric landscape. Silbury Hill provided one obvious viewpoint; the tower of Avebury's medieval church afforded another. [*Private collection*]

of England in an effort to encourage his countrymen to believe that they did not have to travel abroad in order to make a classical Grand Tour. Stukeley never took the Grand Tour himself, observing that, 'It was ever my opinion that a more intimate knowledg of Brittan more becomes us, is more useful and as worthy a part of education for our young nobility and gentry as the view of any transmarin parts'.[12] Though in part disingenuous – he would have loved to have visited Rome – this sentiment recurred throughout his writings, and both *Stonehenge* and *Abury* may be considered part of a concerted programme to encourage domestic tourism and a better understanding of British antiquities.

In both *Abury* and *Stonehenge*, Stukeley styled himself as tour guide, observer and interpreter. His reader is treated as if he were perambulating the sites in person, and the illustrations to both books are tailored to support this written conceit. In the text to Stonehenge, the reader is invited into the monument as if actually there in person: 'it is time to draw toward the sacred pile', Stukeley writes, 'and fancy ourselves walking upon this delightful plain'.[13] This description extends in its remarkable detail: 'Every step you take upon the smooth carpet, (literally) your nose is saluted with the most fragrant smell of *Serpillum,* and *apium*, which … composes the softest and most verdant turf, extremely easy to walk on, and which rises as with a spring, under ones feet.'[14] In his treatment of Avebury, Stukeley pins his written description in his book to the accompanying plates, proposing to 'take the reader [on] a fine tour along with me quite round the verge of the temple.'[15] The prehistoric bank and ditch around Avebury becomes, in his words, 'an agreeable terrace-walk round the town, with a pleasant view upon sometimes corn-fields, sometimes heath … Part of this pleasant prospect I have given in plate XXIII, as seen from Abury church-steeple' **[Fig. 3.1]**.[16]

Stukeley's descriptive style appealed to writers of the short guides to Stonehenge that were sold at Bath and Salisbury in the years following the publication of his book in 1740. The anonymous authors of *A Concise Account of Stonehenge, for the use of Travellers* (c.1750) and *A Description of Stonehenge, Abiry &c. in Wiltshire* (1776) both happily plagiarized his descriptions of the monuments; but this simply served to further disseminate Stukeley's proto-Romantic interpretation and vision of the prehistoric landscape. His account of Avebury also regularly pointed out the opportunities for views and prospects: he noted, for example, that from Overton Hill, 'The view here is extensive and beautiful', or that from Runway Hill we 'contemplate the most agreeable prospect'. He concluded with the remark that he had 'observed many of these studied opportunities in this work, of introducing the ground and prospects, to render it more picture like'.[17] John Smith, who published a work on Stonehenge in 1771, accurately remarked in passing that Stukeley's monograph on that monument 'gives many beautiful and just descriptions of the country that surrounds this temple'.[18] The many works about Avebury published in the years following 1740 clearly indicate its growing popularity as a tourist spot, with short guidebooks fulfilling an explanatory function similar to those published for visitors to the houses and gardens at Stowe and Blenheim.[19]

'A small part of the whole': monuments pictured in their landscape

None, however, were as well illustrated as Stukeley's lavish monograph. These images, as we have seen, were key to the text and undoubtedly reflected Stukeley's personal interest in, and familiarity with, the printed image.[20] (The Society of Antiquaries was already making a name for itself as a publisher of prints, and Stukeley's friends there included the artists Samuel and Nathaniel Buck and George Vertue, the Society's official engraver.) Catherine Levesque has shown how Dutch printmakers of the seventeenth century conformed to descriptive conventions whereby 'as in numerous map collections, descriptive geographies, and poetic sequences, landscape depiction is presented to the reader or spectator as part of an encompassing journey theme'.[21] To paraphrase Levesque, by presenting or inviting the reader of prints and images 'to enter into and proceed through the texts or images', and by placing him in the role of traveller or spectator, the objectivity and truthfulness of knowledge observed experientially was stressed, thus ensuring the 'active participation' of the observer 'in extracting information'.[22] As a work of travel literature, it

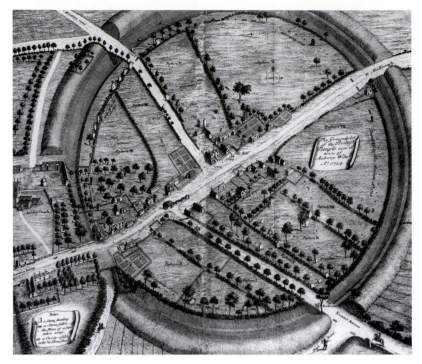

3.2: Elisha Kirkhall, print after a drawing by William Stukeley, *The Groundplot of the Brittish Temple now the town of Avbury Wilts* (1724), from *Abury* (1743). Stukeley made numerous versions of this aerial view of Avebury as it looked during his antiquarian visits in the late 1710s and early 1720s. The final version formed a spectacular frontispiece to his book, and provided a record that continues to be of use to modern archaeologists. [*Private collection*]

was appropriate for Stukeley's printed images (based on his own original sketches) to follow the same convention in the *Itinerarium*. This journey, or tour, style was used to greater success in his descriptions and illustrations to *Stonehenge* and *Abury*. In keeping with the text, the plates to both books gradually draw the reader into the landscape of the 'temples'. The first few prints depicted the roads leading to the sites and the more distant views as one gradually approached. These were followed by detailed, close prospects from various compass points and then, finally, again more distant views – for example, of the avenues, surrounding features, and other details as one drew away.

These images, which were generally described either as 'views' or 'prospects', were clearly intended to guide the reader around the whole landscape of the site. Stukeley's engraved frontispiece to *Abury* even offered a panoramic, three-dimensional bird's-eye view of the site, as if the viewer were literally hovering a couple of hundred feet above the modern village of Avebury **[Fig. 3.2]**. This is a most dramatic and imaginative introduction to the work, and one to which Stukeley devoted considerable care and attention in the various versions and amendments he made between 1721 and 1724.[23] It provided a detailed and attractive plan for the reader unable to actually visit the site in person. Together with the information of their captions and the accompanying text, Stukeley's illustrated books offered a

3.3: J.B. Rigaud and B. Baron, 'View from the Brick Temple', from Sarah Bridgeman's *General Plan of the Woods, Park and Garden of Stowe, the Seat of the Right Honorable, the Lord Viscount Cobham, with Several Perspective Views in the Gardens* (1739). Richard Temple, Viscount Cobham, started work on re-landscaping his gardens at Stowe in 1711. The royal gardener, Charles Bridgeman, and the architects Sir John Vanbrugh and then James Gibbs, assisted him. This landscape is thus exactly contemporary with Stukeley's interpretations of Druid temples, and it reflects similar concepts in its design. [*The British Museum*]

perception of the whole context of the 'Celtic' landscape that easily outrivals even modern guidebooks.

More importantly, of all the commentators on Stonehenge, Stukeley was the first really to step away from the stones themselves in both his written and his visual descriptions. He even included views from Stonehenge, with the viewer's back to the monument itself – an apparently original innovation for an antiquarian image. Again, this emphasised the idea that Stonehenge was a point to look from as well as to be looked at – something that even the modern visitor still fails to realise. We may see this same idea expressed in the context of the eighteenth-century garden; for example, in Sarah Bridgeman's 'View from the Brick Temple', from her *Views of Stowe* (1739), it is the view rather than the structure that is significant in the printed image **[Fig. 3.3]**. (Though it may be noted that the view still focuses on a distant object – in this case a stone obelisk – and it is interesting to compare this view with Stukeley's 'A direct View of Stonehenge from the union of the two Avenues' **[Fig. 3.4]** and 'Prospect from Bushbarrow' **[Fig. 3.5]**.)[24] Like Stukeley's *Stonehenge* and *Abury*, Bridgeman's collection of fifteen printed views, signed by Jaques Rigaud and 'Baron', also adopted the plan of a tour around the grounds which began with the first view of the house and the arrival of a visitor's coach, followed by views in the garden and park becoming increasingly distant from the house.

The incorporation of spectator and landscape into the whole picture of 'Celtic' temples was therefore an important one,

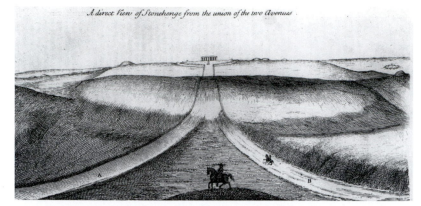

3.4: William Stukeley, 'A direct View from the union of the two Avenues', from *Stonehenge* (1740). Stukeley was the first person to identify the earthwork 'avenue' at Stonehenge: this image clearly shows how he interpreted prehistoric monuments as features in the landscape that were to be approached and viewed from sometimes a considerable distance. [*Private collection*]

and, as Stukeley noted, it was a relationship that had not really been recognised before, though it was frequently observed in his own writings. Thus at Stonehenge, he was the earliest observer really to draw all of the surrounding countryside into his interpretation of the site, even beyond the barrows and ancient hill-fort that had led earlier commentators to believe that Stonehenge commemorated an ancient battle ground. In remarking, for example, upon the two-mile earth 'cursus' that neighbours Stonehenge, which he believed had been the site of ancient chariot races, Stukeley rightly commented: 'This likewise is a new unobserv'd curiosity belonging to this work, and very much enlarges the idea we ought to entertain, of the magnificence and prodigious extent of the thing'.[25] Whilst modern archaeologists consider the purpose and function of the prehistoric avenue and cursus enigmatic and open to speculation, Stukeley is credited as the first person to recognise and comment on them.[26]

Through his discovery of the complex landscaping of the site at Avebury, Stukeley observed: 'The temple which we have hitherto been describing, considerable indeed as it really is, in itself; yet now appears as a small part of the whole.' He then explains that he will 'describe all these parts separately, to render them more intelligible: and then show their connection, and what relation they have, to one another, as well as I can. But it is not easy', he then adds, 'to enter at once, into the exceeding greatness of thought, which these people had, who founded it; bringing in all the adjacent country, the whole of nature hereabouts, to contribute it part to the work'.[27]

'This lovely prospect may your busy mind': gardens for private meditation and reflection

It appears that this new perception of the landscaped site was clearly influenced by conceptions of the early eighteenth-century landscape garden, whereby any physical construction existed only as part of a broader conceptual framework or pattern. To Stukeley, it is clear that Stonehenge and Avebury were to be interpreted as man-made landscapes, modelled with the intention of being interpreted by the knowledgeable spectator, who interacted with the site. Therefore, the spectator was more than simply an observer. This point is emphasised by the staffage figures added to Stukeley's (and, notably, Bridgeman's) images. As John Dixon Hunt has observed, influenced by Italian gardens, early eighteenth-century English gardeners, 'saw their designs in terms of the theater' and that the fabricated scenes of gardens like Stowe and Rousham 'were unthinkable except as stages for human action'.[28] As Stukeley observed in his field notes at Avebury, this site was 'a fine scituation … for you descend to it from on all sides, from hills which overlook it two or three miles distant, so that it is a sort of large Theater, admirably well chosen for the magnificent purpose'.[29] The intervening centuries might have diminished the quality of this landscaped theatre, and the memory of its original meaning might have been lost; but Stukeley prided himself on his 'rediscovery' of it, and applied his skill and diligence in revealing and restoring it to his contemporaries, who were quite accustomed to this idea of the garden as a place of potentially complex cultural meaning.

His perception of his readers touring and interpreting the site also appears to have been related to the growing popularisation in the eighteenth century of the circuit walk. As already discussed, in this period public and private gardens were becoming increasingly fashionable as a mode of pleasure and social entertainment amongst the middling and upper classes. Public landscaped walks such as St James's Park had first developed in London in the mid-seventeenth century, and were followed by examples at Tunbridge Wells, Exeter, and at some

3.5: William Stukeley, 'Prospect from Bushbarrow', from *Stonehenge* (1740). Again, in this image Stukeley reveals the prehistoric landscape as both prospect and stage. The trees were presumably a recent addition, and link the prehistoric landscape neatly into eighteenth-century ideas of garden design. [*Private collection*]

Oxford and Cambridge colleges. By the mid-eighteenth century many other urban centres, spas and resorts likewise boasted commercial pleasure gardens, following the lead of Vauxhall and Kensington Gardens in London. It is in this context, then, that we can best understand Stukeley's suggestion that, 'If it be not impertinent, a small journey into country, at leisure' to visit Avebury, would be a useful diversion for the 'pleasure, health & gratification of the publick'.[30] For, as Hunt has argued, the English landscaped garden 'asked to be explored, its surprises and unsuspected corners to be discovered on foot'.[31] Furthermore, Hunt also notes how 'the "action" of the garden's painting [i.e. its design] is supplied by the visitor, stimulated by the scene and its allusions; the garden visitor becomes a protagonist by his act of reading these devices'. That is, 'verbal commentary was needed not only to amplify the visual but to make explicit other literary sources of a body of literary theory'.[32]

Max Schulz has also shown how the 'practice of organizing the eighteenth-century garden as a circuit tour or a rural paradise' was already well defined by the early part of the century.[33] He suggests that such a circuit design at gardens like Stowe, Stourhead, Rousham and Chatsworth allowed the visitor to follow 'a paradigmatic action which lent itself to a secularized and (if you will) faintly frivolous parody of the soul's circuitous passage in this world from its earthly to heavenly home'.[34] Given Stukeley's interpretation of the Avebury complex as a religious symbol for the Druidic conception of the Trinitarian deity, this analogy is interesting. In addition to the comparison with journeying or touring around the Avebury site, Stukeley developed the idea that Avebury was a 'picture' landscape that would have been read by its 'Celtic' builders and users like an 'hieroglyphic … made in stonework'.[35] As the Druids had built their landscape complex to be read, so Stukeley provided the interpretative text to accompany and decipher it. Although his interpretation may appear eccentric today, many readers of his books were impressed by it. Thus in the summer of 1744 the Quaker physician John Fothergill, who owned copies of both Abury and Stonehenge, travelled from London on a trip to Bath. As he wrote and explained to a friend after his brief tour around the site:

> I just took a transient view of the remains of the celebrated ancient temple at Avebury on Marlborough Downs, which, if it was what Dr Stukeley says it was, has been a most astonishing performance, and by what appears it seems not unlikely.[36]

This association between the eighteenth-century man-made rural and urban landscapes and the landscape of the 'Celtic' temples may be illustrated by the poem *The Country Seat*, written in the late 1720s by Stukeley's friend Sir John Clerk of Penicuik. John Dixon Hunt has described Clerk, a Scottish baronet who had travelled widely in Italy, as 'among the leaders of the landscape movement' in eighteenth-century Britain.[37] In his poem Clerk offered verse advice and instruction for more perfectly situating a country seat. He was particularly concerned with the relationship between house and garden, but his text tellingly illustrates the observations Stukeley made on the religious design of the temples at Stonehenge and Avebury:

> Come now ye rural deities and show
> What form will beautify the neighb'ring Plains.
> The verdant Banks, and meads, that so they may
> With never fading Charms allure our Eyes.
> Stretch out the Lines of every Avenue
> With spreading trees in many stately Rowes …[38]

To the educated eighteenth-century observer who had read John Locke and Joseph Addison, garden landscapes with their temples and hieroglyphs and inscriptions were not simply static vistas to be enjoyed solely for their beauty and design. Rather, like the gardens of Stowe with their Elysian Fields, Temples of Ancient and Modern Virtues and British Worthies, they were expected to inspire a meditative, reflective or associative response.[39]

Michael Charlesworth has suggested that the eighteenth-century garden also had a clear sacred and political character, and that the example of Stukeley's private gardens with their hermitages and Druidic temples 'suggests that the sacred idea was a great floating signifier for the eighteenth century, in which individuals could lodge the signified of their choice'.[40] Charlesworth, though, does not fully extend upon the implications of this suggestion for Stukeley's writings on Celtic temples. To illustrate the point further, we can return to Sir John Clerk's poem, and his perception of the private, religious purpose of the avenue in the landscape:

> That Avenue will most delight the Sight
> That on some beauteous object shapes its way.
> Such is a temple, whose high towering Spire
> Divides the hov'ring Clouds, and seems to be
> A lofty Pillar to support the Heavens.
> This lovely Prospect may your busy mind
> With useful Speculation entertain;
> Consider first, that all you do enjoy
> Is owing to the God, whose awfull Shrine
> Those sacred walks enclose, and where
> With thankful Heart you often should resort.
> And if that here your Fathers lye entombed,
> Your stately house and pleasant fields at last,
> With other charms of Life you must forgo,
> And this way travel to the shades below.[41]

'A temple of the druids': the clergyman in his sacred grove

Stukeley was ordained as an Anglican clergyman in 1728, and it comes as no surprise, therefore, to encounter the presence of the divine in his 'Celtic gardens'. In Stukeley's interpretation, at Avebury 'fountains[,] Rivers & Mountains are introduced as scemically, to make an sepulchre'.[42] Similarly he wrote of Stonehenge that:

> it must be own'd, that they who had a notion, that it was an unworthy thing, to pretend to confine the deity in room and space, could not easily invent a grander design than this, for sacred purposes: nor execute it a grander manner. Here space is mark'd out and defin'd: but with utmost freedom and openness … Here the variety and harmony … presents itself continually new. [E]very step we take, with opening and closing light, art and nature make a composition of their highest gusto, create a pleasing astonishment, very apposite to sacred places.[43]

Gardens have a long-standing tradition as places of thought and meditation, from Eden onwards. For many in the seventeenth and early eighteenth centuries, the Civil War poet and scholar, Abraham Cowley, served as a paradigm for the desire to withdraw from politics and pursue a philosophic life in the garden. This was likewise much the case for John Aislabie, Chancellor of the Exchequer during the South Sea Bubble crisis, who retreated to his estates near Ripon in North Yorkshire following that financial scandal in 1720 and worked there on remodelling his gardens at Studley Royal. Aislabie's avenue of trees, aligned with the distant towers of Ripon's medieval Minster, clearly evinced a patriotic, religious sentiment; it was also plainly analogous with Stukeley's image of the cursus sited on Stonehenge, and the advice given in Sir John Clerk's poem.

For Stukeley, Celtic temples served, in their present form, to illustrate the temporality of man's existence, but in their original form would have served to draw the ancient viewer's thoughts up to the contemplation of the divine. Furthermore, Stukeley's Druids were not mere idolatrous pagan priests, but rather proto-Christians who had brought the true faith to Britain long before the Roman mission of St Augustine. There, according to a manuscript written some time in the 1720s:

> In Bryttish Oak Groves, our old Naturalists Poets & Priests the Druids inculcated the Precepts of Religion, Studyd the Celestial Sciences, reasond of Fate, Providence, Freewill, the Immortality of the Soul, & in all History sacred or profane the Groves were places more immediately consecrate to the attention of the Supreme Being …[44]

It is by now apparent that, in Stukeley's opinion, Celtic monuments had an aesthetic appeal associated both with their religious function and their location. This fact was recognised by at least one of his contemporaries, a Charles Gray, who wrote to Stukeley from Colchester on 28 July 1749. Remarking upon several tumuli thereabouts, Gray observed how some of them were 'in such fine situations as would please your taste, *and prove the taste of those who built them*' [my emphasis].[45]

Furthermore, as well as being apparently motivated to encourage good taste in the eighteenth-century garden, Stukeley's publications in turn inspired others in their own

3.6: Portrait of Dr William Stukeley, FRS, attributed to Richard Collins, *c*.1726-9, oil on canvas. By 1728 Stukeley had begun landscaping a circle of trees in the grounds of his vicarage at Grantham into what he called 'a temple of the druids'. This portrait may well show us a glimpse into that garden, on which he worked so hard, and of which he was justifiably proud. [*The Society of Antiquaries of London*]

construction of physical, landscaped 'temples'. By 1728 Stukeley had already begun landscaping a circle of trees in his own garden at Grantham into 'a temple of the druids', at the centre of which, he informed his friend and fellow antiquary Samuel Gale, there was 'an ancient apple tree overgrown with sacred mistletoe; round it another concentric circle of 50 foot diameter made of pyramidial greens … [which] are in imitation of the inner circle of Stonehenge'.[46] It was possibly standing in front of this garden that he had his portrait painted [Fig. 3.6]. At the grand country house at Wilton, meanwhile, Stukeley's friend and patron the Earl of Pembroke had a 'fine and costly model of Stonehenge' set up in the garden, where, Stukeley told him, 'it shines amidst the splendours of *Inigo Jones's* architecture'.[47] Stukeley was well aware that, in the early seventeenth century, Jones had confidently identified Stonehenge as a Roman construction, so its juxtaposition at Wilton would no doubt have amused him.[48]

The potential criticism that the Druids were known, according to classical sources such as Julius Caesar, to have worshipped in groves and not stone circles posed no problem for Stukeley, since stones and trees were intricately linked in his theory of the origin of architecture. He believed that the Druid order had been established by Abraham, and that in Britain the Druids had planted groves of trees 'in regard to their great founder'.[49] As he famously observed of Gloucester cathedral in the *Itinerarium Curiosum*, its gothic design was 'the best manner of building, because the idea of it is taken from a walk of trees, whose branching heads are curiously imitated by the roof'.[50] Additionally, as the circular stone temples of Stonehenge and Avebury had developed out of the original circular motif of the wooded grove, so likewise the pillared 'Forum & Avenues of Athens & Rome' had been 'inspired by rows of trees, providing shade, & also the cloisters of religious houses'.[51] Indeed, twentieth-century archaeological excavations at Stonehenge indicate that the final stone monument we know today was preceded in earlier phases by a complicated construction made of wooden posts.

The idea that trees could be used to build sacred structures can be illustrated by Gilbert West's poem on Stowe of 1736, where he described how 'Batavian Poplars here in ranks ascend: /Like some high Temples arching Isles extend.'[52] Such ideas directly inspired a young Yorkshire landowner named Mr Crow. In a letter to Stukeley of January 1743-4, Roger Gale wrote informing him of how Mr. Crow

> has been much studying your Abury, & has begun a plantation of elm trees upon that plan. There will be two winding avenues to the house … the head of the snake will be a rising tumulus, planted with several rows of trees, one above another, among which will rise an obelisk of stone for the eye.[53]

In another curious interpretation by a reader of Stukeley's book, Stukeley records how the Duke of Montagu, who in the 1730s had projected some seventy miles of elm avenues at Boughton, subsequently 'honor'd all the greatest oaks in his beautiful Chases, with the names of Druids, stampt in lead, and fastened to the trees'.[54] When, on top of Silbury Hill, Stukeley unearthed the ashes of what he believed to be the ancient king who had ordered the building of Avebury, the digging had not been for speculative archaeological purposes, but 'in order to plant trees for a visto'.[55] These examples clearly illustrate the relationship between ancient temples and the eighteenth-century garden.

Conclusion

Finally, it has been suggested that John Wood's Grand Circus at Bath, an architectural first, was inspired by Stonehenge, and thus provided an appropriate ornament for a town that Wood considered to be the ancient metropolitan seat of the British Druids. We may note here that Stuart Piggott believed that the influence of Stonehenge on Wood's design for the Circus had, before his own observation, 'not hitherto' been suggested.[56] In fact, an anonymously published tract on Stonehenge of 1776 made this connection by quoting from the text on Lord Burlington's collection of Inigo Jones's drawings: 'And I believe it will scarce be doubted that Mr. [Wood], the architect of Bath, took from this, our oval [at Stonehenge], the plan of the beautiful *Circus* at the end of Gay-street, which is one great ornament of that city.'[57]

As the century progressed, and as James Macpherson's fabricated ancient Scottish poems *Ossian* and *Fingal* fanned the flames of Gothic revival and the vogue for all things Druidic, the idea of constructing Celtic monuments in the landscape became more inventive.[58] The most extravagant of these must be the example of General Henry Conway, the governor of Jersey. When in 1785 a small stone circle was discovered on the island near St Helier, the townsfolk donated it as a gift to Conway, who removed it to adorn his garden at Park Place in Berkshire. According to Conway's cousin, Horace Walpole, the circle was known as 'little Master Stonehenge', and Walpole observed in a letter of 1781 how 'Dr. Stukeley will burst his crements to offer mistletoe in your Temple'.[59] It appears that we may intimately link the popular later eighteenth-century Gothic and 'Druidic' landscape with the name of William Stukeley in a way that has not been previously considered.

4

Thomas Rickman's Handbook of Gothic Architecture and the Taxonomic Classification of the Past

Megan Aldrich

Thomas Rickman, FSA (1776-1841), the Gothic Revival architect and scholar of British medieval architecture, pursued a multi-faceted career **[Fig. 4.1]**. Born into a large Quaker family in Sussex, he initially trained with his father, an apothecary and surgeon, before leaving to become a corn factor in London in 1803.[1] By 1807 this business had failed, leaving him with debts he was eventually able to clear after relocating to Liverpool, a seaport then beginning its period of rapid growth and prosperity. There Rickman forged a successful career as an accountant and laid the foundations of a later, highly successful career as a self-taught antiquarian scholar and architect. He produced a key architectural text which reflected the intellectual climate of the Enlightenment and its associated scientific discoveries, a climate in which he was fully immersed during his early years in Liverpool.[2] This 'text-book for the architectural student', as he described it, first appeared in 1817 under the title, *An Attempt to Discriminate the Styles of English Architecture*. There were six subsequent editions, the last in 1881, ensuring it remained a classic text on the subject of medieval architecture throughout the nineteenth century.

'An Attempt to Discriminate the Styles of English Architecture'

An Attempt was nothing less than the first accurate account of the development of medieval architecture in the British Isles, and it set out Rickman's simple and accessible system of nomenclature that is still in use today – namely, Norman (for English Romanesque), Early English Gothic, Decorated Gothic, and Perpendicular Gothic. Although only the last term is recognised as original to Rickman,[3] nonetheless he selected this terminology carefully from a confusing mass of conflicting information on the subject, and defined each term on the basis of easily observed visual characteristics.

His system quickly became canonical. It is important to appreciate the somewhat chaotic state of knowledge of medieval architecture before the advent of Rickman's book. Horace Walpole had been deeply interested in the development of Gothic architecture and had encouraged its investigation. He famously resigned from the Society of Antiquaries in the 1730s over what

4.1: Portrait sketch in pencil of Thomas Rickman by Charles Barber, c. 1819. Rickman was described by his contemporaries as short and stoutly built, with a very lively, congenial personality. His characteristic broad-brimmed hat and ever-present umbrella have been captured in this affectionate sketch by his friend Barber. [*The Liverpool Athenaeum/Author*]

he saw as the Society's excessive emphasis on Roman Britain at the expense of investigation into the medieval period. Walpole must have been deeply sympathetic to the view expressed in 1754 by William Borlase, in *Observations on the Antiquities of Cornwall*, to the effect that Grand Tourists 'return captivated with the Medals, Statues, Pictures, and Architecture, of Greece and Italy', but that interest in the non-Roman antiquities of Britain was limited. Walpole also was in part reacting to theories like that of Christopher Wren, who proposed that the pointed arch was Saracenic, derived from the Middle East.[4] As late as 1797, James Hall, the enthusiastic amateur, had a small wicker cathedral built in his garden in order to test his theory that the Gothic originated from the woodland architecture of the Druids — he had doubtless derived misguided inspiration from reading William Stukeley on the subject.[5]

To crack the code of Gothic, therefore, was one of the key challenges facing the scholarly architectural world of the later eighteenth and early nineteenth centuries. In order to solve this tantalising puzzle, scholars and antiquaries attempted to unravel the history and development of Gothic architecture by studying the layers of historical documentation in cathedral libraries, most of it in Latin, and by examining commemorative monuments and reading their (Latin) inscriptions. Such evidence emphasised the histories of the great churchmen and their deeds, rather than architectural developments. Although Quaker sons and daughters could attend special 'Latin schools', provided their parents could afford the fees, Thomas Rickman had not received a classical education. The fact that he was unable to read this layer of Latin literature, combined with his quasi-scientific background, led him intellectually towards an empirical and overwhelmingly practical approach to his research.[6] Through examining minutely the properties of different stones and other building materials within their geographical and topographical context, and through constructing ornamental vocabularies from the close visual observation of architectural details, Rickman could begin to classify this minute detail into types. From then, by means of some skilful deductive reasoning, he developed his chronology of medieval architectural styles.

His method of approach was more or less in place by 1812, when he wrote an account of the varied periods of medieval architecture visible in the fabric of Chester Cathedral. Rickman had, at this point, been living in Liverpool for nearly five years, during which time he worked as an accountant, latterly for the Case brothers. Thomas and J. Ashton Case were local worthies in Liverpool who were clearly sympathetic to Rickman's passion for Gothic architecture. They allowed him to take study leave in which to carry out sketching excursions to architectural monuments. The hundreds of observational drawings of architectural features he made in the course of these excursions enabled him to develop, eventually, his chronology of Gothic, and the walled, medieval town of Chester became a favourite weekend retreat for Thomas Rickman. He had forged a close friendship with a client of the Case firm, the Chester ironfounder, George Harrison. Rickman met Harrison in 1808 while in the grip of a deep depression resulting from the death of his first wife. Harrison, too, had been widowed early, and his brother was an open-minded Anglican clergyman who greatly enjoyed his discussions with the Quaker accountant from Liverpool. Rickman returned on numerous occasions to stay as a guest of the Harrison family and to study Chester Cathedral and its precinct. On occasion he attended Anglican services there, including midnight mass on Christmas Eve. He must have made a striking addition to the congregation in his 'plain Quaker' dress.[7] By June of 1811 Rickman had delineated a list of thirty ornamental features by which he could analyse buildings, as given in his diaries for this period. After an initial look at the surrounding towns, parishes, trees, population, and natural phenomena of the area, Rickman then began with features such as steeples, naves, aisles, transepts, windows, arches, fonts, and monuments, before ending with a final assignation of 'style'. His professional background as an accountant was undoubtedly useful in allowing him to develop his systems for organising the architectural data he collected in the field.

Rickman was already, in his diaries for 1811, using the stylistic terminology he went on to publish in *An Attempt*.[8] He used ornamental details such as the shapes of windows and their tracery (if any), or the decoration used on mouldings and capitals, as a means for identification and classification. Rickman certainly used contextual information as another tool to assist him in dating buildings, particularly when he was trying to work out the evolution of a structure over time. He was acutely aware that medieval buildings were rarely constructed in one architectural period, as was glaringly evident at Chester Cathedral, which ranged from Norman to Perpendicular. The sensitivity Rickman displayed in appreciating the progressive construction and reconstruction of medieval architecture over often quite lengthy periods of time sets him apart from his contemporaries.

'Founder of the modern science of Gothic Architecture'

Rickman's account of Chester Cathedral, written in 1812, was published posthumously in 1864 by Canon Blomfield, who remarked in his Introductory Memoir that:

> The name of Thomas Rickman is familiar to every student of Gothic Architecture, as the author of the clearest and most comprehensive text book on the subject. He was the first to elucidate the true characteristics of Gothic architecture, and reduce them to a simple and intelligible system. The nomenclature which is now universally received, was first brought into use by him.[9]

Canon Blomfield goes on to say that Rickman's history of Chester Cathedral, 'affords a valuable specimen of the accuracy of this observation, and the clearness [*sic*] of his discriminative judgment . . . he became the . . . founder of the modern science of Gothic Architecture.'[10] That Blomfield should speak of the science of Gothic is indicative of the intellectual climate in which Rickman was working. Rickman, too, saw himself as something of a scientist when investigating medieval architecture, and his diaries make it clear that his method was borrowed directly from the natural sciences. In July 1810, for example, Rickman paid an evening visit to Thomas Binns, a fellow Quaker with antiquarian and architectural interests. In examining his drawings of churches, Rickman remarked, '. . . his collection is large but as yet it is unarranged and there is less of Science … than I would wish.'[11]

On 20 February 1810, Rickman remarked with excitement in his diary entry for that day: 'I attended tonight the first of a Course of Lectures on Chemistry by Dr Traill', and it was 'very good.' Thomas Stewart Traill was a native of the Orkney Islands and represents the kind of polymathic figure thrown up by this period, as does Thomas Rickman, himself. A distinguished medical man and scientist who founded the Literary and Philosophical Society of Liverpool, Traill studied medicine at Edinburgh University and practiced as a doctor in Liverpool for thirty years, before returning to Edinburgh in 1832 to take up a Professorship at the University. He befriended the American ornithologist John James Audubon on his arrival in Liverpool in 1826 and helped him to publish *The Birds of America*. The bird Traill's Flycatcher is named after him, as is Traill's Island in Greenland.[12] Rickman's delight in meeting such a scientific heavyweight is clear from his diary entries for 1810. In March, he attended Traill's lectures on electricity, combustion, galvanism, and hydrogen. On 30 March was the lecture on mineralogy, which moved him to observe: 'How well indeed may it be said that the Lords [*sic*] works are above all Works.' Like most thinking men and women of his time, Rickman saw no conflict between science and faith. Instead, the many scientific discoveries of the age served to confirm faith by revealing the underlying order of the universe. In April 1810 Traill was lecturing on geology and rocks. Rickman wrote to Traill at the end of the month and on 1 May was invited to pay a visit to Traill. His diary entry for that day records that they discussed Kirwan's theory of the creation of matter.[13]

A warm friendship developed between the two men, and Traill assisted Rickman with the next step in his education – that is, making the transition from private, amateur study to a public forum by becoming a member of a learned society. On 24 May 1811 Rickman noted in his diary a meeting at the house of the Liverpool schoolmaster, John Bradley, about forming 'a sort of Philosophical Society which I should much like to forward if Possible'. On 9 August he records that he spent some time at the lecture room of the Philosophical Society, drafting a circular for publication. He was in the company of James Smith, who was to become his first publisher. Later in the month, a series of lectures on geology were given by one of the Society members called Bakewell, although Rickman found them inferior to Traill's. On 18 September Rickman notes that Bakewell lectured in a repetitive style and lacked 'method.' Nine days later Rickman gave his inaugural lecture on the subject of medieval parish churches and their dating: 'at first I was a little confused but got on better when I got into the Subject.' He used the drawings he had prepared from his travel sketches to illustrate his talk.

On 27 December Rickman lectured again, although he noted the audience was small. He was having difficulties with some of the other Society members, whose conduct he did not approve of, although his reasons for this disapproval are not entirely clear from his diary entries.[14] By April 1812 he had decided to apply to join Dr Traill's Literary and Philosophical Society, and give up membership of his own. In order to prepare for his election, Traill presented to the Society a paper by Rickman on Gothic architecture, and it was favourably received by the membership, which included a prominent local architect called John Foster. Rickman was elected a member shortly afterwards. By this time he had begun his career as an amateur architect, providing designs for Gothic tracery to a local ironfounder named John Cragg who was becoming involved in building new churches with cast iron windows.[15] In September of 1812 Rickman was acting as a consultant to Foster for the design of Gothic tracery at the church of St Luke, Berry Place, in Liverpool **[Fig. 4.2]**.[16] Rickman's amateur architectural career, therefore, arose directly out of his antiquarian pursuits in exploring the development of Gothic architecture.

From Linnaean method to meteorology

In October 1811, Rickman recorded in his diary that he took tea with a Swedish traveller, Mr A. Nordblad, who was considering settling in Liverpool. Little is known about this transient figure in Rickman's diaries, except it is clear that Nordblad's interests were scientific and, particularly, botanical.[17] Nordblad and Rickman became good friends, and it is most likely that his Swedish friend introduced him to Linnean method. However, Rickman's diaries contain just two references to Linnaeus – for 24 and 29 April 1813 – when he attended two lectures by Traill that summarised 'Linnean Classification', as Rickman termed it. Carl Linnaeus, later ennobled to Carl von Linné, was born in 1707 to a Swedish Lutheran clergyman and developed 'natural theology', a system by which one could come to an understanding of God through studying his creation in the natural and empirical world. The tool for doing so was the natural sciences (and, perhaps by extension, antiquarian study). This is more or less the concept being expressed by Rickman

4.2: Church of St Luke, Liverpool, built 1811-31 by John Foster the Elder and John Foster the Younger. Window tracery designs were supplied by Thomas Rickman in 1812. Foster was the leading light of the Liverpool style of classicism in the early nineteenth century but produced a creditable essay in the Gothic style here, with Rickman's assistance. [*Author*]

in his diary for 1810, as a result of attending Traill's lectures. Linnaeus studied medicine at the University of Uppsala and developed the binomial system of naming all known plants and animals by genus and species. His publications included *Fundamenta Botanica* (1736) and *Classes Plantarum* (1738), but his great contribution to intellectual history was the *Systema Naturae*, first published in 1735 and subsequently revised and augmented in a number of additions. In it he proposed a simple, hierarchical system for classifying all living things which, as Jenny Uglow has observed, 'offered a map of nature to suit everyone from scholars to schoolgirls.'[18] Linnaeus had died in 1778, when Rickman was two years old; in 1783 his collections and papers were purchased and brought to London in order to found the Linnaean Society, and an English-language biography had been published during the 1790s.[19] There is no evidence to suggest that Rickman actually consulted the papers of Linnaeus directly, but the idea of natural theology was in the air during the later eighteenth and early nineteenth centuries, and Rickman certainly breathed in this air.

Luke Howard, the father of modern meteorology, was directly inspired by Linnaeus, and his career presents some interesting parallels to that of Thomas Rickman. Another self-taught Quaker, Howard was born in 1772, making him only four years older than Rickman. He became a successful businessman who manufactured pharmaceuticals in Pontefract, Yorkshire, while becoming interested in weather and – especially – in cloud formations. He produced a series of beautifully observed watercolours of clouds based on studies taken directly from nature,[20] and he developed a simple, four-part system of nomenclature that is still in use today. These terms are: cirrus, cumulus, stratus, and nimbus. Howard published two key works which are still referred to today in histories of meteoreology. The first, *On the Modification of Clouds*, appeared in 1804 and is known to have inspired the painter John Constable.[21] *Clouds* was first delivered as a lecture to the Askesian Society in 1802; publication followed two years later.

This was a very similar pattern to the development of Rickman's knowledge of Gothic architecture, whereby he first lectured in 1811, based on his studies 'in the field'. This resulted in a lengthy article in 1815 in the *Panorama of Science and Art*, which was published in Liverpool by his friend, James Smith. The article developed into a book, the first edition of his *Attempt*, in 1817, appearing just one year before Howard's influential study of London weather patterns, *The Climate of London*, in 1818.[22] Although there is no firm evidence in Rickman's diaries for this period to suggest that he read Howard's books on clouds, he nonetheless showed great interest in recording the appearance of the skies. There were brief notations on the weather made nearly every day at the end of his diary entries, and there are striking similarities between Howard's system of classification of clouds, and that devised by Rickman for medieval architecture. Howard's simple, four-part system of nomenclature translates readily into Rickman's four-part system for naming medieval architecture. Moreover, it is the simplicity and transparence of Rickman's system of classification, in common with the systems devised by Linnaeus and Howard, which was recognised as one of its great strengths.

Widening participation in 'Gothic'

Writing in the introduction to the first edition of his book, Rickman remarked:

> The object of the present publication has been to furnish, at a price which shall not present an obstacle to extensive circulation, such a view of the principles of Architecture, more particularly that of the British Isles, as may not only be placed with advantage in the hands of the rising generation, but also afford the guardians of ecclesiastical edifices such clear discriminative remarks on the buildings now existing,

4.3: Church of St Martin, Horsley, Gloucestershire, retaining the medieval tower and west wall. Thomas Rickman and R.C. Hussey rebuilt the rest of the church in 1838–39 with an Early English Gothic nave and Decorated Gothic apse. Private parish churches formed a considerable part of Rickman's architectural output. [*Author*]

> as may enable them to judge with considerable accuracy of the restorations necessary to be made in those venerable edifices that are under their peculiar care.[23]

In other words, Rickman wanted to achieve several things. Firstly, his book was to be affordable and, in today's parlance, 'accessible' to a wider public. Next, he wanted to address the 'rising generation' of youth, in order to inspire them to care for the historic built environment they had inherited. Finally, it is clear that Rickman, perhaps following on from the conversations he would have had with his friend, the Rev. Harrison of Chester, wanted to both awaken the clergy to the built heritage that was in their care, and to facilitate their making informed choices concerning the maintenance and restoration of those buildings.

The rapidly growing town of Liverpool and the newly industrialised cities in the north of England provided Rickman with plenty of examples of the threats which medieval buildings were already facing. Rickman makes note in his diaries of going on sketching expeditions to record old churches before they were to be pulled down. Indeed, part of Rickman's own future career as an architect involved rebuilding medieval churches which, in some cases, were too far gone to be repaired according to the technology of his day. For example, in the parish church at Horsley, in Gloucestershire, Rickman kept the medieval tower remaining from the ancient structure, in addition to the original west wall. He rebuilt the rest of the church with a nave in the Early English style, developing into a Decorated Gothic apse, thus giving the appearance of a medieval church which had been built over several centuries – a phenomenon he himself had identified on numerous occasions **[Fig. 4.3]**.[24] Such an assured approach to designing Gothic Revival churches could only be possible thanks to the confidence he acquired through his thorough study of the ornamental and structural characteristics of medieval architecture, as set forth in *An Attempt*.

Delineating architectural styles

Rickman was particularly interested in transitional periods in architecture. One great interest was how Norman architecture, with its round arches, evolved into Early English Gothic, with its high, narrow, sharply pointed windows, and why so many Norman towers and doorcases with their bold geometrical mouldings were retained in later periods of rebuilding. In the section on Norman architecture he remarked, 'The general appearance of Norman buildings is bold and massive. Very few large buildings remain without much alteration and mixture with other styles'; and in the section entitled 'Norman Doors', he observed, 'There seems to have been a desire in the architects who succeeded the Normans, to preserve the doors of their predecessors.'[25] He cited the church of Iffley, near Oxford, a building he knew well, for he had made a special trip from Liverpool to study it in 1812.

In *An Attempt*, Rickman included his own plates to clarify his discussion about the architectural styles and made frequent reference to existing buildings he had studied. However, as in Plate VII, 'a Norman Composition' **[Fig. 4.4]**, his plates did not illustrate actual buildings, but rather were his own compilations of what he saw as typical features of each style. Therefore, it was round arches and dog-tooth mouldings for Norman, while

4.4: Thomas Rickman, *An Attempt to Discriminate the Styles of Architecture in England* (1835), Pl. VII, 'A Norman Composition'. This is one of the plates original to the first (1817) edition that was included in subsequent editions of the book. It shows a composite exterior view on the left, and an interior on the right, both displaying the round arches and distinctive geometrical mouldings of the Norman style without reference to a specific example.

4.5: Thomas Rickman, *An Attempt to Discriminate the Styles of Architecture in England* (1835), Pl. IX, 'A Perpendicular Porch'. The left side of this plate is original to the first (1817) edition of the book, and illustrates an idealised Perpendicular Gothic porch with a doorcase. On the right, however, a group of moulding profiles taken from examples of Perpendicular architecture has been added in order to bring the plate up to date for the fourth edition.

Early English Gothic (Plate VIII of the first edition) shows tracery, lancets, and flying buttresses. Rickman makes the astute observation that the progression from Norman to Early English was gradual, and that it is the numerical combinations of pointed lancet windows which characterise the style, as at Salisbury and Lincoln. He also added that Early English towers were taller than Norman examples, and, 'Some of our finest spires are of this age, and the proportions observed between the tower and spire, are generally very good.'[26] Early English was graceful, where the Norman was bold. The text continues in a similar vein through Decorated Gothic, rich in lace-like tracery and stone details, through to that eccentric and original late phase of English Gothic which Rickman aptly named Perpendicular for the grid-like tracery of horizontal and vertical lines in its broad, shallow arches. As he remarked of Perpendicular English windows, 'These are easily distinguished by their mullions running in perpendicular lines.'[27] Plate IX of the first edition illustrates another of Rickman's compositions for 'A Perpendicular Porch' **[Fig. 4.5]** including twenty-five profiles of mouldings which could readily be copied by a craftsman, thus serving one of the stated purposes of the book as a useful source for restorers and modern church builders, alike. Towards the end of his life, Rickman realised that a weakness of his book lay in the fact it did not include illustrations of actual buildings. He was at work on a well-illustrated, fifth edition of his book when his health began to decline in the later 1830s, and he did not live to finish this project.[28]

Rickman's handbook contained the first accurate chronology to show when the medieval styles, from Norman to Perpendicular – and, even, Elizabethan – developed. In it Rickman even correctly hypothesised that the curious architecture of churches like Earls Barton in Northamptonshire dated to the pre-Norman, or Anglo-Saxon period **[Fig. 4.6]**. This, alone, was a great accomplishment and a result of Rickman's careful, empirical study of hundreds of examples he observed during his travels, and to which he applied his considerable powers of deductive reasoning. In keeping with the spirit of the day, he was able to adapt the scientific systems of taxonomy being developed to explain the natural world, and apply these to his study of ancient architecture. Scientific methodology was applied to antiquarian study, and the result was simple, clear and effective – so much so, that Rickman's nomenclature has survived to the present day.

Rickman's legacy

Rickman's handbook almost immediately became a standard text in the architectural world. His system of classification and his terminology, although sometimes challenged, was never eclipsed. Writing in 1849, eight years after Rickman's death, the thoughtful architectural historian Edmund Sharpe observed:

> It is to Mr. Rickman that we are indebted for that classification of the styles of English Architecture, and that system of Nomenclature which has been almost exclusively used by recent writers on the subject. The excellence of the Classification and Nomenclature, and their sufficiency for the purpose for which they were intended, are best evidenced by the fact, that, although the attempts to

4.6: Thomas Rickman, *An Attempt to Discriminate the Styles of Architecture in England* (1835), Pl. XIII, 'Long and Short Masonry' in Anglo-Saxon Churches. This lithograph was specially prepared for the fourth edition of Rickman's book, by which time he was illustrating actual examples of architecture. From left to right, he illustrates the tower of Whittingham Church, Northumberland; the chancel of North Burcombe, Wiltshire; and the door and tower of Barton-on-Humber, Lincolnshire.

supersede them have been both numerous and persevering, Mr. Rickman's 'Attempt to discriminate the Styles of Architecture in England,' still remains the best guide of the Architectural Student in his first inquiries into the History of Art, and the principal text-book from which most of the popular publications of the day on the subject have been compiled.[29]

Writing at the beginning of the twentieth century, the architect Thomas Atkinson confirmed the use of Rickman's terminology, while in the 1960s Alec Clifton–Taylor remarked that Rickman's terminology was, 'now impossible to reject.'[30] One recent author, James Stevens Curl, has stated the case for Rickman's achievement thus: 'He was of great importance in the history of the Gothic Revival as he was the first [to apply] simple scientific methodologies to a subject that had up to then been treated with vagueness.'[31]

Nor was Rickman's fame confined to Britain. In 1836, not long after Rickman had undertaken his second study tour to northern France to investigate the origins of French Gothic, the eminent French antiquary Arcise de Caumont acknowledged the work of English antiquaries as pioneers in the study of Gothic,[32] and in particular he acknowledged the 1825 (third) edition of Rickman's *Attempt*:

> One must not forget Mr Rickman's essay which contains very extensive statistical information on the historic monuments of England and an enumeration of the characteristics which distinguish the principal styles of architecture as they developed in that country; the work forms a volume of 400 pages illustrated with 14 plates: the last edition appeared in 1825.[33]

In fact, de Caumont was mistaken, for in 1835, the year before he wrote these remarks, Rickman had published the fourth edition of *An Attempt,* which contained even more numerous illustrations and examples of the styles of medieval architecture than the third edition, which the French antiquary had praised, above. Finally, when a young architect of the New World was training in the Gothic tradition of the Old World, to whom should he turn but Mr Rickman. There was simply no other reasonable option, even at the end of the nineteenth century. Henry Van Brunt, an aspiring American architect, made a close study of the seventh (1881) edition of Rickman's *Attempt* and copied out the relevant text for his purposes, interspersing beautiful pencil drawings of architectural details in his own hand with some of his own notes and commentary at the back.[34] It was a method of attacking the subject that was pure Rickman. The resulting seventy-five pages of Van Brunt's 'Synopsis of Rickman's Gothic Architecture' create a visually elegant testament to the power and longevity of Thomas Rickman's system to 'discriminate the styles of English architecture.'

5

Antiquarianism and the Creation of Place: the Birth of Japanese Archaeology

Simon Kaner

The history of Japanese archaeology has tended to be one of 'great men', a story of pioneers and 'fathers' of Japanese archaeology.[1] In this regard, historians of archaeology have argued over the respective contributions of these pioneering individuals, the impact they had on their contemporaries and successors, and on the subsequent 'emergence' of the discipline of archaeology. Accounts of the early development of the study of the ancient past and its material traces have set these individuals in their intellectual context, and recent studies have considered the political and institutional constraints within which they were operating.[2] On occasion, the motivations of these often inspirational characters have been addressed. Understanding the history of a field of enquiry is essential to developing the self-reflexive, critically aware discipline that archaeology now is in this very post-modern world. This need is partly driven by a recognition that an unreflexive archaeology is open to both overt and covert political manipulation, resulting in occasional and regrettable excesses of justificatory interpretation, such as using the questionable inscriptions on the fifth-century King Kwangaett'o stele found in Korea in 1883 to justify, in part, the annexation of the Korean peninsula by the Japanese in 1911.[3] Some of the controversies that still dominate Japanese archaeology have very early manifestations: To Teikan's claims that the great mounded tombs of the Yamato elite were occupied by Korean nobles presage current debates over access to the same tombs being restricted and controlled by the Japanese imperial household agency.

In the early seventeenth century, the rulers of the Japanese archipelago decreed that Japan would isolate itself from the rest of the world under a policy termed *sakoku*. The ensuing two and a half centuries witnessed the development of a distinctive culture which gave rise to something of a golden age in Japanese art and culture. At the same time as the West was wrestling with the revolution of ideas that came to be known as the Enlightenment, scholars, *literati* and the cultured classes in Japan were forging a set of concepts about Japan, its origins, and their place in it. These concepts included the development of ideas about objects from the ancient past, in indigenous Japanese terms, from the 'Age of the Gods'. Interest in these objects, which ranged from stone arrowheads to ceramic figurines, roof tiles and bronze bells, all dug out of the soil of the archipelago, generated a Japanese antiquarian phenomenon. Scholar-politicians such as Arai Hakuseki, To Teikan and their circles collected and studied these objects. Antiquities came to the attention of some of the most influential intellects of the age, notably Moto'ori Norinaga, and came to feature in the *kokugaku* discourse, or the native study of Japanology.

Japan's self-imposed isolation came to an end with the arrival of the West off the Japanese coast in the form of the American Commodore Perry, aboard his infamous 'black ships' in 1853. Within fifteen years, the rule of the Tokugawa Shoguns was over, the Emperor restored as true head of state, and the country was embarking on a period of rapid assimiliation of western ideas and practices. Under the auspices of its new Constitution, Japan set out to become a thoroughly modern national state, able to hold its own among the world powers of the late nineteenth century. Along with the foreign specialists and knowledge imported into the archipelago at this time came a number of individuals who brought western knowledge and an interest in the material remains of the past which fell under the rubric of the newly emerging disciplines of archaeology and anthropology. These included Edward Sylvester Morse, William Gowland, Romyn Hitchcock, and, a little later, Neil Gordon Munro. Although all were professional men in their own right (a zoologist, engineer, photographer and doctor, respectively), their interest in archaeology and antiquities was amateur.

Within Japan itself, however, a series of academic archaeologists emerged, including Tsuboi Shogoro and Hamada Kosaku, to lay the foundation of the academic disciplines of archaeology and anthropology. This happened at the same time as many of the institutional structures relating to antiquities and their preservation and conservation were established, including the National Museum, complemented by a legislative framework based on western models. Antiquarian interest in objects from the ancient past, however, continued. Indeed, the first exhibition of Japanese antiquities, in 1871, was organised by one Baron Kanda Takahira, who was influential in the establishment of the National Museum.

The interaction between the antiquarians and the newly emerging archaeologists is of considerable interest as it provides insight into broader cultural networks at this time. Many authorities who have written on this have set these individuals and their activities in the context of an emerging national identity.[4] The approach adopted here is a little different to this. It posits that one of the major issues facing Meiji nationalism was how to weave a new national identity out of various competing regional and local identities. The Meiji restoration was achieved at the expense of much bloodshed and a series of violent encounters between forces loyal to the imperial throne in Tokyo, and those with allegiance to the regional powerhouses including Satsuma, Date, and so forth. These regional and local influences have continued to exist beneath the veneer of national identity. This paper argues that there was a creative dialectic between national and regional forces that had, and continues to exert, a major influence on the ways in which the 'archaeology of Japan' is constituted and understood.

Furthermore, one of the most significant ways in which these regional archaeological debates have been developed is through the activities of local antiquarians, and then local archaeological collectors, whose collections and objects often form some of the most significant parts of regional and prefectural museums. Examples include the Flame pots in the possession of the Nagaoka City Museum and the Furindo Collection in the Aomori City Museum of Archaeology, or Aomori Kyodokan. This antiquarian tradition builds on the earlier collection and appreciation of antiquities by figures such as Masumi Sugae, Minomushi Senjin and Kimura Kenkado. These collectors and antiquarians were part of a cultural network which also involved those concerned with the procurement and sale of antiquities, who were supplying both the domestic and foreign markets.

At the same time as new vistas on the Japanese past were being opened up, the territory of the archipelago was being subjected to unprecedented scrutiny. Map-making had been introduced, and there are a large number of extant maps from the Edo period. With the Meiji peiod, however, a new emphasis was placed on understanding the structure of the landscape. Japan was to be surveyed for the natural resources required to turn it into a modern industrialised nation state. William Gowland (1842-1922) was an English mining engineer who, when not working at the Osaka Mint, could be found exploring the Japanese countryside, making detailed observations of the many mounded tombs he encountered in the Osaka region, and also seeking the metallurgical sources which were needed to allow Japan to mint its own coinage.[5] This interest in surveying also led him to the mountain fastnesses of central Honshu, for which he is credited with coining the name 'the Japan Alps'. An active member of the Japanese mountaineering community (a new pastime as, during the Edo period, the step-sided Japanese mountains were regarded as the homes of devils and other evil spirits), Gowland contributed to works designed to open up the Japanese countryside to foreign travellers.

In this spirit of geographical pioneerism, Gowland was similar to Minomushi Senjin (1836-1900), whose record of travels through what was to become Akita Prefecture is a truly remarkable account of late Edo and early Meiji domestic exploration. Minomushi was born in Bizen Province, later to become Gifu Prefecture. Leaving his hometown for the first time in 1849, at the age of 14, over the next forty-eight years he travelled extensively around Japan. His travels to Akita from 1877 (intriguingly, the year of Morse's excavations at the Omori shell midden) are of particular interest in the current context as they involved him in some archaeological investigations of his own. In 1887 he was involved in excavations at the Kamegaoka site in Kizukuri town, Aomori, which was reported in the new archaeological and anthropological journal, *Jinruigaku Zasshi*, and held an exhibition of ancient objects at Misawa. Returning to Tokyo in August that year, he met Baron Kanda Takahira at the Office of Culture. In 1888 he reported his collecting of stone tools from Chojayashiki to Baron Kanda. While he was there he kept in regular communication with local notables. He displayed his journeys and discoveries in a record kept in a Nagoya temple. His journals, accounts and watercolours provide a unique insight into the atmosphere of these far reaches of the Japanese empire in the early years of the Meiji government.

Early interest in the ancient past

The earliest account of ancient remains in the Japanese archipelago, even if they were not explicitly referred to as 'prehistoric', can be found in the *Hitachi Fudoki*, an account of the Hitachi District, now Ibaragi Prefecture, dated to 713 AD, which describes, 'a large deposit of shells … at a place called Ogushi Hill and that these shells are the remains of food gathered and eaten by ancient giants'.[6] Also mentioned are descriptions of stone arrowheads in the *Zoku Nihon koki* of AD 869. In this account, these objects were considered to have fallen from the sky, a notion picked up in the early tenth century account, *Sandai Jitsuroku*, which considered such artefacts to have fallen with rain, resulting from thunder, as they were found in the fields after thunderstorms.[7] In an interesting manifestation of the parallel evolution of ideas, such interpretations were also found among western antiquarians (see, for example, chapters 1 and 3 of this volume).

It was not until the Tokugawa period, however, that interest in artefacts from the ancient past really developed. Peter Bleed has identified three spheres of interest in Edo Japan: historical scholarship, practical scholarship and avocational scholarship. Historical scholarship, rooted in the Neo-Confucian philosophy that underpinned much of Tokugawa period intellectual development, developed a rational approach to explanation, removing the causal significance of the supernatural. This was tied to a burgeoning interest in history as the best place to seek for, 'examples and explanations for human affairs'. At the same time, however, a separate and conflicting school of thought, the *kokugaku*, or 'National Learning School', as embodied by figures such as Moto'ori Norinaga, rejected Confucianism, basing their approach to Japanese history entirely upon detailed readings of the ancient chronicles, the *Kojiki* and the *Nihongi*. This approach was reflected in major histories of the time such as the *Dai Nihonshi*,[8] whose author, Tokugawa Mitsukuni, was involved in the investigation of ancient burial mounds in Ibaragi Prefecture.

Bleed argues that most Edo period writers had little or no interest in or awareness of antiquities. He singles out two figures, Arai Hakuseki (1656-1725) and To Teikan (1731-98), 'who made genuine advances in the direction of prehistoric archaeology'.[9] Arai drew on his extensive knowledge of the ancient chronicles to argue that stone points he was sent from northern Honshu had been made by a group of people called the *shukushinjin* whom Chinese records describe as inhabiting Manchuria, and who are mentioned in the ancient Japanese chronicles as having invaded northern Japan around the sixth century AD. Arai's major contribution was, therefore, to make a strong case that these stone tools were made by historically attested humans, rather than being of some supernatural (or natural) origin.

To Teikan wrote extensively on history, and his books contain illustrations of 'excavated stone and bronze artefacts, prehistoric pottery, antique porcelains and architectural remains',[10] and developed a particular interest in roof tiles. He used antiquities to support his discussions on ancient Japanese customs and history. This included an account of ancient dress based on designs on the terracottas (*haniwa*) set up around ancient tombs, which led him to address similarities between early Japanese and early Korean dress, and, more controversially, that the 'founders of the Japanese imperial line were Korean nobles' and that 'the formation of the Japanese imperial line must have taken place some 600 years after the recorded date of 660 BC'.[11] These opinions led other, more influential scholars, notably those of the *kokugaku* school, to dismiss To Teikan as a 'lunatic'.

Towards the end of the Tokugawa period, travelogues became a popular genre among this Early Modern literate population. Bleed describes the contribution of one Sugae Masumi (1754-1829), whose practical curiosity, 'led to the recognition and investigation of prehistoric remains'.[12] Masumi travelled throughout Japan from 1783 and published illustrations of ancient pottery from northern Japan, mainly from Kamegaoka (literally, the Hill of the Jars), a location known since the earlier seventeenth century as a rich source of ancient pottery vessels, in his *Shinko Shukuyohin-rui No Zu [Illustrations of Old and New Ceremonial Vessels]*. Bleed considers that Masumi's work was of importance for two main reasons: firstly, his books were successful, suggesting a broadening interest in antiquities. Secondly, it is significant that, by this stage, even a non-Confucian supporter of the *kokugaku* school of thought espoused by Moto'ori Norinaga, such as Masumi, was adopting a rational, historical approach to understanding antiquities, rather than the supernaturalism of the ancient chronicles from which the *kokugaku* school drew so much inspiration.

As well as this developing interest in the natural and cultural geography of the archipelago, fed by the popular travelogues produced by men like Masumi, the later Tokugawa period witnessed a growing fascination with collecting rocks and stones. Bleed identifies Kiuchi Sekitei as one of the most important practitioners of this hobby.[13] Sekitei organised a club, the *roseki-no-sha* or 'Rock Handlers Club', which had a national membership, and, by the early nineteenth century, 'rock collectors had developed a body of literature dealing with the typology and distribution of prehistoric stone tools'.[14] Representative of this *oeuvre* was Sekitei's own *Unkonshi*, published in sections between 1773 and 1801. As Bleed points out, Sekitei was part of a network of collectors which also included Tamura Sanzo (1759–1806), a *Samurai* from Aizu (modern day Fukushima Prefecture) with whom Sekitei maintained a 'friendly correspondence', and whose own work on different forms of stone tools and their distribution perhaps exceeded that of Sekitei.

For the most part, however, as exemplified by the *dilettanti* attentions paid to them through groups such as the *Tankikai*, or the 'Oddity Enthusiasts Club', who met to display and discuss antiquities in Edo in 1824 and 1825, objects from the ancient past remained as, 'interesting curios rather than material reflections of past cultures'.[15] Masumi, Sekitei and Sanzo, although their descriptions, accounts and illustrations are of interest to historians of archaeology, were all restricted in their interpretations by the historical sources available to them.

Therefore, although this Edo period interest in antiquities had a limited impact on the historical consciousness and understanding of the period, nonetheless the networks of collectors and travellers that existed provided the background for some developments towards the end of the Tokugawa shogunate that, combined with the arrival of the concept of 'archaeology' as the systematic study of the material traces of the human past after the Meiji restoration, gave rise to early institutional concerns with preservation and conservation. These institutional concerns related in particular to the enactment of legislation designed to protect ancient remains, and the establishment of museums to house the material traces of the ancient past.

Early modern developments

In the years following the arrival of Commodore Perry, but prior to the establishment of the Meiji state, a number of Japanese travelled overseas. Amongst these was Machida Hisanari, a liberal-minded *samurai* who studied for two years in England in about 1866.[16] While there, he visited the British Museum and, in 1867, attended the Fourth World Fair in Paris. He returned to Japan on the eve of the Meiji Restoration. The new Meiji state identified itself firmly with Shinto, the indigenous religious system of the Japanese archipelago, which since the arrival of Buddhism in the sixth century had developed a syncrenistic symbiosis. The Meiji iconoclasts, however, regarded Buddhism as a foreign imposition, and the period following 1868 saw the destruction of many Buddhist temples and the export of many Buddhist art works. Even the Great Buddha of Kamakura was considered for selling off. This activity was met in some circles with concern about the destruction of so many art treasures.[17] It was in this context that the government put forward an edict which, albeit in a rather weak form, proposed protection for historical records, collections and objects.[18]

These calls for the preservation of historical monuments were, however, not entirely new. As Walter Edwards has expertly demonstrated, the authorities towards the end of the Tokugawa period were paying increased attention to the conservation of some of the greatest monuments of ancient Japan, the burial mounds of the ruling classes at the time of the emergence of the Japanese state in the Kansai region. These tombs were under threat not only from the natural forces of erosion and ground movement, exacerbated by earth tremors, but also from looters. Indeed, the increased regularity of repair works to the tombs in the Ansei period (1851-55), during which Perry's black ships were arriving off the coast of Tokyo Bay, were prompted by the arrest of four culprits who were accused of robbing some of the tombs. Edwards gives the following account, which leaves little doubt as to the intentions of the authorities at this time:

> The culprits were eventually given the extraordinarily harsh sentence of first being publicly paraded through the streets as criminals, and then crucified – a grizzly form of execution that in the late Edo period consisted of tying a person to a cross and repeatedly stabbing the torso. Conditions in *bakufu* jails not being very favourable, three of the four had already died during the six-year lapse prior to sentencing. Their execution was nevertheless carried out to the letter: on their corpses, which had been preserved in salt.[19]

To risk such punishment, it must have been economically worth the while of these unfortunate looters to be involved in these practices, indicating the significance of the networks through which their ill-gotten gains would subsequently have circulated.

At the same time as these early institutional developments were taking place, Bleed's 'avocational archaeologists' continued to be active. One of the most famous is Negishi Bunko (1831-1902), a wealthy landowner and major collector of antiquities. Edward Morse, two years after arriving in Japan to join Tokyo Imperial University, visited Negishi in 1879 and was shown his extensive pottery collection and a series of ancient locations. Bleed suggests that Negishi actually undertook recognisable archaeological excavations, perhaps inspired by Morse's interventions at Omori.

Edward Morse undertook and published archaeological excavations at the Omori shell mounds, between Yokohama and Tokyo; he also ensured that the specimens and artefacts he collected were displayed in a museum within the Science Department at the University. Morse's considerable contribution to the development of Japanese archaeology can be summarised as follows: the introduction of the words 'archaeology' and 'prehistoric' to the archipelago; recognition of the legitimacy, credibility and importance of archaeology as an intellectual field worthy of support at the premier intellectual institution in Meiji Japan, Tokyo Imperial University, where he taught; the introduction of systematic excavation and collection of artefacts and other data; a concern with what are now termed assemblages; the use of a function-based nomenclature for artefacts; and the inference of behaviours from artefacts not found in the historical chronicles, notably (although mistakenly) cannibalism. Bleed also attributes the introduction to Japan of the 'idea of prehistory' to Morse, even if he did not fully appreciate the significance of this.[20] Along with the date of publication on the cover of the first excavation report from the Japanese archipelago, that of his investigations of the Omori shell mounds (1879), Morse placed the date according to the mythological founding of the Japanese imperial line (2539). Morse was first and foremost, however, a zoologist interested, *inter alia*, in evolution. His impact on the subsequent development of Japanese archaeology has been questioned, as apart from work undertaken by his students, his approach to archaeological investigation and analysis was not pursued by later Japanese archaeologists.

Five years prior to Morse's arrival in Japan, the Englishman William Gowland had taken up a position at the Osaka Mint. A mining engineer, while in Japan Gowland began to investigate and record the ancient mounded tombs which were found in large numbers in the area around Osaka. He began his investigation of the tombs in 1876, and came to be assisted by Romyn Hitchcock from the Smithsonian Institution in the United States. Gowland brought his engineer's training and assiduousness to investigating these mausolea, introducing innovations such as photography and a method of recording artefacts using a grid, but he was also a passionate collector. The artefacts and archives that he sent back to Britain were purchased for the British Museum by the pioneering curator Augustus Woollaston Franks. Gowland must have encountered Tsuboi Shogoro (see below), but also, through his governmental connections, he clearly had access to bureaucratic sources that gave him volumes such as the *Seisekizushi*. The paper archive at the British Museum shows that he was in direct receipt of many important documents. This was another aspect of the cultural network at this time of the emergence of Japanese archaeology. Gowland returned to Britain in 1888 and is best known in British archaeological circles for his work at Stonehenge in 1903, and for his important studies of Roman metallurgy. His contribution to Japanese archaeology is underestimated and, indeed, until recently his archaeological work in Japan was unrecognised.[21] Further, Gowland is a significant figure because of his important work in surveying Japan. He epitomised the late Victorian explorer–antiquarian.

Tsuboi Shogoro (1863-1913) was the first Japanese scholar to take a very proactive interest in anthropological archaeology, and was a successor to Morse at Tokyo University. He disagreed with Morse's hypotheses about the early Japanese inhabitants. Tsuboi is an interesting if somewhat unsympathetic character, and it is worth our while to consider him in the context of the predominant antiquarian activity of the time – collecting. Tsuboi, who established the earliest courses in archaeology and anthropology at the University of Tokyo, is most often referred to in the context of the racialist theories which related who was whom in East Asia. Tsuboi was the major early influence on Torii Ryuzo, who pioneered ethnographical and archaeological explorations throughout the developing world of the East Asian Co-Prosperity Sphere. Tsuboi is of the greatest importance for the theme of this essay, as he represents the transition from antiquarian to archaeologist, and an anthropological archaeology at that. Through one of his major vehicles, the Anthropological Society of Tokyo, and its organ, *Jinruigaku Zasshi*, Tsuboi laid the foundations of archaeology that was to last through to 1945, and has had major repercussions ever since.

Torii Ryuzo (1870-1953) represented a new generation of scholar-explorers. Born in Tokushima on the island of Shikoku, he was influenced by the new school of East Asian studies developed by Shiratori Kurakichi. He was familiar with the Chinese classics and with 'the imported western disciplines of geography, geology, paleontology, archaeology, art history, physical anthropology and ethnography'.[22] Torii was an ethnologist, anthropologist and folklorist. He travelled to Manchuria in 1894 and 1895, sent by the Tokyo Anthropological Association, to study the 'Manchurian races', and is credited with being the first to identify prehistoric materials from Manchuria and the Korean Peninsula.[23] In Korea, he followed Yagi Sozaburo from the Tokyo University Anthropological Research Institute, who worked on traces of later archaeology on the peninsula from 1893. He was also the precursor to Sekino Tadashi from the Department of Architecture of the same university, who studied many of the historical monuments. Over the coming years, theories were propounded about the racial connections of the Manchurians, Koreans and other East Asian populations, and their relationship with the Japanese. Discoveries such as that in 1883 of the King Kwangaet'o stele caused a furore, as it mentioned Japan some four centuries prior to the dates of the early Japanese chronicles.[24] Torii went on to excavate sites in Korea, including a fortress of the kingdom of Koguryo in 1905. He had always been passionate about collecting.

While Torii was exploring Taiwan, Korea and Manchuria, the Scottish doctor Neil Gordon Munro (1870-1942) was investigating archaeological sites around the Kanto and elsewhere in Japan. Munro arrived in Japan in 1891, 'having long been interested in archaeology'.[25] He is thought to have taken part in excavations in Europe during vacations in his medical course at Edinburgh University. Munro was also a great collector, and the more than 2,000 Jomon and Ainu objects, along with traditional Japanese musical instruments which he sent to the Royal Scottish Museum (now the National Museums of Scotland) between 1909 and 1914 form one of the great collections of Japanese antiquities outside Japan. Munro was particularly interested in finding evidence for the Palaeolithic in Japan. His major contribution to the field was his book *Prehistoric Japan*, published in 1908, which followed on from a paper delivered to the Asiatic Society of Japan in 1906. Munro's interest in Japanese antiquities was fostered through a passion for collecting coins.[26]

He was very interested in the racial questions which were so fascinating to his Japanese contemporaries, and *Prehistoric Japan* contains a long account of the physical anthropological remains for what Munro termed the 'Prehistoric Races'. Munro was in contact with Koganei Yoshikiyo of the Anatomy Department of Tokyo University.[27] This interest was encouraged by the discovery of human skeletons at the Mitsuzawa shell midden, excavated by Munro in 1905-6. He was aided by the archaeologist Yagi Shozaburo, and Munro's new wife, Takahata Toru, the first woman to be mentioned in regard to archaeology or antiquarianism in Japan, who directed the excavations in Munro's absence. According to correspondence at the Society of Antiquaries of London, Munro paid £20 for the land on which the site of Mitsuzawa was located. His investment provided a handsome return. Probing beneath the shell layers, Munro and his associates discovered the first pit house from a prehistoric context in Japan, the first of many tens of thousands which have been excavated subsequently. This interest in archaeological features rather than only objects represented a major advance over the methodology of Morse. In *Prehistoric Japan*, Munro also drew on the new information available about the numbers and distribution of archaeological sites across the archipelago. The maps included within Munro's volume show patterns that are still commented upon today.

Conclusion

In 1974 Hoffman discerned four themes in the rise of antiquarianism in Japan and western Europe: the role of emergent nationalism and the political stabilisation associated with the unification of Japan under the Tokugawa Shoguns; the aristocratic patronage of *dilettanti* antiquarianism; the rise of anti-Chinese nationalism and an antiquarian Neo-Shinto philosophy; and the influences of European ideas, in particular the 'Dutch learning' that was coming in through Nagasaki.[28] This gave way in the later nineteenth century to the development of a scholarly tradition of prehistoric antiquarian research within a context of intellectual generalisation and comparative cultural studies, emphasising accurate fieldwork and recording.

However we define 'antiquarianism' and 'archaeology', we can see various connections between the two, and the 'emergence' of the latter as a 'scientific' discipline in the later nineteenth century. It is true that concerns with national identity were important for many of the individuals involved in this transition, and yet a passion for collecting, and serious attempts to understand ancient Japan in the context of emerging new western 'modern' discourses, were also very important. Tsuboi, Hamada and Machida spent considerable time in the West before returning to Japan to shape the intellectual and institutional structure of archaeology. Just as previous generations of antiquarians, Arai Hakuseki, To Teikan, and so on, were fascinated by the *rangaku*, or Dutch learning, so Tsuboi and others wanted to know what their foreign counterparts were thinking. They interacted with the leading western scholars of the time, and with westerners based in Japan such as Morse, Gowland and Munro, who were also fascinated by the objects and sites from ancient Japan. The contribution of Gowland and Munro was in terms of moving interest from objects, alone, to a more recognisable archaeological concern with context and synthesis of data. Gowland waited to publish his major work on the tombs he had investigated until he had painstakingly assembled all of the available information and completed his metallurgical analyses. Munro chose to embed his report of work at Mitsuzawa into the first synthesis of Japanese prehistory to appear in a western language, and, indeed, one of the first in Japanese, as well.

The geopolitical context was one of 'soft colonialism' in the later nineteenth century, which was gradually transformed into the real colonialism that drove the expansion of the Japanese Empire at a time when Japan was a very important ally of the western powers. The activities of these men were, however, underpinned by an extensive cultural network that procured and exchanged antiquities from all over Japan. Were these 'fathers' of Japanese archaeology complicit in the fostering of nationalist ideologies, or did they unwittingly allow their ideas and discoveries to be used and manipulated by shady political powers with their own agendas of national advancement? Within, or perhaps underlying, any such manipulation lay a web of local and regional tensions, and it is, perhaps, this dialectic between national endeavour and local pride and identity that was one of the driving forces behind modern Japanese archaeology. Without understanding this dialectic, it is difficult to appreciate fully the significance of the attention paid to the massive investigations of the late twentieth century at sites such as Sannai Maruyama,[29] and Yoshinogari.[30] These two sites, located in provincial and somewhat remote areas at either end of the archipelago, generated enormous public interest when discovered and excavated, and demonstrate the power of the ancient past in contemporary Japanese imagination, as well as the potential archaeology has for contributing to the rediscovery of regional identities within Japan, and the accompanying benefits of cultural tourism.

6

Recording the Past: the Origins and Aims of the Church Monuments Society

Simon Watney

In his introduction to the catalogue of the 2007 Royal Academy exhibition celebrating the third centenary of the foundation of the Society of Antiquaries of London, the exhibition's curator, Dr David Starkey, pointed out that the Society's origins lie in a period long before the existence of modern public museums and galleries, and that its broad goal of recording historic monuments of every kind effectively laid the foundations of much of the modern conservation movement.[1] Britain is often accused of being obsessed with its own past, but it should, however, be appreciated that the study of our national heritage is particularly important because so much of the physical evidence of our past cultural achievements has proved uniquely vulnerable. To take just two random examples, the last, major, early seventeenth-century domestic building in central London, Northumberland House, was demolished as long ago as 1874 to be replaced by the uniquely pointless Northumberland Avenue, whilst the last surviving fourteenth-century domestic building in Essex, the Old Chaplaincy at Hornchurch, was demolished as recently as 1970.

Writing on the history and origins of the Royal Commission on the Historical Monuments of England, Andrew Sargent has shown how far Britain lagged behind the rest of Europe, and even the British Empire, in the legal protection of historic monuments.[2] It was, moreover, only the direct threat of bombing which lay behind the establishment of the National Buildings Record (NBR), set up in 1940 in order to photographically record buildings recognised to be at risk from enemy action. In this context the study of the history of English sculpture is quite unlike that of the study of English painting, in so far as historians of painting generally take it for granted that their primary materials are held in museums or private collections, or in the care of dealers and auction houses, and are thus on the whole well documented and cared for. This certainly cannot be said of the great bulk of British historic statuary, and this difference has had major implications for the history of the Church Monuments Society and other associated bodies and organisations. Events such as the destruction of the sculptor Rachel Whiteread's east London *House* in 1994, and the restoration of Windsor Castle after the disastrous fire of 1992, have generated a certain amount of public discussion of monuments in modern Britain, yet by and large the subject of church monuments and memorials has been marginal to most mainstream cultural debate.

Origins

This chapter concerns the origins and aims of the Church Monuments Society, founded in 1979 as the International Society for the Study of Church Monuments (ISSCM), and given its present name in 1985. It is instructive in this context to consider the dates of the emergence of some of the other surviving national historic heritage organisations, many of which have also changed their names for a variety of reasons. These include the British Archaeological Association, founded in 1833; the Society for the Protection of Ancient Buildings, founded by William Morris in 1877; the Ecclesiological Society, founded in 1879, though with an ancestry dating back to the formation of the Camden Society in Cambridge in 1839; the Monumental Brass Society, founded in 1887; the National Trust, founded in 1895; the Royal Commission on the Historical Monuments of England, founded in 1908; the Ancient Monuments Society, founded in 1924; the Historic Churches Preservation Trust, founded in 1953; the Friends of Friendless Churches Trust, founded in 1957; the Redundant Churches Trust, founded in 1969 and renamed the Churches Conservation Trust in 1994; the Living Churchyard Project, founded in 1986; the Scottish Redundant Churches Trust, founded in 1996; the Society for Church Archaeology, also founded in 1996; and the Mausolea and Monuments Trust, founded in 1997.

These organisations vary greatly in scale and remit, collectively reflecting a strong scaffolding of overlapping aims and objectives. Together with many other societies they display a wide range of specialist interests and accumulated knowledge, as well as an indication of newly evolving and emerging areas of expertise and concern. The original mission statement of the Church Monuments Society stated that: 'The Society aims to promote, for the public benefit, the study, care and conservation of funerary monuments of all periods and of all countries'.[3] The current mission statement explains that:

> The Church Monuments Society was founded in 1979 and offers a focus for all who have an interest in church monuments of all types and periods. It was conceived to encourage the appreciation, study and conservation of church monuments both in the UK and abroad. The Society organizes biennial symposia, biannual study days, an AGM and monthly excursions whenever possible. The Society also organizes study groups and an information service. The Society publishes an annual academic journal *Church Monuments* and a less formal, informative twice yearly Newsletter. These publications are provided free to members, but may be purchased separately from the

Membership Secretary. Please note that the Church Monuments Society is not able to offer grant aid.

As is often the case in the history of specialist learned societies, there was at least one false start, namely, the Society for Preserving the Memorials of the Dead, which was founded in 1880 and which lasted for some ten years under the patronage of the archbishop of Canterbury.[4] It was, perhaps, initially over-ambitious, with plans for 'secretaries' in no less than twenty-seven towns, and it eventually closed down as a result of debilitating financial wranglings. A similar society in Ireland ran more successfully from 1888 to 1933. The Church Monuments Society's original mission statement was an ambitious and inclusive manifesto which remains close to the Society's present aims and activities, which are amicably divided between the goals of scholarship, conservation, and organised excursions and visits. Before looking at these in more detail, it may be of interest to consider something of the circumstances of the Society's origins. It is generally agreed that the Society came about as the result of discussions between the late A V. Norman, master of the armories at the Tower of London, Claude Blair, and Philip Lankester, following a symposium on historical effigies held in 1978 at the Tower of London. As his widow has explained, A V. (Nick) Norman:

> came to the study of monuments from his underlying interest in historical arms and armour, the study of which was enjoying a revival in the 1950's following the foundation of The Arms and Armour Society by James Mann and his colleagues at the Tower of London Armories. A distinguished career in museology led to his appointment in 1963 as Assistant to the Director of the Wallace Collection where he was put in charge of their remarkable European and Asian arts & armour collections, which he effectively re-catalogued. An author of seminal books and articles, a Fellow of both the Society of Antiquaries of London and of the Royal Society of Antiquaries of Scotland, he became Master of the Armories in 1977. His work was multi-disciplinary in approach, drawing on art history & manuscripts as well as brasses and effigies.[5]

Writing in 1989, Claude Blair and Richard Knowles observed that: 'It would be no exaggeration to state that without Nick, we would not have the Church Monuments Society or the Journal'.[6] Norman provided it with its original postal address c/o the Armories at the Tower of London. A founding meeting took place on 15 September 1979, where the original Council was elected, with Claude Blair (president); Robin Emerson (secretary); Margaret Scott (assistant secretary); Philip Lankester (membership secretary); Dennis Corble (treasurer); Nigel Ramsay (bulletin editor); John Blair (bulletin production); and John Physick (V&A) and Peter Burman (secretary of the Council for Places of Worship and subsequently of the Council for the Care of Churches) as ordinary members, and Nick Norman as vice-president. Philip J. Lankester recalls that:

> The focus of the first symposium was on monumental effigies (though the papers ranged a little more widely and at least one didn't mention effigies at all). I think Nick and Claude were partly prompted by the realisation that a number of people other than themselves who had been working on British medieval effigies had only recently become aware of each other's existence. The first step was a symposium and the idea of a society (though more broadly based than the symposium title) was the next logical step … And so it came to pass that the meeting at the end of the symposium voted to start a society: the only cracks in an otherwise solid consensus appeared when it came to decide what it should be called – the result was the long and rather pompous name which was, to general relief, abandoned a few years later. I think we were all aware of the problems of preserving monuments (and John Larson gave a paper on conservation) but, in my memory, the emphasis of that first symposium was more on academic study. However, the early issues of the ISSCM Bulletin contain a number of notes on the loss, deterioration or abuse of monuments.[7]

Claude Blair notes that he became involved:

> at a very early stage and was, of course, very enthusiastic about the project, not only for its own sake, but also because I had for years been concerned about the fact that monumental brasses had a flourishing society of their own, which insisted on treating them as though they were somehow different from effigies in the round, and that the latter had nothing but the local societies.[8]

He further notes that:

> We had no idea what sort of response we would get for the symposium, and were pleasantly surprised when it turned out to be an enthusiastic one. Another pleasant surprise was the discovery that the late Enoch Powell was an enthusiast for medieval effigies, and he offered to give a paper. I agreed to chair the meeting, and I shall always remember his paper, not for its contents – which were about cross-legged effigies – but because he orated it, something I had never experienced at any kind of antiquarian/archaeological meeting before, nor have I experienced it since! Powell was a brilliant scholar, and a very nice man. He became a member of the Society when it was eventually formed and was very helpful in using his influence to save Buslingthorpe Church, Lincolnshire, from being messed up by the diocese instead of being invested in the Churches Conservation Trust, and, above all, over the Abergavenny monuments conservation scheme. This last was started at the Society's instigation, though everything else was done by the locals.

I think that this must be the Society's greatest achievement to date, apart, of course, from the publication of a very successful academic journal.[9]

A founder-member, John K. Bromilow, points out that from the initial symposium:

> came the *International Society for the Study of Church Monuments*, the first president being Claude Blair, the first vice-president Nick Norman and the first secretary Robin Emmerson. This society with its somewhat unwieldy name became, of course, in 1983 the *Church Monuments Society* after much discussion and a ballot of the members. The ISSCM produced a biannual *Bulletin,* with articles, news etc, the editor being Nigel Ramsay. This was an A4 typewritten and duplicated production which today looks remarkably primitive although at the same time rather friendly. In 1985 the *Bulletin* 'split' its function into two new publications which we still produce today: the annual *Journal* whose first editor was again Nigel Ramsay and the biannual *Newsletter* whose first editor was Pam King. These publications have developed and improved over the years. A small subgroup was also formed in these early days to produce the *Medieval Effigy List Project*, gathering and collating relevant material. This group consisted of Nick Norman, John Blair (Claude's son), Philip Lankester, Harry Mayo and myself; we met in the Tower and I have to say it was a great delight both meeting in the Tower when the visitors had gone home and especially meeting these interesting and delightful people. This list was never completely finished but may well be one day. The Society began its biennial symposia, its annual AGM and weekend coach tours. At this early time too the Society produced a Society Tie and even Christmas Cards'.[10]

Early members who played an important role included Pamela King, who edited the first newsletter, a role subsequently taken on by Moira Gittos from 1987 to 1999; Richard Knowles and Anthony Wells-Cole, who edited the journal; Moira Gittos as the first publicity officer, followed in 1987 by John K. Bromilow (a post he still holds); as well as the late Peter Fairweather and others including Dr Adam White who was for many years the Conservation Cases Recorder (in whose illustrious footsteps I ventured to follow in 2000). Robin Millerchip also played a crucial role in organising the Society's public excursions programme from 1986 to 2008. Writing on the first page of the first edition of the *Church Monument Society Newsletter* in June 1985 (replacing the former A4 *Bulletin*), its editor, Pamela King, explained that: 'We are not, and cannot aim in the foreseeable future to be, a grant-aiding body in the field of church monuments' conservation, but we have considerable potential as a pressure and advice group'. This remains the case today.

6.1: The Beauchamp Chapel, (c.1475), the Collegiate Church of St Mary, Warwick, demonstrating an exceptionally fine ensemble of monuments to complement the rich, late medieval architecture. [*Author*]

The table of contents of the first issue of the newsletter is illuminating and includes reports of excursions, the excursion programme, conservation advice for the layman (on damp, heat, accidental damage, theft, decorative repainting); monuments in churches under threat of redundancy; an open forum (e.g. Notes and Queries); the minutes of the 6th annual meeting of the society, held on 22 September 1984, under the presidency of Claude Blair; and the minutes of the extraordinary general meeting, 10 November 1984, which record something of the 'lively discussion' surrounding the proposal by Brian Gittos to change the society's name from the International Society for the Study of Church Monuments, to the Church Monuments Society, 'in order to appear less pretentious, to attract more members and more accurately reflect its actual work'. It was pointed out by John Physick that the shorter name was already widely colloquially in use, and the resolution was passed by 28 to 13 votes, with a related change from the *Bulletin* to the journal *Church Monuments*, with an additional *Newsletter*. Finally the advance minutes for the 1985 AGM were included, together with a notice concerning a proposed symposium on the subject of 'Antiquarian Enterprise: the Study of Church Monuments' to be held in September 1986.

Precursors

The subject of this initial symposium serves to provide a useful reminder of the wider historical context which informed and motivated the society's origins, responding to a long-established interest in medieval funeral monuments and sculpture as reflected in the pioneering publications of Fred H. Crossley, Arthur Gardner, E S. Prior, and Lawrence Stone, amongst others. Writing in the Society's journal in 1986, John Physick and Nigel Ramsay discussed the significance of Mrs Katharine Ada Esdaile (1881-1950), concluding that: 'It can probably be stated without contradiction that the Church Monuments Society would not have been founded if her writings had not generated an increasing interest in the subject during the forty years since the end of the Second World War'.[11] It would be difficult to overstate the significance of Mrs Esdaile's writings in her lifetime, from her pioneering published surveys of church monuments, to her many letters to *The Times* and other campaigns on their behalf.[12] Her scholarly enthusiasms led her to being asked to edit Vertue's *Notebooks* for the Walpole Society, the first volume appearing in 1930. Much of her work was concerned with identifying clusters of monuments which might be attributed to particular workshops or individual mason-sculptors.

It is certainly true that Katharine Esdaile did not closely consider mainland European parallels, that many of her attributions do not stand up to close scrutiny, and that she sometimes contradicted herself. Her methods contrasted strongly with the emphasis of later scholars, who took a much more restrictive line on attributions, understandably preferring textual evidence such as contracts. This should not, however, lead one to underestimate her central role in the stimulation of popular interest in the subject, and her emphasis on the physical condition of monuments, together with questions of their conservation and care. This pioneering dual attention to issues of artistic significance and conservation was unusual and prescient.

Whilst almost anything inside a church may be a monument or memorial, from stained glass windows to pulpits or stalls given in memory of a named individual, the notion of church monuments is generally selectively applied to the history of carved or otherwise sculpted memorials. Such monuments frequently speak eloquently of the craftsmen who made them and the individuals and families whom they were designed to commemorate. They assume distinct architectural forms, and require a technical language of explanation which has its own fascination and beauty, from 'gadrooning' to 'swan-necked curly broken segmental pediments', which those interested in Baroque monuments could perhaps usually more easily draw than describe in words. Funerary monuments moreover may be divided into various distinct formal categories, from hanging wall monuments, tablets and cartouches to standing wall monuments, and so on. Most, but by no means all, of these derive from mainland European sources, mediated within local traditions.

Obstacles

Something of the neglect surrounding the subject of church monuments may be related to the widespread tendency to talk about churches in exclusively architectural terms, as if they were entirely distinct from their fittings and furnishings. Many architectural historians tend to celebrate architectural achievements in singularly abstract terms, as if houses or churches were best imagined purged full of all movable and distracting things such as furniture or monuments; yet most churches, like most houses, tend to be above all *ensembles* **[Fig. 6.1]**, brought together over time, with accumulated experience, mistakes, changes of mind and so on, sometimes utterly of one brief period, but far more often subject to slow growth with constant minor changes and modifications **[Fig. 6.2]**. There is no substitute for the direct, first-hand experience of looking closely at monuments *in situ,* not least because until the invention of the internet there was no easily accessible body of photographic reproductions. However, since most historic statuary remains in the churches for which it was intended, it is ironically far less known than secular sculpture and decorative art, since nowadays historic houses are far more widely visited than historic churches.

Unlike works of art in public galleries or private collections, the future survival of church monuments is not secured, and

6.2: Detail of the monument to Richard Blisse (died 1703) and family, Southwark Cathedral, London, showing anachronistic modern gilding on the cherubim and architectural details. [*Author*]

they are frequently vulnerable to accidental damage or worse. Sadly, this does not necessarily attract the subject to many contemporary art historians, whose concerns are either focused on more accessible and better protected classes of objects, or whose work is largely theoretical in outlook. Unfashionable and poorly documented, the careers of most mason-sculptors are difficult to square with the main trends of contemporary Anglo-Saxon art historical research, which tend to be grounded in a heady mixture of Foucauldian theory and Gramscian Marxism, as developed in post-war Britain by the late Raymond Williams, and others. Primarily sociological, such analysis tends to be highly skeptical of notions of human nature or artistic identity, or ideas about historical continuity, let alone the role of art and religious beliefs in our personal and collective senses of belonging. With few exceptions, the academic study of church monuments in recent years has thus focused on their ideological and political significance, and the class and economic circumstances of their patrons, resulting in a highly reductive approach which is largely indifferent to their remarkable aesthetic richness and variety. It is certainly no coincidence that the Church Monuments Society, like other similar organisations including the Monumental Brass Society and the Ancient Monuments Society, has its origins outside the university system, and depends largely on the work of independent scholars.

Largely un-admired, church monuments mainly slumber, patiently waiting to be valued again and treated with the same amount of physical respect we would unthinkingly bring to any surviving secular furniture or easel paintings from the same period. Their long-standing neglect, moreover, carries with it a set of largely unexamined and ossified prejudices, including a general Whiggish hostility to the Baroque as if it were intrinsically un-English and lacking in taste. Such attitudes are particularly pronounced in the influential writings of Margaret Whinney, in whose eyes most British sculpture was almost invariably inferior to that of mainland Europe.[13] As Matthew Craske has recently pointed out, the bibliography of Hogarth's graphic works, alone, exceeds that of all contemporaneous English sculpture.[14] Certainly few areas of British cultural achievement are more neglected than the history of late Stuart Baroque statuary, resulting in a major impoverishment of our sense of our national cultural history.

Unless we can persuade large numbers of people to visit churches, they will not have the opportunity to discover for themselves just how remarkable that history is. In this respect the motives of the founders of the Church Monuments Society were by no means unlike those of the antiquaries of the sixteenth and seventeenth centuries, who were so directly inspired by their acute sense of the recent widespread destruction of monuments, together with the immediate threat of equal or worse to come.

6.3: View of the gravestone to Stephen Wigzell (died 1727), aged six months, at Kemsing churchyard, Kent. Our fine national heritage of carved gravestones is increasingly vulnerable to the effects of weathering. [*Author*]

The issue of conservation is thus a central aspect of the Society's mission **[Fig. 6.3–6]**. The early antiquaries recognised, as should we, that monuments will only finally be protected if there is a popular constituency which cares sufficiently about their fate and recognises the need to protect them. This is precisely why they undertook their largely thankless work. I suspect that most members would agree that the Church Monuments Society attempts to achieve its objectives by encouraging diverse interests, recognising the equal validity of generalists and specialists alike who possess a wealth of diverse interests within and across all periods. In reality the membership combines a number of significant clusters of special interests, including arms and armour, epigraphy, historical costume, heraldry and patronage. These overlap with consideration of monuments as works of art and the craftsmanship involved in their manufacture. The effects of decay and neglect are widely apparent from the most cursory

6.4: View of the De Hilton family monument in the Church of St Mary the Virgin, Swine, East Riding, Yorkshire. This monument was examined during the Church Monuments Society Symposium visit (29 July 2006), when it was found that several of the medieval alabaster monuments at Swine show evidence of damage from the widespread problem of rising damp. [*Author*]

6.5: Detail showing severe cracking and evidence of movement on the monument to Sir John Burgoyne, 3rd Bt (died 1709) and his wife Constance (died 1711), attributed to Edward Stanton, at the Church of All Saints, Sutton, Bedfordshire. [*Author*]

study of surviving church monuments, and this awareness is reinforced by appreciation of past and recent losses.

Vandalism

Putting to one side the inevitable effects of ageing and the

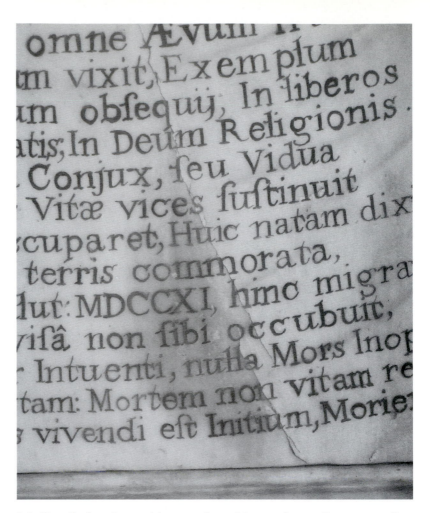

6.6: Detail showing evidence of cracking and rust from corroding internal iron cramps on the monument to Sir John Burgoyne, 3rd Bt (died 1709) and his wife Constance (died 1711), attributed to Edward Stanton, at the Church of All Saints, Sutton, Bedfordshire. [*Author*]

climate, the subject of vandalism is thus inseparable from the study of monuments **[Fig. 6.7]**. Vandals generally seek to damage or destroy objects held to contain some special symbolic value or significance which they actively dislike or disapprove of. It is a violently projective force, to which all societies seem to be periodically vulnerable. Immensely egotistical and self-celebratory, vandalism leaves triumphant concrete traces of the vandal's work, to which it is its own monument. Iconoclastic vandalism is most likely in periods of intended revolutionary social change whose advocates turn against monuments which represent historical continuities with the past from which they wish to forcibly detach themselves. It ranges widely in scale and kind, from individual zeal to the vindictive actions of occupying armies, as well as direct government policy. John Stow's 1598 *Survey of London* provides a rich source of information on vandalised monuments compiled directly in response to such events.[15] Recent church burnings from Ulster to India and Iraq remind us, if we need reminding, of the undiminished potential for violence fuelled by religious and political hatred.

6.7: Detail of the monument produced by Nicholas Stone in 1625 to Sir John and Lady Monson, in the Church of St John the Baptist, South Carlton, Lincolnshire, showing one of the many vandalised kneeling figures, here with the top of the figure's head hacked off. [*Author*]

Vandalism may also be the result of well-intentioned interventions, including the vast amount of damage to monuments associated with the wholesale 'restoration' of churches in the late eighteenth and nineteenth centuries, which triggered the modern conservation movement led by William Morris and his followers, as reflected in the aims of the Society for the Protection of Ancient Buildings.[16] More recent problems include the widespread tendency to garishly repaint monuments in the misguided belief that they were all originally brightly coloured. Westminster Abbey and Southwark Cathedral provide particularly unfortunate modern examples of this kind of damage. Theft is also a serious problem. Ten years ago there were approximately seventeen break-ins to Anglican churches in Britain every single day of the week.[17] This lamentable situation has not improved, and recent years have seen a marked increase in the theft of brasses and other parts of monuments which can be sold as scrap metal.

An increasingly authoritative society

The antiquaries of sixteenth and seventeenth-century Britain such as John Stow (1525/6-1605) and Sir William Dugdale (1605-86) set out to record as many surviving church monuments as possible because they were acutely aware of the scale of recent destruction and the imminent risk of future iconoclasm.[18] In 1631 John Weever contrasted the traditional reverence for monuments to the attitudes of contemporary iconoclasts: 'swearing and protesting that all these are remaines of Antichrist, papisticall and damnable'.[19] Subsequent European history provides countless unfortunate examples of self-styled 'revolutionary' political fanaticism intent on transforming the social order together with its basic belief system, one major aspect of which usually involves the rewriting of history and, in particular, the destruction of monuments and memorials to those variously deemed 'enemies of the people', or 'class enemies', or whatever.

In this respect the circumstances of the formation and history of the Church Monuments Society may perhaps be compared to the work of our not-so-distant antiquarian forbears, motivated both by direct memories of the Blitz and anxiety concerning the future of our national ecclesiastical heritage. Certainly an interest in and affection for church monuments stands in marked contrast to the widely fashionable contemporary view that the Reformation involved an overnight end to the so-called 'cult of the dead', oblivious both to the richness of pre-Reformation religion and its social roles, and the universal human need to celebrate and mourn which monuments embody. As Society founder-member Clive Easter concludes:

> I think that the principal achievement, other than the journal, must be that we have established ourselves as one of the leading authorities on the subject of commemorative art and that our expertise continues to grow. We have been successful in raising the profile of church monuments and this we continue to do whether the interested individual is concerned with costume, architecture etc. I feel that the coming years will see us as an increasingly authoritative society at the forefront of art historical debates on the subject. Equally important is the increasing awareness that the church has in preserving and maintaining its historical legacies and we have been instrumental in helping in this process. I feel that the future is essentially a bright one for us as we continue to be recognised as an authoritative organisation. Unfortunately, the plight of many monuments is increasingly dire and we might be fighting a losing battle in so many cases. We may be a small voice in the darkness but we are being heard.[20]

We should also recall that, whilst some types of monument are neglected in contemporary Britain, others are the subject of widespread growing popular interest, especially standing stones, and stone circles. The growth of popular interest in genealogy and family history, together with the success of the 'living churchyards' movement, which has brought many neglected churchyards into use as well-tended nature reserves, both have potential lessons for those interested in the future of historical church monuments. The afterlife of prehistoric monuments has attracted much thoughtful archaeological attention in recent years, and Richard Bradley has written eloquently on the ways they continued to function meaningfully in centuries and even millennia after their original functions were forgotten.[21] We might similarly consider church monuments as embodiments of important historical continuities which are all the more important in an age which has little or no long-term historical memory. In an age fascinated by hybridity of every kind, it seems important to emphasise that the study of church monuments involves a twin attention to matters of artistic value and meaning as well as to conservation issues in a manner quite distinct from most contemporary art history. The Church Monuments Society seems well positioned to prioritise and articulate these issues alongside and in relation to one another.

Living societies, like individuals, are able to constantly integrate and learn from the past in relation to the always unpredictable future. Things go badly wrong for societies, like individuals, if this process breaks down. Looking back, we gradually come to understand ourselves in relation to our families, not judging our younger selves too harshly for having not all along known the lessons that only accumulated experience can teach us. Much the same is true for societies as a whole. If we know nothing at all of our own family histories, our knowledge of ourselves is radically impaired. What would consciousness amount to, if we had no memory at all of who we were, where we come from, and used to be, and how we grew into the people we are today? Much the same question might be asked of societies as a whole. As Nadezhda Mandelstam asked in *Hope Abandoned*, the second part of her remarkable personal history of life in Russia in the Lenin and Stalin eras: 'What can we expect to happen in a country with a disordered memory? What is a man worth if he has lost his memory?'.[22]

Conclusion: monuments and cultural memory

Churches, together with the fittings and furnishings they house, including monuments, play a quiet but central role in the work of cultural memory.[23] It therefore seems regrettable that the main tone of recent discussion within the Church of England concerning the future uses of redundant historic churches has focused almost entirely on wholesale re-functioning into offices, galleries, private dwellings and so on, to the virtual exclusion of serious consideration of how church visiting might be encouraged on a par with other forms of cultural tourism. The most extensive discussion of the role of monuments in modern Britain has been related to the question of how best to commemorate the late Diana, Princess of Wales, with suggestions ranging from the making of new memorial gardens and the naming of hospitals, schools, and play-grounds, to the water-feature installed in her memory in Hyde Park in 2004. In all of this, surprisingly little attention has been paid to the distinction between memorials and monuments, nor has much attention been paid to questions of mourning, or to the enduring significance of the transmission of the stories and legends of great lives and great events which lies at the heart of the testimonial impulse to memorialise. Instead, throughout the debate, there has been a tenacious strand of hostility to the very idea of monuments, as if they were some kind of luxury which we would do well to do without in their entirety, though of course such puritanical hostility is to be found in every age.

Surely few claims are more insidiously wrong and misguided than the oft-quoted words of Brecht's Galileo concerning the supposed unhappiness of the land in need of heroes.[24] This is not to question the need to enlarge our sense of exemplary public and private heroism. Should we, therefore, conclude that monuments can no longer be made? Such pessimism is not borne out by the plethora of new public monuments which strongly suggest that we do not nowadays lack sufficient confidence in ourselves, or our values, to be able to envisage making works of art intended largely for the future. Equally significant is the recent widespread revival of interest in the subject of war memorials, and concern for their protection. The question, however, remains how such concerns and interests might be connected to the larger question of protecting existing monuments which so frequently commemorate individuals of whom little or no other record survives, or whose names are not even recorded. The future of the Church Monuments Society depends in large part on our ability to convincingly articulate such aims, building on the recognition that our past successes seem closely related to our equal attention to questions of conservation and church-visiting as well as to the unique qualities of monuments themselves, and the skills of countless generations of largely anonymous craftsmen whose legacy so vividly and poignantly continues to bring the past to life.

Acknowledgements

I am grateful to Sally Badham, Claude Blair, John K. Bromilow, Clive Easter, and Philip J. Lankester for information provided in the preparation of this chapter.

7

Modern Antiquarians? Pagans, 'Sacred Sites', Respect and Reburial

Robert J. Wallis

The link between paganism and antiquarianism is not new: following John Aubrey (1626-97), William Stukeley (1687-1765) linked Stonehenge in Wiltshire to the Druids and styled himself the Archdruid Chyndonax.[1] More recently, the punk musician turned modern antiquary, archaist and pagan, Julian Cope, published *The Modern Antiquarian: a Pre-Millennial Odyssey through Megalithic Britain* in 1998, a widely celebrated volume soon followed in 2004 by *The Megalithic European: The 21st Century Traveller in Prehistoric Europe*. The former volume, particularly, linked British prehistoric archaeology to ancient paganism and so inspired contemporary pagans to make their own pilgrimages to sites. Today's pagans and others have been making such visits for some time, of course: nearly one thousand members of the Grand Lodge of the Ancient Order of Druids held a ceremony at Stonehenge in 1905,[2] and ceremonies ceased in 1985 (until 'managed open access' from 2000) after travelers clashed with police at the infamous 'Battle of the Beanfield', when the Stonehenge Free Festival was stopped.[3] Arguably, though, Cope's work, alongside the 1990s journal *3rd Stone: Archaeology, Folklore and Myth – The Magazine for the New Antiquarian*, galvanized a pre-millennial fascination with ancient sites. My recent work, both independently,[4] and in collaboration,[5] over the last decade or so, has attended to these contemporary pagan interests in the past, focusing on 'sacred sites' and the representation of the past. The most extensive published output on this topic over the last decade has been from the 'Sacred Sites, Contested Rites/Rights Project',[6] co-directed by myself, an archaeologist, and my colleague Jenny Blain, an anthropologist.[7] While my earlier work argued that pagans should not be seen as 'fringe' and eccentric, but as serious and equal stakeholders in our heritage, and that dialogue between the interest groups is crucial to resolving differences,[8] our more recent research indicates the climate is changing and such dialogue is now taking place in some instances.[9] Tensions endure, but pagans are now often viewed as a minority interest group whose views must be engaged with and taken seriously. Site access, site welfare and site management are of concern to pagans, as is ancestor welfare, and the reburial of prehistoric British human remains is now on the heritage agenda. As such, some pagan interests in things antique may qualify them as antiquaries or archaists themselves, while in other instances they disrupt these categories. In many ways, pagan practices re-enchant the past and, as such, fit Nietzsche's concept of antiquarian history as a form of history which seeks to create a feeling of connection to one's past.[10] Through their beliefs and practices, pagans feel connected to the prehistoric monuments of the British Isles and the 'ancestors' who built them. Such a re-enchanted past may challenge how heritage sites are managed, bringing pagans into conflict or dialogue with archaeologists and others who curate the past, with access to sites and calls for the reburial of human remains, being contested issues. There are also implications for how prehistoric material culture is curated, but while some aspects of paganism challenge orthodox archaeology, many pagans, campaigning for the protection of sites, for instance, are also a resource for heritage managers.

Earth mystics – modern antiquarians

I borrow the title of my chapter from Julian Cope, a punk musician with *The Teardrop Explodes*, who published an imaginative and practical gazetteer of ancient sacred pagan sites in Britain entitled *The Modern Antiquarian*.[11] Cope is a self-styled modern antiquary, who might also be termed an archaist, with a passion for the megalithic past and the pagan religions of antiquity. He describes how, 'Before the Romans foisted their straight lines upon us, these isles undulated with all that was the wonder of our Mother Earth'.[12] Further, 'The evidence of a spiritual basis to these sites – probably a goddess-based one – is overwhelming'.[13] The power of the sites today is also held to be significant, as they 'can offer healing', Cope says, and he advises that visitors should 'always hold shamanic experiments' at megalithic sites.[14] In earlier work Cope identifies himself as a pagan, although it isn't clear where the boundaries lie between what is pagan and what is not, since he claims 'Cliff Richard is a Pagan … Cliff is a Pagan for Christ, but he's still a Pagan'.[15] More recently, however, Cope's interests, always unconventional and idiosyncratic, have moved away from and are critical of the contemporary paganism I discuss here.[16] This does not detract from the fact that Cope's very successful books on archaeological sites have promoted pagan pilgrimages to them and respect for them, and as such the titles of modern antiquarian and archaist for him seem fitting. His areas of interest are broad, from prehistoric archaeology and the past in the present, to paganism and mysticism. Where modern archaeology might be perceived by some to demystify the past and approach it in scientific terms, the work of Cope, among other earth mystics, attempts to re-enchant the British landscape with goddesses and other deities, spirits, wights, mystical energies, ancestors, mystery and imagination. The success of these alternative archaeologists begs serious engagement from those engaged professionally with the past.

7.1: Druids process ritually around the Neolithic monument of Avebury Henge, Wiltshire. Druid and other pagan rituals at Avebury are commonplace, particularly at festival times celebrating the wheel of the year – in this instance, Beltane (Mayday, the first day of summer, 1998). [*Author*]

Other alternative archaeologies include the work of Michael Dames and Terence Meaden, who again focus on goddesses in prehistory. Dames' work, *The Silbury Treasure* (1976) followed by *The Avebury Cycle* (1977), interprets the megalithic complex of Avebury in Wiltshire as evidence of a Neolithic goddess religion.[17] These ideas have their origin in earlier academic research of the 1950s, when O.G.S. Crawford, Gordon Childe and Glyn Daniel proposed the existence of Neolithic mother goddesses, an idea popularised very successfully (if problematically, for many archaeologists) from the 1970s by Marija Gimbutas.[18] Dames' contribution was to tie these goddess interpretations to the megalithic complex of Avebury, particularly Silbury Hill, seeing the hill and its landscape setting as a three-dimensional expression of 'the harvest goddess', with the hill itself embodying the pregnant belly of the goddess.[19] Terence Meaden's work, *The Secrets of the Avebury Stones* (1999), also takes an interest in Neolithic goddesses, extending his thesis to consider fertility in general, arguing for a Neolithic fertility cult.[20] Meaden sees the shapes of the stones of the Avebury circles as purposely sculpted to be male or female, with irregularities in their surfaces revealing fertility symbols. This once again recalls earlier academic archaeological work, this time associating megalithic sites with fertility cults. As one reviewer commented, 'There are breasts, vulvas, various orifices, phallic stones and their shadows. It's a provocative parade of lithic seduction'.[21]

Imaginative as these goddess and fertility approaches are, re-enchanting the past as they do so, there is no evidence for a coherent prehistoric 'goddess religion' or indeed a fertility-focused religion. Nor should we expect there to be one: ethnographic examples evince diversity of belief, animic ontologies and polytheisms, rather than overarching 'goddess religion', and in line with this, the archaeological data indicate a broad range of – for want of finer terms – religious, ritual, social and economic activities, undergoing constant change over time. My interest here, though, is not so much in the veracity of these alternative archaist archaeologies, as the way in which they are attractive to and indeed inspire a number of interest groups, and contemporary pagans in particular.

Pagans today

Paganism today is a generic term referring to a number of recognised and coherent sets of beliefs and practices.[22] There is such diversity that we might rather speak in the plural of 'paganisms', comprised of a variety of allied or associated 'paths' or 'traditions' such as Wicca or modern witchcraft;[23] Druidry **[Fig. 7.1]**, drawing on Iron Age and other Druids as well as 'Celtic' and Medieval sources;[24] Heathenry **[Fig. 7.2]**, engaging with Anglo-Saxon, Norse and other Scandinavian archaeology and literature;[25] and Goddess Spirituality, with a specific focus on ancient goddesses.[26] All of these paths, despite their differences, are united by a perception that nature can be understood and directly engaged with as deified, sacred or otherwise animated by 'spirit', or forming a living community of human and non-human people. There are archaist pagans who see their 'traditions' as stretching back into prehistory, taking little account of historical change and the difficulties of

7.2: A Heathen performs a ritual at Wayland's Smithy long barrow, a Neolithic funerary monument in Oxfordshire, in the late 1990s. Many Heathens, whose practices draw on Northern folklore, mythology and archaeology, regard this site as especially significant due to its association with the figure of Wayland the Smith. [*Author*]

interpreting what ancient paganisms looked like. The notion of an unbroken tradition of witchcraft in Britain (and other parts of Europe) from prehistory through the medieval witch trials to the present in some forms of Wicca, marks one example, largely drawing on the outdated if popular and stimulating works of Margaret Murray.[27] Other pagans are more sensitive to the issue of historicity, situating themselves and their practices and beliefs very much in the present, but drawing on the past in a process of re-enchantment, reinvention and reconstruction. While there are 'capital P Pagans', those who use the term themselves, there are others who avoid it, preferring the title of their respective path (Druid, Heathen, and so on), or a loose understanding of pagan which cannot be pigeon-holed. Such diversity makes it difficult to pin down what paganism is, and as the examples discussed here indicate, while there is agreement on certain issues, pagans tend to resist the idea of a coherent, organised 'Paganism'.

For some pagans, such antiquaries as William Stukeley **[Fig. 7.3]** are important 'ancestors', not only for recognising the significance of megalithic remains but also for associating himself with ancient paganism. Stukeley became the first secretary of the Society of Antiquaries of London in 1718 and, following John Aubrey, linked Stonehenge to the Druids. The ancient Druids, for Stukeley, comprised a priesthood professing a fragment of the one, true Patriarchal religion, of which Christianity was the most recent manifestation. He went on to style himself as the Archdruid Chyndonax of Mount Haemus, and in the 1720s drafted a number of books outlining his theories, preaching, as the historian Ronald Hutton has put it, a 'pagan religion embodied in the old monuments which was actually valid,

7.3: 'A peep into the sanctum sanctorum' of Stonehenge in Wiltshire, an engraving by Stukeley dated 1724. Stukeley's 'druids', robed, with staffs and sagely beards, engage reverentially with an idealised version of the site. [William Stukeley, *Stonehenge* (1740)].

and reflected cosmic truths'.[28] There is no evidence for Iron-age Druid ritual at Stonehenge, of course, and Stukeley went on to convert back to Christianity, popularising as a vicar the idea that the Druids were emissaries sent by Abraham to bring the Patriarchal religion to Britain;[29] yet Stukeley's archaist interpretation of Stonehenge as an ancient pagan Druid temple has become a resource which some pagans today draw upon to inspire and, in some instances, legitimate their practices.

The idea of Stukeley as marking a historical precedent has been picked up on by some contemporary pagan Druids. Ross Nichols, for instance, founder of the Order of Bards, Ovates and Druids in 1964, claimed, misleadingly, that Stukeley was in his time the head of a Druid order.[30] Nichols is probably imaginatively referring to Stukeley's credentials as a freemason, having been initiated as such, according to his diary, on 6 June 1721. Pagan Druids today tend to distance themselves from Stukeley's Christian connections, and see themselves and ancient Druids as pagans. It is interesting to note how, in their engagements with the past, some contemporary pagans – there are plenty who are more careful in their interpretation of the past – creatively select information which suits their tradition-building most appropriately, associating Stukeley and Stonehenge with Druidry, on the one hand, but on the other distancing Stukeley's Christian persuasions and his appropriation of ancient Druidry as monotheistic and patriarchal. Such convenient attention to certain details but neglect of others is not necessarily intentional but a form of 'cognitive slippage', and creates a new tradition out of material which itself favoured certain views over others. A convergence is therefore evident between antiquarianism and certain paganisms today, particularly Druidry.

Ritual at 'sacred pagan' sites

Looking beyond historical material, pagans engage with megalithic sites in various ways today, most visibly in the form of pilgrimage and ritual. With pagan ceremonies such as those at Avebury now a tradition stretching back at least two decades, they are a part of Britain's heritage. Postcards available at sites have, in recent years, depicted Druid ceremonies: the example illustrated **[Fig. 7.4]**, available from tourist shops at Avebury, is comprised of a montage of photographs including examples of Druid ceremonies, and is accompanied by the following text on the reverse which clearly glosses meaning into the images: 'Avebury, Wiltshire: Midsummer Day. The stones seem eternal, but traditions change. Thus we find meaning in the lost beliefs of all our ancestors'. Also in the last year or so, pagan festivals such as summer solstice, as well as the dates of specific rituals, have been listed on menus in the Red Lion pub. Tourists have come to expect to see a pagan handfasting (marriage or joining of partners) or child-naming (or child blessing) ceremony,

AVEBURY

7.4: A postcard available from tourist shops at Avebury, showing druid ceremonies, accompanied by the following text on the reverse: 'Avebury, Wiltshire: Midsummer Day. The stones seem eternal, but traditions change. Thus we find meaning in the lost beliefs of all our ancestors'. Tourist culture foregrounds the mystical nature of such monuments and uses imagery of pagan ritual to emphasise this association. [*Mike Pitts*]

and during my ongoing fieldwork at the site, tourists remark disappointedly if there is no ritual at the time of their visit.

Traces of ritual may remain after the event, however; a convention for many pagans is to make votive offerings **[Fig. 7.5]**. This may take the form of a garland of flowers, a piece of bread, a candle, incense, or less permanent substances such as mead, ale or cider. These instances of material culture are valuable in understanding the nature of pagan rituals at archaeological sites, with such offerings intended to honour, respect, invoke or placate the non-human beings thought to dwell or make presence there. The remains of ritual can, though, include broken glass, plastic bottles, fire debris and other 'ritual litter' which someone has to clear up and which can be damaging to a site – unsightly scorch marks on the sarsen stones inside West Kennet long barrow caused by the lighting and placing of candles are an ongoing problem. While pagan interests in the past present problems for heritage managers, they can also be allied to heritage preservation. Pagans approaching archaeological sites as sacred may regularly visit those close to their homes, forming a sustained connection to them, and so site welfare is an important issue. An example is the National Trust Guardianship scheme instituted in the 1990s, under which local pagans and others joined forces with the National Trust to clear up ritual litter, monitor impact on sites, and provide on-site guardianship during annual pagan festivals.[31] This organised approach to site welfare, involving pagans, has been re-instituted since 2005 as part of the 'Avebury Sacred Sites Forum' (ASSF). Pagans involved in site welfare, then, can be seen as allied to the aims of heritage management.

Much of the pagan activity at archaeological monuments I have discussed may be regarded as, for the most part, safe, tame and perhaps quintessentially, eccentrically, English. Pagan interests in archaeological monuments can be far more challenging, however, not only in terms of ritual litter and instances of intentional or unintentional damage to sites, but also with regard to site access. Stonehenge crystallises many of these issues, with ongoing tensions and negotiations over summer solstice 'managed open access' with 30,000 attendees in 2008,[32] and at Avebury unease between pagans, local people (some of whom are pagan), the National Trust and Kennet District Council are magnified at pagan festival times in the summer.[33] Furthermore, site welfare for some pagans extends to ancestor welfare, and the issue of respect for and the reburial of prehistoric human remains is a burgeoning issue.

A British reburial issue

Stukeley and other antiquaries are key figures in the development of field archaeology, yet their interventions at sites were often problematic in the light of today's excavation techniques and non-invasive investigative procedures. It is

7.5: Pagan votive offerings at West Kennet long barrow, a Neolithic monument which comprises a part of the Avebury complex in Wiltshire. These offerings were left in the main chamber at the time of Beltane, 2009, and include seasonal foliage tied with a ribbon, and a loaf of home-made bread – all of which may be classed as 'ritual litter'. [*Author*]

interesting that despite these advances, archaeologists are viewed by some pagans as nothing more than grave-robbing antiquarians under a different name. Archaeologists excavating in the Avebury region in recent field seasons have often had to deal with protests from Druids, for instance, and their rites at megalithic tombs and related sites involving (perceived) direct communication with prehistoric 'ancestors' prompts many pagans to feel a responsibility not only to the sites but also to the ancient peoples themselves; site welfare extends to ancestor welfare, as expressed by the voice of one Druid:

> Every day in Britain, sacred Druid sites are surveyed and excavated, with associated finds being catalogued and stored for the archaeological record. Many of these sites include the sacred burials of our ancestors. Their places of rest are opened during the excavation, their bones removed and placed in museums for the voyeur to gaze upon, or stored in cardboard boxes in archaeological archives … I believe we, as Druids, should be saying 'Stop this now. These actions are disrespectful to our ancestors.' When archaeologists desecrate a site through excavation and steal our ancestors and their guardians … It is a theft … We should assert our authority as the physical guardians of esoteric lore. We should reclaim our past.[34]

In a tone reminiscent of calls for reburial among indigenous communities, Davies is associating his archaist claims to the past with those of such claimants as Native Americans and Aboriginal Australians. Precisely how this sort of pagan concern over reburial can be addressed is unclear, but during discussion of the proposals for implementing the management plan for Stonehenge, Philip Shallcrass ('Greywolf'), wrote a letter to English Heritage and the National Trust:

> I expressed my concern that any burials found might simply end up in boxes in a museum basement. I asked for access to burials on site when they were uncovered, for permission to make ritual before burials were removed, and also whether it would be possible to re-bury the ancestral remains after a suitable period of study, preferably within the Stonehenge area … Both English Heritage and the National Trust replied very promptly and favourably.[35]

While their views may be contrary to the preservation ethos of heritage discourse, it is interesting that pagan voices are being taken seriously by heritage managers, indicating that pagan viewpoints are respected alongside other commentators on the heritage of Britain.[36] The future of Stonehenge is far from resolved:[37] in December 2007 proposals for a road tunnel past Stonehenge and other aspects of the proposed management plan for the Stonehenge landscape were scrapped by government, looking instead towards 'possible small scale improvements'[38] in the future. Pagans concerned over the excavation and treatment of human remains in the Stonehenge environs have therefore focused their attention elsewhere.[39]

Druid claims for reburial at Avebury

Speaking as 'Reburial Officer' for the Council of British Druid Orders, or COBDO,[40] Paul Davies has, among other actions over the last two years or so, collected signatures calling for the reburial of certain high profile human remains at the Alexander Keiller Museum in Avebury, particularly the child known as Charlie (excavated by Harold Grey in the early twentieth century from the southern ditch of Avebury henge), on display in the museum. Davies made contact with the National Trust at Avebury and Devizes Museum in Wiltshire, initiating dialogue, and organised a small protest at the Alexander Keiller Museum in January 2007,[41] which caught the attention of the local press.[42] A document entitled 'Guidance and Request for the Reburial of Druid Ancestral Remains at Avebury' authored by COBDO was submitted to heritage organisations and the COBDO West website has an online (undated) document entitled 'Reburial Officer Statement' outlining the order's standpoint on reburial. Interestingly, this document draws on recent UK legislation on human remains. A working group, established in 2002 by the Department of Culture, Media and Sport (DCMS), examined 'the current legal status of human remains within the collections of publicly funded Museums and Galleries in the United Kingdom', and produced a 'Human Remains Report' which made recommendations for dealing with requests for the return of human remains.[43] Neither the panel nor the report made explicit recommendations with regard to British prehistoric material, but the onus in the case of claimants is to demonstrate a 'close genetic' link to the remains at issue. Identifying this as of potential import to pagan claims for the reburial of prehistoric human remains in Britain, the COBDO West 'Reburial Officer Statement' suggests:

> The human remains of Charlie and the Kennet Avenue ancestors are everyone's family and belong to us all. Modern research on mtDNA from the University of Oxford clearly proves an unbroken genetic link between people today indigenous to Europe and our long dead. Statistically, these range between 43% and 2%. Women therefore carry our ancestral line from our deep past and into the future. Oxford also state that male DNA traces back through deep time. Until this research is disproved I will assume that members of the Council, like all people indigenous to Europe, have a 'close genetic' claim for reburial as stated in the DCMS Guidance (ibid: 26). We all have a close and unbroken cultural and spiritual relationship with the human remains of our ancestors. It is time to remember who we are – the ancestors reborn. This genealogical claim therefore informs

and underpins the main points of our request for reburial that are based upon ethics and belief.[44]

How ancestors are constituted is, of course, a construction, and how 'close' an ancestral link there needs to be, based on DCMS guidelines, is as yet untested. Davies' argument, based on unspecific genetic inheritance, may well be less strong than a religious argument given that Druidic religious claims are as authentic as those of any other religion. Interestingly, Davies' argument is also based on Druid traditions regarding initiatory connections to landscape and ancestors,[45] as well as the idea that 'putting things back is as important as taking things away.' All of these many efforts on the part of Druids calling for reburial have not gone unrecognised, and the respective museums have responded, with English Heritage and the National Trust announcing a public consultation on reburial of the Avebury material in addition to quarterly meetings with COBDO to discuss the reburial issue, and permitting two Druid ceremonies over the remains. Furthermore, David Thackray, head of archaeology at the National Trust, and Sebastian Payne, Chief Scientist for English Heritage, commented jointly that:

> Human remains have a unique status within museum collections, and should always be treated with respect … These are sensitive issues with wide implications. To date, these new guidelines are untested and their scope goes beyond the individual case we will be considering at Avebury, with implications for museums across the country.

Thackray added that COBDO's claim would indeed 'be assessed under Department for Culture Media and Sport's (DCMS) guidelines'.[46] The language of heritage management here carefully chooses 'respect' in response to pagan claims to the contrary, to indicate that respect is integral to the process of excavating and storing human remains. Also, the language makes it clear that the DCMS guidelines will be followed. It will be interesting to see how the remit of a 'close genetic' link is tested. Meanwhile, Davies has recently expanded his scope and made a formal request for the 'reburial of 50 ancestors taken from West Kennet long barrow to the Duckworth Laboratory [the Leverhulme Centre for Human Evolutionary Studies] at the University of Cambridge', 'nine ancestors from Stonehenge', as well as the 'Wookey Witch', the remains of an allegedly 1,000 year-old Anglo-Saxon witch found in the Wookey Hole caves and now displayed at Wells and Mendip Museum.

Honouring the ancient dead

Arguably, the claims for reburial from COBDO are intentionally confrontational. The call for respect for prehistoric human remains and permission to perform pagan ceremonies over them as they are excavated, from a different quarter, has subtler and likely more sustained implications. Honouring the

Ancient Dead (HAD) is an organisation founded by the Druid Emma Restall Orr, and although HAD is not exclusively pagan, it is committed to 'honouring the ancient dead',[47] and aims to 'ensure respect for ancient pagan remains' with 'clear interactions between archaeologists, historians, landowners, site caretakers, museums and collectors ... and the pagan community':

> The purpose of this interaction is clear and positive communication that will inspire a broader and deeper understanding of the sanctity of all artefacts (notably those connected with ritual, sacrifice, burial and human remains) sourced from the Pagan eras of the British Isles. HAD will be seeking assurances that there will be communication and consultation on matters relating to such artefacts and remains.[48]

With a broad and long-term view (rather than calling for immediate reburial), HAD is particularly concerned with furthering dialogue and establishing consultation between the interest groups during excavations as well as the opportunity for pagans to 'make ritual in appropriate ways, honouring the spirits involved'. As with 'ancestors', how 'appropriate ritual' is constituted is at issue since, obviously, we do not know what sorts of rituals, if any, were associated with these remains. As such, HAD proposes a 'rite of committal of human remains' for potential use by museum personnel and others, which takes care to specify how much is 'not known' of either the persons committed or their 'religion' and ritual.[49]

The aims of HAD to promote dialogue and respect resulted in collaboration with the Manchester Museum (linked to the University of Manchester) and the Museums Association in a conference entitled 'Respect for Ancient British Human Remains: Philosophy and Practice' (November 2006), which brought archaeologists, museum professionals and pagans into dialogue. This demonstrates the ways in which heritage managers and museum professionals are addressing a timely issue with respect to all involved. There are challenges to this sort of dialogue, though:[50] the British Association for Biological Anthropology and Osteoarchaeology (BABAO) sent a letter to the Museums Association requesting that it withdraw its support from the conference, and in their 'Response to the DCMS Consultation Document *Care of Historic Human Remains*' BABAO states:

> Guidelines for determining the legitimacy of claims on behalf of a religious community, in the absence of direct family relationship to the deceased, must address the question of how frivolous claims are to be discerned and rebutted. As one example, in the UK there are already new-Age and neo-Druid claims for the reburial of prehistoric remains, but no demonstrable continuity across the intervening millennia in

terms either of genealogical descent or of recognition and care of the original burial location.[51]

A clear, problematic distinction is made here between what is 'frivolous' (seemingly, here, pagan interests) and what is 'legitimate' (scientific research), with the axiomatic assumption that the former can be dismissed as wrong while the latter is common sense; indeed the issue of 'demonstrable continuity' speaks to the earlier discussion of 'close genetic' connection as well as how paganism can demonstrate its authenticity if not, of course, unbroken links with the past. Indeed, pagans have thought carefully about this issue; Restall Orr states:

> In terms of reburial, there is no sense of reaching for some authentic ancient rite, or even some ritual that is close to what would have been done in the past. The connection to the dead, to the ancestors, is what is important. Nor is this some special relationship with the ancient dead that Pagans claim: it is simply a religious obligation, integral to Pagan reverence for nature, for spirit, for life (past, present, future).[52]

The viewpoints from Davies/COBDO and HAD make clear that pagans are not of one mind, and, indeed, there is an expanding voice challenging the COBDO viewpoint on reburial. Yvonne Aburrow points to how respect can be offered in other ways, such as through memory and narrative,[53] and her recently-formed group 'Pagans for Archaeology' argues:

> [W]e are opposed to the reburial of ancient human remains, and want them to be preserved so that the memory of the ancestors can be perpetuated and rescued from oblivion, and the remains can be studied scientifically for the benefit of everyone. Of course we want human remains to be treated with respect, but respect does not automatically mean reburial. Respect should mean memory, which involves recovering the stories of past people.[54]

This diversity of opinion in the pagan community is a good sign, evidencing a climate of difference and debate.

Save Tara

A further example, the 'Save Tara' campaign, illustrates the way in which calls for the reburial and the respectful treatment of prehistoric human remains is increasingly affecting archaeology in a broader European context.[55] In Ireland, calls for reburial are part of wider protest over the construction of the twice-tolled M3 motorway[56] through the archaeologically sensitive Gabhra (Skryne) Valley in County Meath.[57] The Hill of Tara and its monuments (including the remains of the inauguration site of early medieval Ireland and a Neolithic passage tomb, the Mound of the Hostages) are the best known of the sites in this region and while the Hill itself will not be damaged by the physical construction of the road, the surrounding Valley will be irrevocably changed including the destruction of archaeology; this destruction includes both known sites and those newly discovered as part of the building project – for example, the major sites of Lismullin Henge, ironically, declared a National Monument, and the Rath Lugh Iron-age hill fort. In a recent article, Maggie Ronayne highlights problematic circumstances in which archaeologists are employed by the National Roads Authority (NRA);[58] that is, those concerned with the conservation of the past are simultaneously involved in its destruction. This circumstance is not new since, in England, rescue archaeology due to road building and other construction is commonplace; but excavation there is conducted by regional units operating independently from the state, in Ireland archaeologists are directly employed by the NRA. Ronayne claims a conflict of interest and raises concerns over the privatisation of archaeology in the Irish Republic, and this setting a precedent for archaeology elsewhere.[59]

At Tara there are claims that archaeological practice has been ethically compromised, with, allegedly, pre-dawn excavations of a burial ground so as to avoid confrontation with protesters. As a result, the claim goes, human remains were poorly recorded and even lost, and if such is the case, the issue of respectful treatment of remains is begging. In their press release, the Save Tara campaign state:

> Tara Campaigners worldwide are supporting a petition to the Irish Government calling on them to re-inter the remains of individuals whose graves have been desecrated by the ongoing construction of the M3 ... The petition went live on Saturday 19th July. Campaigners demand that the ancient remains be reburied in a dignified manner and as closely as possible to the ceremonial layout of the original graveyards. It is estimated that over 60 bodies were disturbed and removed from the Collierstown site and over 27 from Ardsallagh.[60]

Tara was a controversial topic at the recent Sixth World Archaeological Congress (in a further layer of irony, the Congress was sponsored by the NRA) where a plenary session invited the different stakeholders to contribute. My notes record that speakers did not agree on the number of burials excavated, an anomaly which may vindicate protestors' claims regarding ethically-compromised archaeology and disrespectful treatment of human remains. As a result of this plenary, the World Archaeological Congress stated:

> Following the largest ever international gathering of archaeologists in Dublin, Ireland, the World Archaeological Congress has released a statement expressing its opposition

to any further development alongside the new stretch of motorway in the wider landscape zone surrounding the historical site of Tara in Co Meath, Ireland. 'Tara has significance far beyond Ireland itself,' said Professor Claire Smith, President of the World Archaeological Congress. Its iconic significance derives from its unique cultural character, as situated in a broader landscape. The World Archaeological Congress strongly encourages the Irish Government to instigate formal protection measures for this area, and to consider nominating Tara for inscription as a World Heritage site.[61]

In an interesting move for the largest professional body of archaeologists, WAC made a specific statement on reburial:

> Recognising that the reburial of ancient remains in Ireland is subject to the provisions of the National Monuments Act and the agreement of the National Museum of Ireland, the World Archaeological Congress also draws attention to the Vermillion Accord on human remains and suggests that any human remains excavated from the cultural landscape of Tara should be re-interred with due respect as close as possible to their original locations, as this is where these people would have wished to be buried.[62]

One of the organisers of the reburial petition on the Save Tara website is Carmel Diviney of the Hibernian Order of Druids, who said:

> We hope that this petition is the beginning of a debate on the ethics of this archaeological 'resolution' of our ancestors, the indigenous people of Ireland. This debate and respect for our own indigenous people, ourselves, is long overdue and [we hope] that this puts added pressure on the Irish Govt. [sic.] to re-inter the bodies.[63]

Issues raised in the words of Diviney on the construction of indigeneity, and use of this standpoint to make archaist truth-claims about the past, reflect those discussed earlier regarding Davies.[64] Pagans in Ireland, like pagans elsewhere, are key figures mobilised by their passion for site and ancestor welfare.

The re-presentation of Lindow Man
I close with discussion of an example of effective dialogue between the interest groups which built on the success of the 'Respect for Ancient British Human Remains: Philosophy and Practice' conference at the Manchester Museum, involving negotiations over the display of the bog body known as Lindow Man. Originally found at Lindow Moss near Manchester, Lindow Man is on permanent display at the British Museum. On two occasions in the past, in 1987 and 1991, Lindow Man returned to the northwest of England for exhibitions at the Manchester

Museum. Preparation for a third exhibition between April 2008 and April 2009 involved ongoing consultation with various interest groups, including pagans. The 'Consultation Report' of a meeting held on 10 February 2007 includes a section (3.2) entitled 'Spirituality':

> There was broad agreement that the approach taken to Lindow Man needed to reflect that he had been a living human being and that he was most definitely a 'he' and not an 'it', that he was an ancestor and that he must be treated with sensitivity … People felt that there is a spiritual dimension to Lindow Man and how he is treated on display, which also extends to allowing visitors to demonstrate their respect for him as an ancestor. The Museum should explore the option to create a shrine near the Lindow Man exhibition where people could make offerings to the ancestors, of which Lindow Man is a representative but not make offerings *to* Lindow Man. A Pagan perspective on Lindow Man is very important. We want to emphasize his humanity. He certainly is not a museum object. Lindow Man's discovery and excavation was an intersection of then and now, of us and him, that is still on-going, evolving and certainly not over.[65]

As a result, the exhibition includes the display of objects from local residents and other interested parties in order to show that interest in Lindow Man, since his discovery, has its own history. These objects include one woman's 'Care Bear' and, from a pagan, some crow feathers.[66] Furthermore, in a collaboration involving pagans and Bryan Sitch, head of Humanities and curator of the exhibition, opening events at the Manchester Museum in April 2008 involved ceremonies conducted by pagans, and an area has been set aside for people (particularly pagans, though not exclusively so) to make offerings. These negotiations over the re-display of Lindow Man mark a clear example of inclusive and sensitive museum practice,[67] with an apparently successful outcome for the interest groups – which is not, however, to say all voices are satisfied. Reaching understanding through dialogue can only be a positive development. As a further example, the HAD website describes negotiations relating to production of the current *Draft Code of Practice for The Care of Human Remains in Museums*, where differences in understanding were discussed:

> During a meeting between HAD and the Drafting Group, the Chair expressed a lack of understanding as how or why bones or other remains retained their significance even when the 'spirit left the body'. It was only when the non-dualistic world view of many animists and other Pagans was explained, together with notions of tribal song and the webs of land and ancestry, that he grasped the relevance, validity and importance not only of British Pagan sensitivities but those of Pagan traditions around the world.[68]

The case of the representation of Lindow Man, then, indicates how constructive dialogue between museum curators, pagans, archaeologists, local people and other interest groups can be established successfully, leading to the sensitive and respectful display of human remains.

Conclusion

There is a great diversity of contemporary pagan engagements with the past, from those who contest the preservation ethos and challenge archaeological practice, to those who may be archaeologists themselves, or who work with heritage management for the conservation of archaeological sites. These and other alternative interests in the past which might easily be dismissed as eccentric, and without consequence for the practice of archaeology and its allies, are now very much on the agenda. My earlier work pointed to the significance of pagan interests in the past to archaeologists and related interest groups and attempted to initiate dialogue; my more recent research indicates the climate is indeed changing and such dialogue is in effect, with pagans addressed in heritage management literature, in museum policies and at the government level. After an article on pagans and reburial in the Council for British Archaeology's journal *British Archaeology*,[69] one reader wrote in the *Letters* column:

> 'Pagan mysticism' may have 'no place in serious archaeology' (Letters, September) but pagans (like every other interest group) certainly have a role to play in the management of the archaeological resource. As a community heritage officer for a local authority, I work on many heritage and archaeology-related projects. There are as many outlooks, prejudices and hidden agendas as there are groups, but all are passionate about their heritage and committed to working for the benefit of the archaeology. They all have something of value to bring to the table and all deserve the common courtesy of respecting their views – even if we do not agree with them.[70]

Pagans are increasingly viewed, alongside other minorities, as serious if not yet equal stakeholders in our heritage, and these developments are of ongoing interest to the Sacred Sites project which is moving into its second decade of research. There are, then, ways in which some pagans might indeed be termed 'modern antiquarians', of the sort Julian Cope represents, who powerfully re-enchant the past; and there are ways in which the interests of pagans today sit well with or, of course, are problematic for, today's antiquaries. Those archaist pagans who consistently impose the present on the past without awareness of historicity, overlooking or creatively embellishing key evidence as they do so, mark a problematic example. As a newsletter of the Society of Antiquaries opined in 2007, however, antiquaries have been accused of being too morbid in their fascination for funerary remains, they have been accused of being too general in their scope, encompassing all things antique, and they have been accused of being elitist in their studies, blinkered to public interests. Reflecting on the consistently multidisiplinary and interdisciplinary nature of antiquarian studies, however, it is pertinent that paganism and the study of paganism offers a significant intellectual, spiritual, visual and material landscape of some relevance to antiquarian interests.

8

Continuity and Revival in Modern Chinese Culture: the Woodblock Prints of Wang Chao

Anne Farrer

Introduction: tradition and continuity

The significance of China's past in its contemporary art is largely obscured at a time when western-influenced ideas and modes of production dominate academic scholarship, art criticism, exhibitions, and the market.[1] Many leading artists and art movements have developed since the death of Mao Zedong (1893-1976), when the influx of new ideas into China has provoked reactions against cultural traditions, history and politics. Their work, based on ideas drawn from western conceptual art, now constitutes the core of the art market both in China and worldwide. Known collectively as 'Chinese contemporary art,' this work comes from a body of artists, some of whom have left China, but the majority of whom are still working in China as independent artists and as teachers affiliated to Chinese art academies.[2] An important part of this contemporary field is the work of a body of artists who rely on the continuation of traditional techniques and the revival of ideas from China's cultural past.[3] Many of these artists are recognised within the artistic community in China and are known to specialists in the academic and curatorial circles outside China, but their work does not receive the critical or commercial acclaim of contemporary Chinese conceptual artists. This paper sets out to explain the context of continuity and revival in Chinese culture, and how the past plays an essential role in the development of printmaking of the twentieth century – in particular, in the work of the print-artist Wang Chao (b. 1974).

Although the creative output of modern China has been extended far beyond the artistic scope of the past to include media such as oil painting, printmaking, sculpture, textiles, photography and installation,[4] modern artistic creativity is underpinned by a strong cultural continuity in which past models are valued and regenerated.[5] These models are part of a much wider continuity of knowledge of historical, political and philosophical processes, intellectual ideas and visual forms that have been transmitted from one millennium to the next. One of the major forces in creating a continuity of ideas in political and intellectual life in Chinese culture has been through the continued use and value associated with a body of texts, including poetry, history, ritual, divination, and annalistic works compiled during the first millennium BC which were supposedly edited by Confucius (550-479 BC).[6] In the Han dynasty (206 BC-221 AD), these texts became the focus of scholarly enquiry and were recopied and engraved in stone.[7] Recognised as the basis for Chinese society, politics and intellectual life, these texts became known as the Confucian Classics. The texts became the standard works for the education of candidates aspiring to become government officials, and as early as the second century BC candidates were tested on their knowledge of the classics. In later centuries, the official examination required the memorisation of large tracts, which ensured the continued importance of these texts as the core of political and intellectual life in Chinese society over nearly two millennia, until the abolition of the official examination system in 1905.[8]

Antiquities, meaning and legitimacy

China's emperors and rulers have ensured the continuity of knowledge of antiquities and historical artefacts by acquiring them over a period of more than three millennia. For China's rulers, historical artefacts carried a highly important symbolic significance in which they were central to the ritual establishment and recognition of the power of the ruler. Historical records document the myth of the Nine Tripods cast in bronze by a virtuous emperor of the Xia dynasty (c. 2000-1600 BC),[9] and that the acquisition of the bronze tripods was central to the establishment of subsequent rulers of the first millennium BC.[10] Later on, the creation of imperial art collections which included historical artefacts and court-sponsored art represented a complex set of symbolic meanings establishing the legitimacy of the ruler and the glorification of the state.[11] On the establishment of a new state or dynasty, the acquisition of a collection of antiquities, calligraphy and paintings from the past was central to the ritualised process of the emperor assuming the mantle of rule. This often involved sending envoys in search of antiquities and art collections from private collections and other sources. The seizure or dispersal of the imperial art collections was an important stage symbolising the fall of the dynasty.[12] Calligraphy, paintings, and, occasionally, artefacts from the imperial collection were inscribed with poems, colophons and seals by the emperor or his official calligraphers, creating an historical association with the past and adding to the 'body' of historical association carried by the object.[13] The collecting and connoisseurship established by the court were emulated outside the court from the Six Dynasties period (220-589), onwards. Collections were assembled by scholar-officials, aristocrats, and newly-gentrified merchants who contributed to the growth of connoisseurship, thereby reinforcing the continuity of knowledge of antiquities.[14]

In China, an important process in promoting continuity

with the past for the scholar, artist, or artisan is learning through the copying and memorisation of models. In the field of painting, the process of copying as a method for study is first mentioned by the painter and theoretician Xie He (*fl. c.* 479-502), whose Six Canons (*Liufa*), presented a list of criteria which constitute a good quality painting. His sixth canon recommends, 'transmission [of the experience of the past] in making copies', implying that the principles of good works of art should be learned by copying past artists, and, once the basic style and methods are established, the artist could evolve his own style.[15] This approach is illustrated in the biographical details of countless artists who, while working under a tutor, learned different styles of painting through copying paintings by past masters. In this way the compositions and brush-styles of painters who had lived over a millennium before continued as part of living traditions of the past.[16]

The continuity of China's cultural and artistic systems is marked by particular periods of antiquarianism in which archaic models are selectively revived and interpreted in different ways. Antiquarianism in the Song period (960-1279) was regarded as a means by which the emperors could renew their cultural heritage and legitimise their rule.[17] The Song emperors instigated a search for the sources of Chinese culture after centuries of foreign influence and political division under the Tang (618-906) and Five Dynasties (900-960). In the early Song period, objects for court ritual, were manufactured from descriptions based on the study of texts dating back to the Han dynasty. From the eleventh century, antiquarian study was based on researching the antiquities, themselves. After the Mongol conquest of China in the late thirteenth century, a new wave of antiquarianism emerged among scholar-painters who revived archaic painting styles of the Tang and pre-Tang as a means of expressing their regret for the Mongol conquest and their loyalty to the Song imperial line.[18] Their antiquarianism established the beginnings of an 'orthodox' tradition of painting models that was fully realised in the theoretical writings of the artist and scholar Dong Qichang (1555-1636).[19] In the early seventeenth century, a new trend in 'primitive' archaistic figure painting emerged which reflected a cynical reaction to the decline of the imperial administration of the late Ming emperors.[20]

The preservation of classical knowledge

Although the major trend in China's history from the late nineteenth century has been the modernisation of China through the adoption of political, cultural and educational systems from the West, there has remained an underlying connection with China's past and respect for its cultural heritage which has remained a subtext in the history of modern China. Antiquarian interests, revived under imperial patronage in the reign of the

Qianlong emperor (1735–96), were followed by new research amongst private scholars into inscriptions on bronze vessels and stone *stelae* in the late eighteenth and nineteenth centuries.[21] This brought a revival of archaic scripts and seal-carving, and the use of archaic characters as decoration on more popular media.[22] The discovery of oracle bones and plastrons in 1908 which were inscribed with divination texts in burials of the late Shang (*c.* 1500–1050 BC) period inspired further research into early ritual texts and the origins of Chinese writing.[23] In the early twentieth century, scholars loyal to the former Qing dynasty after its fall in 1911 maintained their interest in classical learning and the study of antiquities. They promoted the preservation of their cultural heritage and, for the first time, began the publication of collotype books with reproductions of Chinese antiquities for a wider audience.[24] The publication in 1911 of the *Art Treatises Series* (*Meishu congshu*), made important texts of art theory and connoisseurship available for scholars and students researching Chinese art history.[25] From the 1920s, ancient sites began to be excavated by Chinese archaeologists trained in western scientific methods. From the 1950s, archaeological excavations were state-regulated operations which were regarded as providing China with a renewed legitimisation and identity with its past.[26]

The regeneration of Chinese culture was an important motive behind the initial introduction of western ideas and systems in the early twentieth century. Western models of art education were intended to revive systems of art education and technical practice.[27] From 1902, art instruction was included in an educational system modelled on that of the West. The teaching included oil painting, drawing, design, mechanical drawing, perspective and projective geometry. In the new art academies which were subsequently opened in Shanghai (1912), Beijing (1918), Hangzhou (1928), and in other major cities, the approach was to encourage the co-existence of western and Chinese art taught in the parallel departments of oil painting (*youhuaxi*) and traditional painting (*guohuaxi*) and to bring about a synthesis of the two traditions. In the teaching of traditional Chinese painting, the learning of composition and brushwork by copying reproductions of classic works from the past has continued up to the present, continuing the methods advocated by Xie He in *c.* 500, and displaying the continuation of an underlying attachment to the past.

The Modern Woodcut Movement

The Modern Woodcut Movement (1930–1950),[28] initiated in the late 1920s, synthesised the ideals of modernisation through the introduction of western art with new educational theories devised by the Republic's first minister of education, Cai Yuanpei (1868–1940). Cai Yuanpei proposed that art should be a substitute for religion in forming an ideal society. The new woodcut movement was initiated by the writer, intellectual and collector Lu Xun (1881-1936). Lu Xun had been appointed to the Social Education Office in 1912, where he had given a series of public lectures proposing a programme to disseminate art through all levels of Chinese society. A major factor in the success of the movement was Lu Xun's vision to regenerate and revive the woodcut as the medium for its new function of artistic, social and political expression with a widespread appeal among all strata of the population.[29] The pictorial woodcut had been a familiar element in every level of society in China since its invention in the Tang dynasty (618-906).[30] The pictorial woodcut, previously a multi-staged process carried out by different artisans, was revised by Lu Xun to become a process made by the individual artist who carried out all stages of designing, cutting and printing. Lu Xun introduced socialist realist models from Russia and Europe, and provided formal teaching instruction by a Japanese printmaker, Uchiyama Kakichi (1900-84), to initiate the movement.[31] The woodcuts produced by the artists who participated were innovative, small-sized, black-and-white prints (*heibai muke*) which had immediate success in Shanghai and the surrounding region in the early 1930s. The assimilation of pictorial elements from regional folk art of the north-central region of Shaanxi came about from the late 1930s, when artists at the Lu Xun Academy of Fine Arts in the Communist occupied Yan'an initiated a new regional development of the modern woodcut. Artists combined the black-and-white print, intended for the urban audience, with the visual appearance of the papercut and rural folk art as a means of spreading political propaganda in the mostly uneducated rural audiences.[32] The revival of the coloured folk print genre came about as a result of Mao Zedong's talks at Yan'an in 1942, when the genre was used as a further means for spreading Communist propaganda.[33] In the 1950s, the production of this new genre by urban printing houses and regional workshops is a further indication of the pattern of continuity and the renewal of indigenous traditions in the service of China's modernisation.[34]

In the years following the foundation of the People's Republic of China in 1949, there was a new wave of cultural nationalism in which artists debated aspects of China's native art traditions.[35] As part of this process, and following the success of printmaking in the Modern Woodcut Movement, print-artists in the newly reopened academies relearned the processes of multi-colour printing from woodblocks using water-soluble inks that had originally been devised in the late sixteenth and early seventeenth centuries for book illustrations and sheet prints. In 1954, art academies sent print-artists to the print studio Rongbaozhai in Beijing to learn the colour-printing process.[36] The Rongbaozhai, established in 1894, was the only studio remaining in the Liulichang area that had continued the production of decorative colour-printed stationery using these techniques.[37] Among the art academies represented at this course was the Eastern-China Branch of the Central Academy of Fine Arts (now named the China National Academy of Fine Arts) in Hangzhou, whose director of the printmaking department, Zhang Yangxi, sent the print-artist Xia Ziyi to Beijing to study for six months.[38] The reason for this decision was that Hangzhou in south-east China had been one of the principal printmaking centres several hundred years before, and it was considered appropriate for the academy to introduce a revival of water-soluble colour printing in its printmaking department. When Xia Ziyi returned to Hangzhou, the newly acquired knowledge initiated an important association of the academy's print-artists with water-soluble colour printing that has continued until the present. The academy subsequently opened a section of the printmaking department, the Purple Bamboo Studio (*Zizhuzhai*), for research into the history and practice of processes of colour-printing and for the reproduction of model socialist-realist artworks, paintings, decorative letter-papers, folk prints, compendia of seals and illustrated books.[39]

From the 1950s the woodcut served as one of the important media for the dissemination of socialist realist propaganda under China's newly formed Communist state. The traditional colour woodcuts made with water-soluble inks were amalgamated with techniques of the black-and-white woodcut in larger format prints made in the print departments of newly opened art academies. The illustrated book, significant in pre-modern Chinese culture, was regenerated as a means for spreading socialist realist propaganda. The new picture story-books (*lianhuanhua*) were created using pictures made by artists working for publishing houses in 'illustration' sections of many academy printmaking departments.[40] European oil-based inks, introduced in the 1950s, allowed artists to produce brighter and bolder poster-like images and became the focus of the regional development in printmaking in area of the north-east of China known as the Great Northern Wastes (Beidahuang).[41]

New interest in traditional Chinese culture in the post-Mao period

By the early 1980s, after the death of Mao Zedong and the end of the Cultural Revolution (1966-1976), printmaking gradually lost its socialist realist content and became a conservative medium following printmaking techniques of the previous fifty years.[42] The major artistic movements which followed in the 1980s were not primarily engaged with the development of medium-based art, but were young artists' response to the new philosophical, literary and artistic ideas from the West that had entered China as a result the Open Door policy. The conceptual art that emerged from these young artists addressed issues relating

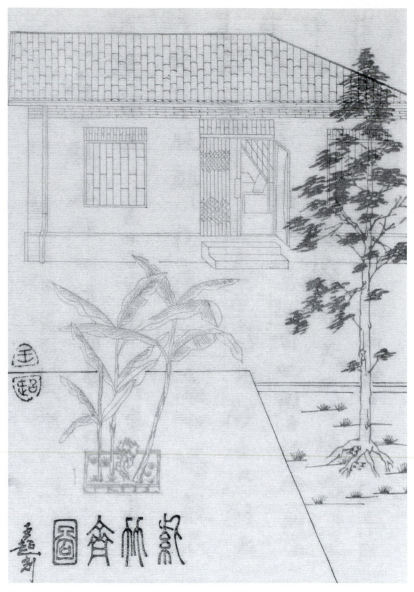

8.1: Frontispiece entitled 'Illustration of the Purple Bamboo Studio' by Wang Chao (b. 1974), from the woodblock printed book, *Foreign Images* (1998), impression 1/26; water-soluble ink on paper; closed book cover: 20 cm x 32.5 cm; frontispiece frame: 16.2 cm x 23.8 cm. The Purple Bamboo Studio at the China National Academy of Fine Arts, Hangzhou, is the only studio of traditional colour woodblock printing in a Chinese art academy. [*Muban Foundation/Artist*]

to history, cultural memory, identity and East–West relationships. From this group, Xu Bing, originally trained as a print-artist, emerged as a leading figure in his work examining language and communication.[43] Trained at the Central Academy of Fine Arts, Beijing, as an undergraduate from 1977 to 1981, Xu Bing produced woodcuts of familiar representational themes of the period with originality and freshness. From the mid–1980s, Xu Bing began to explore conceptual ideas in relation to woodblock printing. His major work, *Book from the Sky* (*Tianshu*), of 1987–91, established Xu Bing as a leading figure of the avant-garde movement in China.

A significant but less prominent counter-movement reviving and re-examining Chinese culture also began in the post-Mao period. The Chinese Communist party relaxed its previously unsuccessful attack on Chinese traditional culture, which had formed a major part of Mao's modernisation programme in the Cultural Revolution, as a means of reasserting its legitimacy. Archaeological discoveries were celebrated, and painters working in traditional media were reinstated. The important place of traditional art during this period can be seen as a reaction against the orthodoxy of the Cultural Revolution.[44] As a result of the new tolerance of traditional culture in China in the 1980s, a new intelligentsia developed made up of the artists and intellectuals who had grown up during the Cultural Revolution and whose education had consisted of Communist indoctrination. These individuals wanted to become knowledgeable in Chinese traditional culture through their interests in calligraphy, painting, poetry and archaeology. In the visual arts, a significant group of artists became interested in re-examining traditional imagery and technical practice. These artists believed that art based on China's native traditions was vital to its future development, in contrast to the westernisation of art and culture that they saw around them.[45] Many of these artists used the traditional media of painting, calligraphy and printmaking in a contemporary manner.[46]

An example of the younger generation of the new intelligentsia in contemporary China can be found in the life and artistic *oeuvre* of the print-artist Wang Chao.[47] Wang Chao is from Heze, Shandong, in north-eastern China, and joined the printmaking department of the China National Academy of Fine Arts, graduating in 1998. Specialising in techniques of colour woodblock printing, he has become a lecturer in the printmaking department and director of the Purple Bamboo Studio. Wang Chao's self-identity and intellectual interests relate to pre-modern and pre-westernised Chinese culture. His prints represent a revival of techniques and subject-matter which predate most other contemporary print-artists who follow the principles established in the Modern Woodcut Movement. As director of the Purple Bamboo Studio, he is heir to traditions of the studio founded in 1954 to research and practise techniques of multi-block colour printing; it is the only studio specialising in colour-printing methods within an art academy in China. Originally situated in its own traditional building within the main campus of the academy, the work of the Purple Bamboo Studio was temporarily suspended during the time the academy was being rebuilt between 2000 and 2003 **[Fig. 8.1]**. The contents of the studio include the woodblocks used for prints made since the 1950s. Wang Chao is now one of the few print-artists in China able to practise these specialist and highly refined printmaking techniques. As a young artist

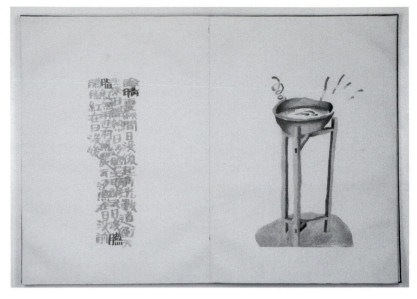

8.2: *Images of Heavenly Phenomena* (1997) by Wang Chao, impression 3/10; concertina album, printed from woodblocks with water-soluble ink on paper; closed book cover: 25 cm x 40.2 cm; main illustration frames: 18 cm x 28 cm. Wang Chao wittily depicts a series of meteorological events with the microcosm of a mundane enamel wash-basin on a stand. [*Muban Foundation/Artist*]

establishing his career in the 1990s, Wang Chao is aware of the importance of developing a personal artistic voice in addition to the representational and technical aspects of his work.[48] He has developed a type of individual antiquarianism in printmaking through which he uses formats, imagery, and techniques drawn from pre-modern China to offer a personal statement about the present. Although, as a developing artist still only in his thirties, the character of this antiquarianism is slowly being evolved and is not yet mature, nonetheless his refined woodcuts represent a significant and unusual achievement in the field of traditional art in contemporary China. Following the practice of artists in pre-modern China, Wang Chao uses different studio names in order to present himself in the guise of a traditional scholar, sometimes humorously. In his print, *The Desk in the Jiuli Studio* (*Jiulifang zhi antou qinggong*) of 2003, he presents himself seated and asleep in the Jiuli Studio with his head on his arms in front of an open book; his glasses are on the table, and an angle-poise lamp is attached to the edge of the table **[Figs 8.5–8.7]**.[49] The table and chair are represented as Ming dynasty furniture, showing the artist's interest in antique furniture.[50]

The work of Wang Chao

The illustrated book is an important element of Wang Chao's printmaking, and he bases his work on formats from colour-illustrated books made between 1580 and 1630 in the late Ming period.[51] Interest in fine, late Ming printing in the twentieth century has been revived through facsimiles produced in the specialist colour-printing studios in Beijing and Shanghai, whose printmaking techniques Wang Chao has studied in depth at the China National Academy of Fine Arts.[52] Through the format of different types of Ming-styled printed book, Wang Chao presents images that give humorously critical reflections about the present through models from the past. *Images of Heavenly Phenomena (Tianhou tuzuan)* of 1997 is a concertina album with image and text imitating the format used in the famous late Ming printed book, the *Ten Bamboo Studio Manual of Calligraphy and Painting (Shizhuzhai shuhua pu)* of *c.* 1619-1633, which reproduces the graded tones of ink paintings and calligraphy in printed form **[Fig. 8.2]**.[53] Wang Chao illustrates a series of meteorological events including sunlight, fog, hail, rain and the falling of a meteorite, inspired by his knowledge of traditional folklore of weather-casting within the microcosm of a mundane enamel wash-basin on its stand. The illustrations, printed in graded tones of ink and colour simulating painting, are accompanied by text in closely printed characters in blocky script with important characters highlighted in darker ink. The series of nine illustrations ends with the destruction of the wash-basin and its stand. Inspired by the weather Wang Chao viewed from the window of his studio one day, this album puts forward a metaphorical comment on the somewhat destructive interchange between the manipulaton of natural resources in modern times and the resulting turbulent changes of the world's climate.

A further printed book, *Foreign Images (Yangxiang tu)* of 1998, relates to the format and subject matter of two famous compendia of finely printed letter-papers in book form, published in 1627 and 1644, which have survived from the late Ming period.[54] Letter-papers with colour-printed decorative images, sometimes with embossing, were printed and sold by stationery shops from the late Ming dynasty until the twentieth century. Wang Chao emulates the format of these works in *Foreign Images* with traditional stitched binding and blue covers, a printed calligraphic label, printed calligraphic introduction and index. These are followed by illustrations within ruled borders, beginning with an illustration of the original Purple Bamboo Studio in delicate translucent colours **[Fig. 8.1]**. The principal pages of this work have exquisite colour-printed representations against a blank background of objects introduced from abroad including a bicycle, sewing machine and lounge suits accompanied by a further embossed image giving a contemporary commentary. Wang Chao uses the abbreviated pictorial imagery of late Ming printed letter-papers which represented well-known literary and historical themes. In the late Ming period, these pictorial vignettes are believed to have been produced as a visual puzzle to test the knowledge of the upwardly mobile merchant classes.[55] In a similar vein, Wang Chao presents in *Foreign Images* simple pictures of modern innovations in China with an ironic

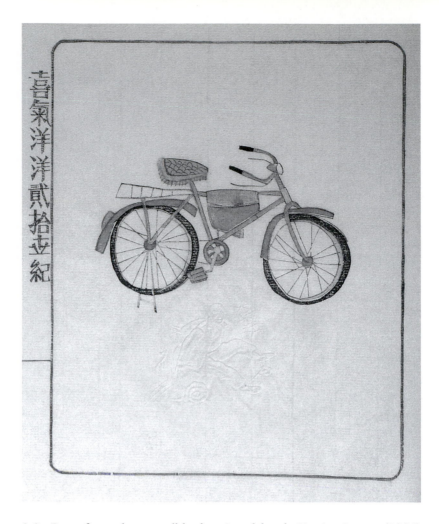

8.3: Page from the woodblock printed book *Foreign Images* (1986) by Wang Chao, impression 1/26; water-soluble ink on paper; closed book cover: 20 cm x 32.5 cm; illustration frame: 14.6 cm x 18.2 cm. Wang Chao portrays pictures of modern innovations in China. The twelfth innovation is a bicycle, printed in colour, accompanied by the embossed image of a peasant who has fallen from the bicycle and is plunging through the clouds with the embossed caption 'Great Leap Forward'. [*Muban Foundation/Artist*]

twist under the title, 'The Twentieth Century Bursting with Happiness', printed outside the ruled border of each illustration. The illustrations consist of finely colour-printed images of each innovation, which are accompanied by a pictorial response in the embossed image. The twelfth innovation is a bicycle, printed in colour, accompanied by the embossed image of a peasant who has fallen from the bicycle, and is hurtling through the clouds, accompanied by the embossed caption, 'Great Leap Forward', which refers to the political movement initiated in 1958 **[Fig. 8.3]**. Here Wang Chao light-heartedly comments that westernisation and innovation in China have also brought discomfort and unhappiness.

The sheet print is a further important aspect of Wang Chao's *oeuvre*. Several of his prints represent images of domestic interiors showing objects that evoke strong cultural symbolism associated with vernacular life in traditional China.[56] The print *Reminiscence* (*Zoujin mouri*) uses the auspicious imagery found in folk prints of pre-modern China **[Fig. 8.4]**.[57] Made in 1999, the print is inspired by the artist's sense of *fin-de-siècle* nostalgia at the end of the twentieth century. Its function is to present aspects of traditional culture, suggesting regret at their passing in the modernisation of China. The print shows the interior of a traditional Chinese house, with a view of the altar table and the images on the back wall in the principal room.[58] This room is the centre of the Chinese house and the place where all domestic rituals relating to the honour of the family's ancestors and seasonal festivals took place.[59] The objects represented carried symbolic meanings. The horizontal section at the bottom of the print corresponds to the surface of the long, narrow table which served as an altar table. Standing up-ended on the table is an ornamental rock of eroded limestone, regarded as a precious decorative object representing a microcosm of landscape scenery, and representing longevity.[60] The two crickets, one having jumped out of a lidded soup bowl and the other sitting on the rock, have been added to enliven the static composition and bring a note of personal recollection for Wang Chao, who, as a child, collected crickets in the countryside every autumn and kept them as pets. In the centre of the print, the vase of flowers on the table corresponds to the picture that was placed above the altar table in the principal room of the house, which here is represented without an edge or frame. It stands in the place that the ancestor portrait would have occupied in pre-modern times. The vase of flowers recalls a well-known composition from a folk print in which the vase of flowers would have been surrounded by auspicious elements relating to success and good fortune. Wang Chao appears to have borrowed this image from a coloured folk print originally from Suzhou which was recut and reprinted at the Purple Bamboo Studio, and whose image would have been familiar to him.[61] All the images in Wang Chao's print have auspicious associations. 'Vase', pronounced *ping* in Chinese, is a homophone for 'peace'; the lotus flower, *lian*, is a homophone for 'to connect', suggesting here a shared harmony; and the lotus seed pods are symbols of fertility.[62] The arc-shaped section at the top of the print containing porcelain dishes corresponds to the painting or plaque hung at the top of the wall in traditional houses which bore the name of the room, or which depicted further auspicious elements.[63]

An important feature of Wang Chao's prints is the variety of small, intricately depicted objects associated with aspects of traditional Chinese culture which serve as focal points in his compositions. Although fine descriptive detail is a feature inherent in the book illustration which Wang Chao has studied at the Purple Bamboo Studio, his prints display a significant originality in capturing design, pattern and texture in the

8.4: *Reminiscence* (1999) by Wang Chao, impression 4/25; multi-block woodcut with water-soluble ink on paper; image: 68.2 cm x 137.3 cm. This print is inspired by Wang Chao's *fin-de-siècle* nostalgia at the end of the twentieth century. The print shows the back wall of the main room in a traditional Chinese house where the family altar is set. [*Muban Foundation/Artist*]

8.5: *The Desk in the Jiuli Studio* (2003) by Wang Chao, impression 1/150; woodblocks with water-soluble ink; image: 49.8 cm x 35.5 cm. This print shows the objects on Wang Chao's desk and, at the centre, a portrait of the artist asleep engraved on a pear-shaped stone with the images from his nightmare portrayed in a dream-bubble. [*Artist*]

representation of small objects. His pictorial description of objects is reminiscent of the imagery in the paintings and book illustrations of the late Ming artist, Chen Hongshou (1599–1652), in which decorative and descriptive detail became an important vehicle in expressing the irony of Chen's archaistic references.[64] In Wang Chao's print, *The Desk in the Jiuli Studio*, the principal elements in the composition are finely delineated tools and equipment from the artist's working table **[Fig. 8.5, and detail in Fig. 8.6, Fig. 8.7]**. These include a table screen, a brushpot made from flecked bamboo containing brushes, a stand in the form of a miniature table for two decorative rocks, a seal carved in the shape of a lion, a woodblock, a pair of scissors and blockcutting and printing equipment. Through this array of accoutrements, Wang Chao alludes to writing equipment and decorative objects associated with the scholar's desk that were particularly esteemed as collectors' objects in the late Ming period, further enhancing Wang Chao's self-image as an artist from a past age.[65]

Wang Chao's printmaking presents a play of pictorial, verbal and technical elements whose significance relies on decoding by the viewer. Inspired by the use of imagery in late Ming printed books and popular visual culture, Wang Chao's approach expresses layers of meaning which often present a humorous comment on modern and contemporary life.[66] *The Desk in the Jiuli Studio* builds up layers of imagery to represent different levels of meaning relating to the print, the subject-matter, and

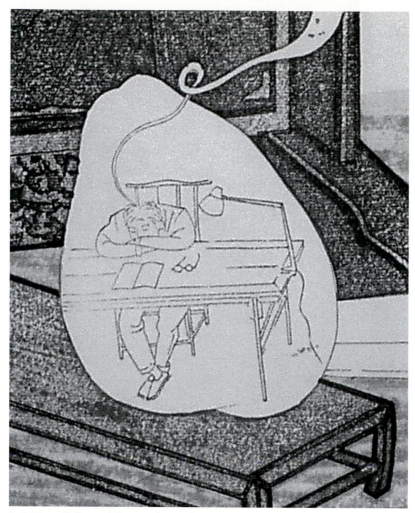

8.6: Detail from *The Desk in the Jiuli Studio* (2003) by Wang Chao. [*Artist*]

the artist. At the front of the composition, the woodblock carved with reversed characters in relief bears the title, 'Contemporary Chinese Woodcuts' (*Dangdai Zhongguo muke banhua*), which is the name of the portfolio of prints for which this print was created.[67] The detailed display of carefully represented objects from Wang Chao's work-table defines in the viewer's mind his identity as a print-artist and his interests in traditional culture. The focus of the print is the image of the scholar, sleeping rather than studying, engraved on the pear-shaped stone together with the humorous fantasy of the pictorial images involving bronzes and broken artefacts of the nightmare which are contained in Wang Chao's dream-bubble [**Figs 8.6-7**]. Wang Chao has carefully selected his pictorial models from the seventeenth century: not only is the dream-bubble a convention of late Ming book illustration,[68] but the play of images-within-images prominently featured in illustrated books of the period, and, in particular, in Chen Hongshou's paintings and woodcut designs which involve the viewer in multiple layers of visual artifice.[69]

The print 'Eight Fragments from the Dust Pile of Brocades [treasures]' (*Jinhuidui zhi bapo tu)* of 2006, translates awkwardly from the Chinese as 'Eight Brokens from the Dust Pile of

8.7: Detail from *The Desk in the Jiuli Studio* (2003) by Wang Chao. [*Artist*]

Brocades,' and represents a play between the real and the imagined **[Fig. 8.8]**.[70] Wang Chao portrays torn and discarded pages and fragments of pages from eight different works which include a label from the outside of a book, a title page, pages of text, a page from a book of rubbings and a sheet of characters in outline to be used by a child learning calligraphy. The haphazard composition of the sheets scattered against the background contrasts with the technical virtuosity of the woodblock printing in which every detail, mark, tear and fold is reproduced with great realism. Wang Chao's composition borrows from a genre of *trompe l'oeil* painting depicting fragments of rubbings, printed pages and calligraphy which began to be produced by commercial artists in China during the nineteenth century.[71] These paintings combined an interest in realism and illusionist effects introduced from the West, antiquarian trends of the period, and subject matter drawn from the scholar-type paraphernalia for the status-conscious middle classes. The *trompe l'oeil* compositions were presented in the form of good luck pictures whose titles were often homophones for characters with auspicious meanings. Elements given in the title of many of these paintings, including the number 'eight,' and the idea of 'broken' objects carry auspicious associations. Often the objects represented carried dual associations. Even the katytid, seen in the bottom left-hand corner of Wang Chao's print, carries an auspicious meaning, conveying the wish for numerous children. Wang Chao's revival of the *trompe l'oeil* composition in the format of his present-day fine art print, transforms its function from the earlier auspicious decorative picture to an intellectual statement about China's past. Wang Chao celebrates scholarly antiquarian interests of the past and implies a regret for declining interest in aspects of traditional culture during recent decades of modern Chinese history. In contrast to the *trompe l'oeil* paintings, Wang Chao achieves a brilliant double visual parody in which he convincingly represents a print of a painting of original printed objects.

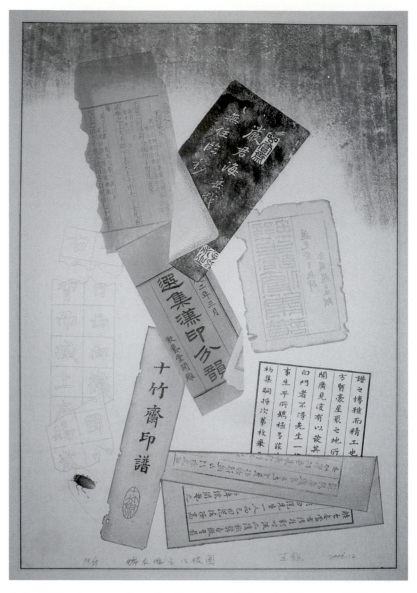

8.8: '*Eight fagments from the Dust Pile of Brocade [Treasures]*' (2006) by Wang Chao, impression 14/25; multi-block woodcut with water-soluble ink on paper; image: 45 cm x 68 cm. Wang Chao represents pages and fragments from eight different finely printed works. The haphazard composition of the sheets scattered against the background contrasts with the technical virtuosity of the printing in which every detail, mark, tear and fold are faithfully reproduced. [*Ashmolean Museum, University of Oxford/Artist*]

The monochrome palette

Wang Chao's use of monochrome and subdued colours in his prints links him to the new revivalism in traditional approaches to painting in China since the 1980s. Reacting against the dominance of imported styles of realist art in China over the last sixty years, many artists have adopted a muted palette of graded ink and colour in their representation of traditional subject-matter in a contemporary manner.[72] The monochrome palette used by these artists carries powerful cultural associations, connecting their work to the large body of highly respected scholar-amateur painting that had existed in China since the eleventh century. Many contemporary print-artists, following the revivalism of traditional painting, have produced largely monochrome prints with landscape and subjects such as prunus, lotus, grasses and insects, in compositions which resonate with painting traditions of pre-modern China.[73] These print-artists have been experimental in their use of materials and techniques, borrowing and adapting elements from both traditional and western-derived traditions to achieve a variety of different effects. Although Wang Chao is part of this group of print-artists, he occupies a separate category of his own in his use of techniques of colour printing associated with the Purple Bamboo Studio, and pictorial formats and subject-matter which are derived from late Ming printing.

Wang Chao is unique as a print-artist in contemporary China in his use of the assembled block (douban) technique printed with water-soluble ink in an unmodified form.[74] His prints involve the use of multiple small woodblocks made from pearwood, each representing linear elements and intricate areas of colour, and blocks, often made from plywood faced with Manchurian ash, giving a woodgrain texture, to build up larger areas of tone in the print. These blocks are printed in sequence, on a traditional Chinese printing table which achieves completely accurate registration. Sheets of paper are clamped in the centre of the table allowing the paper to be held in register during the print run, and the small woodblocks are printed in succession, with individual sheets passed through a gap in the centre of the table. The embossing process used in the printed book *Foreign Images* is part of the colour-printing process and is carried out after the printing of ink and colour. It is achieved by placing the paper over an intaglio block which is rubbed with a wooden burnisher. Using this complex process involved Wang Chao in cutting more than forty individual blocks for the print *Reminiscence*, and twenty-three blocks for *The Desk in the Jiuli Studio*. Although Wang Chao is the only academy artist using the assembled block technique (douban) in a largely unchanged form in China, other artists frequently use the less technically demanding approach of colour printing using a set of blocks sharing the same register (taoban), in combination with other aspects of traditional or western realist printmaking.[75]

Conclusion

The dynamic of the past in Chinese culture is a dominant theme that transcends dynastic and political change. Even when looking in detail at the development of art movements dependent on the absorption of foreign ideas, such the Modern Woodcut Movement in the new art of twentieth-century China, it is evident that revival and regeneration of elements of visual culture from the past are an important component in their success. The work of contemporary artists such as Wang Chao demonstrates how the reworking of past models continues to be a powerful force in the generation of the highest quality traditional art in the twenty-first century.

Afterword

Alex Seago

As the editors explain in the preface, this volume is the result of serendipitous circumstances. Both Robert Wallis and I teach at Richmond the American International University in London, and for a number of years we have been organising field trips for students to the prehistoric 'sacred pagan sites' of Oxfordshire and Wiltshire. I remain very impressed by Robert's gift of bringing the history of these wonderful locations to life and his ability to place this history in contemporary context. As I also lecture on an occasional basis at Sotheby's Institute of Art in London, and have been friends with Megan for many years, it occurred to me that Robert's research interests might combine with Megan's antiquarian scholarship to produce a heady and original intellectual brew. Several meetings in pubs combined with a memorable trip to Uffington Castle, Wayland's Smithy and Avebury resulted, and these helped lay the foundations for the October 2007 Burlington House conference and, ultimately, for this book.

As a cultural historian with an interest in the 1950s and 1960s, the subject matter of this volume poses interesting and intriguing questions for my own research. Although some traditional academics might baulk at the suggestion, it seems to me that British discussions of antiquarianism and archaism, particularly those focusing upon topics such as paganism, sacred sites, landscape and heritage, inevitably raise associations with 1960s counterculture and its contemporary successors – in the form of New Age travellers, Spiral Tribe ravers, free festival organisers and their ilk. Indeed, as Robert Wallis points out, the recent history of major British, sacred, pagan sites such as Stonehenge and Avebury has been characterised by the ideological, and sometimes physical, conflict between mainstream and official *versus* counter-cultural interpretations of the meaning of these sites and their relationship with landscape and national heritage. In recent years a particularly interesting characteristic of these struggles has the been the ways in which counter-cultural meanings (for example, regarding holistic interpretations of the significance of 'sacred' sites and their importance as spiritual locations and sites of pilgrimage) have become incorporated into official discourses – the result, perhaps, of yesterday's hippies becoming today's civil servants!

A fascination with prehistory – the ancient, the archaic, the pagan and the occult – has, of course, characterised the counterculture from its earliest origins as an anti-modernist, anti-rationalist, anti-industrial/capitalist movement. Counter-cultural pioneers such as Alan Ginsberg, Gary Snyder and Kenneth Rexroth rejected the consumerism of mid-twentieth century America and turned instead to the religions, mysteries, and rituals of India, China, and Japan for inspiration. Their hippy successors, the Woodstock generation, characteristically identified strongly with Native American culture, often adopting or appropriating the religions, environmental views, clothing, hairstyles, jewellery and hallucinogenic substances of native Americans. Small towns in the United States' South-west with a strong Native American heritage and their own 'sacred sites', such as Santa Fe, Taos and Moab, became sites of pilgrimage and relocation for this counter-cultural generation.

In the light of this volume, it is particularly interesting to consider the national cultural nuances of these counter-cultural affiliations, associations and attachments to specific sites and landscapes. In the United Kingdom during the late 1960s and early 1970s, for example, a strong association developed between a sense of counter-cultural identity and a ritualistic engagement with the British landscape. As Michael Clark has pointed out in his study of the history and politics of pop festivals, the historical development of British festivals during this period of counter-cultural efflorescence can be understood in terms of the subtle differences between commercial festivals (e.g. the Isle of Wight or Reading), 'free' festivals (e.g. the original Glastonbury and Stonehenge Free festivals), and the rather more middle-class environments of 'neo-medieval country fayres' such as the Totnes Festival, the Green Man Festival, or the Rougham Tree Fayre.[1]

In contrast to the United States, a country which since the mid-nineteenth century has been controlled by an urban industrial bourgeoisie, Britain's landowning aristocracy often played a leading if somewhat eccentric and paradoxical role in cementing relations between the British landscape and the rituals of the counterculture. Several of England's major 'official' pop festivals such as Beaulieu and Knebworth were hosted in the grounds of stately homes, while Glastonbury Fayre, the original iconic counter-cultural 'free' festival and now, in its commercial form, arguably as much part of the English summer 'season' as Ascot or Henley, was originally the brainchild of the hippy aristocrat Arabella Spencer-Churchill.

These curious connections between aristocratic interests and counter-cultural concerns remain a distinctive characteristic of British culture and resonate with the history of the Society of Antiquaries – indeed, it has become something of a cultural cliché for successful British counter-cultural entrepreneurs to gain cultural capital and social acceptability by 'buying into' British heritage and landscape. While not motivated by a desire to gain conventional social acceptance, the recent television series on Britain's sacred sites hosted by ex-Teardrop Explodes guitarist and self-styled 'neo-drude' Julian Cope is a case in point. Indeed, Cope's 1998 book, *The Modern Antiquarian* – an exegesis on dolmens, stone circles and barrows such as Long Meg, Callanish, Maeshowe, the Ring of Brodgar, East Aquharthies and West Kennet – has probably achieved more than any other recent publication in engaging a non-academic public with Britain's ancient heritage, its sacred significance, and its relationships to the landscape (see chapter 7).

From a personal perspective I find these connections both fascinating and cathartic. The deep emotional ties to the landscape forged during an adolescence at boarding school in the Vale of the White Horse and frequent visits to local ancient sites such as Segsbury Camp, Wayland's Smithy, White Horse Hill, and Uffington Castle is inextricably linked in my imagination and experience to the feelings of liberation and collective exaltation I experienced at festivals such as Glastonbury. Perhaps this 'collective effervescence', the perceived energy formed by a gathering of people at festivals, rituals or riots and their connections with sacred landscapes, lies at the very roots of religion and human social identity. As such, and to emphasise the scholarly implications of this volume compiled by Megan Aldrich and Robert Wallis, I end by quoting the great sociologist Emile Durkheim:

> Our definition of the sacred is that it is something added to and beyond the real .... In fact we have seen that if collective life awakens religious thought on reaching a certain degree of intensity, it is because it brings about a state of effervescence which changes the conditions of psychic activity. Vital energies are over excited, passions more active, sensations stronger: there are even some which are produced only at this moment. A man does not recognise himself: he feels himself transformed and consequently he transforms the environment which surrounds him. In order to account for the very particular impressions which he receives, he attributes to the things with which he is in direct contact properties which they have not, exceptional powers and virtues which the objects of every day experience do not possess. In a word, above the real world where his profane life passes he has placed another which, in one sense does not exist except in thought, but to which he attributes a higher sort of dignity than to the first. Thus from a double point of view it is an ideal world.[2]

Notes

Introduction: Enchantment, Disenchantment, Re-enchantment

1. David Gaimster, Sarah McCarthy and Bernard Nurse, eds, *Making History: Antiquaries in Britain, 1707-2007* (London: Royal Academy of Arts, 2007). Starkey contributes the Introduction, 'Making History', pp. 11-13.

2. Stuart Piggott, *Ancient Britons and the Antiquarian Imagination* (London: Thames and Hudson, 1989).

3. See Mark Gillings and Joshua Pollard, *Avebury* (London: Duckworth, 2004); Mark Gillings, Joshua Pollard, Rick Peterson and David Wheatley, *Landscape of the Megaliths; Excavation and Fieldwork on the Avebury Monuments, 1997-2003* (Oxford: Oxbow, 2008).

4. John Michell, *Megalithomania: Artists, Antiquarians and Archaeologists at the Old Stone Monuments* (London: Thames and Hudson, 1982).

5. Bruce Trigger, *A History of Archaeological Thought* (Cambridge: University Press, 1989).

6. See Philippa Levine, *The Amateur and the Professional: Antiquarians, Historians and Archaeologists in Victorian England, 1838-1886* (Cambridge: University Press, 1986); Graham Parry, *The Trophies of Time: English Antiquarians of the Seventeenth Century* (Oxford: University Press, 1995); Rosemary Sweet, *Antiquaries: The Discovery of the Past in Eighteenth-Century Britain* (London: Hambledon and London, 2004); Susan Pearce, ed., *Visions of Antiquity: The Society of Antiquaries of London, 1707-2007* (London: Society of Antiquaries of London, 2007); Joan Rockley, *Antiquarians and Archaeology in Nineteenth-century Cork* (Oxford: BAR British Series, 454, 2008).

7. Sam Smiles, *The Image of Antiquity: Ancient Britain and the Romantic Imagination* (New Haven and London: Yale University Press, 1994). See also Smiles' paper, 'The Art of Recording', in *Making History* (2007), pp. 123-41.

8. See, for example, Christopher Tilley, Sue Hamilton and Barbara Bender, 'Art and the Re-presentation of the Past', *Journal of the Royal Anthropological Institute*, 6:1 (2000), pp. 35-62; Colin Renfrew, *Figuring it Out: The Parallel Visions of Artists and Archaeologists* (London: Thames and Hudson, 2003); Stephen Calloway, 'Antiquaries and the Arts', *Making History*, pp. 165-9; Robert J. Wallis, 'Shimmering Steel / Standing Stones: Reflections on the Intervention of Anish Kapoor at the Rollright Stones', in Jon Wood, ed., *Object-Excavation-Intervention: Dialogues between Sculpture and Archaeology*, Subject/Object: New Studies in Sculpture Series (Oxford: Ashgate Press in conjunction with the Henry Moore Institute, 2009), forthcoming.

9. Dana Arnold and Stephen Bending, eds, *Tracing Architecture: The Aesthetics of Antiquarianism*, Art History Special Issues (Oxford: Wiley Blackwell, 2003).

10. See particularly, Richard Bradley and Howard Williams, eds, 'The Past in the Past: the Reuse of Ancient Monuments', *World Archaeology*, 30:1 (London: Routledge, 1998); Richard Bradley, *The Past in Prehistoric Societies* (London: Routledge, 2002); Howard Williams, ed., *Archaeologies of Remembrance: Death and Memory in Past Societies* (New York: Kluwer/Plenum, 2003); Howard Williams, *Death and Memory in Early Medieval Britain* (Cambridge: University Press, 2006); A. Jones, *Memory and Material Culture* (Cambridge: University Press, 2007).

11. See, for example, David Boyd Haycock, *William Stukeley: Science, Religion and Archaeology in Eighteenth-century England* (Woodbridge, Suffolk: Boydell Press, 2002); Stuart Piggot, *William Stukeley: an Eighteenth-Century Antiquary* (New York: Thames and Hudson, 1985).

Chapter 1: Dragons, Elves and Giants: Some Pre-archaeological Occupants of British Barrows

1. Michael Hunter, *John Aubrey and the Realm of Learning* (London: Duckworth, 1975), p.167.

2. *Beowulf*, Michael Alexander, trans. (Harmondsworth: Penguin, 1973). All subsequent quotations are from this translation.

3. Hilda R. Ellis Davidson, 'The Hill of the Dragon: Anglo-Saxon Burial Mounds in Literature and Archaeology', *Folk-Lore,* 61:2 (1951-2), pp. 169-85, esp. pp. 179-81.

4. Charles R. Beard, *The Romance of Treasure Trove* (London: Sampson Low, 1933).

5. *Chronicle of Thomas of Walsingham*, in Henry Thomas Riley, ed., *Chronica Monasterii S. Albani* VII: *Ypodigma Neustriae, a Thoma Walsingham* (Rolls Series, 28vii, 1876), pp. 283-4. My translation.

6. George Lyman Kittredge, *Witchcraft in Old and New England* (Cambridge, Mass: Harvard University Press, 1929), pp. 206-13.

7. See the references under these names in the county volumes of the English Place-Name Survey: Derbyshire, 27-9 (1959), Northamptonshire, 10 (1933), Worcestershire, 4 (1927), Cheshire, 44-8, 54, 74 (1970-97), Surrey, 11 (1934), West Riding, 30-7 (1961-3), Nottinghamshire, 17 (1940), Norfolk, 61, 72, 79 (1989-2002), Lincolnshire, 58, 64:5, 66, 71, 73, 77 (1985-2001), North Riding, 5 (1928).

8. Margaret Gelling and Ann Cole, *The Landscape of Place-Names* (Stamford: Shaun Tyas, 2000), pp. 145, 174, 178.

9. See the reference under this name in the county volume of the English Place-Name Survey: Surrey, 11 (1934).

10. Michael Alexander, *The Earliest English Poems* (Harmondsworth: Penguin: 1966), pp. 30-1.

11. *Sir Tristrem*, George P. McNeill, ed., Scottish Texts Society, 1st ser., 8 (1886), lines 2478-81.

12. Christopher Abram, 'In Search of Lost Time: Aldhelm and *The Ruin*', *Quaestio: Selected Proceedings of the Cambridge Colloquium in Anglo-Saxon, Norse and Celtic* 1 (2000), pp. 23-44.

13. Leslie V. Grinsell, *Folklore of Prehistoric Sites in Britain* (Newton Abbot: David and Charles, 1976), p. 103.

14. Geoffrey of Monmouth, *The History of the Kings of Britain*, Lewis Thorpe, trans. (Harmondsworth: Penguin, 1966), pp. 96-8.

15. *Des Grantz Geanz* in James P. Carley and Julia Crick, 'Constructing Albion's Past: an Annotated Edition of *De Origine Gigantum*', *Arthurian Literature* 13 (1995), pp. 41-114, lines 467-77.

16. *Liber Eliensis: A History of the Isle of Ely from the Seventh Century to the Twelfth*, Janet Fairweather, trans. (Woodbridge, Suffolk: Boydell, 2005), p. 4.

17. Antonina Harbus, *Helena of Britain in Medieval Legend* (Cambridge: Brewer, 2002), p. 68.

18. Ranulph Higden, *Polychronicon*, Churchill Babington, ed., (Rolls Series, 41, 1865-86), pp. 2-78.

19. Ralph of Coggeshall, *Chronicon Anglicanum*, Joseph Stevenson, ed., (Rolls Series, 66, 1875), pp. 280-6.

20. *Andreas*, George Philip Krapp, ed., (Boston: Ginn, 1906), lines 1492-5.

21. G.B. Grundy, 'The Saxon Land Charters of Hampshire: with Notes on Place and Field Names', *Archaeological Journal,* 84 (1930), pp. 160-340, esp. p. 178.

22. Richard Coates, *Hampshire Place-Names* (London: Batsford, 1989), p. 23.

23. William Worcestre, *Itineraries*, J.H. Harvey, ed., (Oxford: Clarendon, 1969), p. 293.

24. William Worcestre, *The Topography of Medieval Bristol*, Frances Neale, ed., Bristol Record Society, 51 (2000), p. 35.

25. T.D. Kendrick, *British Antiquity* (London: Methuen, 1950), p. 24.

26. Arthur B. Ferguson, *Utter Antiquity: Perceptions of Prehistory in Renaissance England* (Duke University Press, 1993), p. 108.

27. John Leland, *The Itinerary of John Leland In or About the Years 1535-1543*, Lucy Toulmin Smith, ed., (London: George Bell, 1906-10), pp. 5-57.

28. William Camden, *Britannia*, Edmund Gibson, ed., (London: Edmund Gibson, 1695), p. lxv.

29. Hugh Owen, 'Peniarth MS 118, fols 829-37: Introduction, Transcript and Translation', *Y Cymmrodor*, 27 (1917), pp. 115-52.

30. Jan Bondeson, *A Cabinet of Medical Curiosities* (Ithaca, NY: Cornell University Press, 1997), pp. 78-88.

31. Leslie V. Grinsell, 'Wayland the Smith and his Relatives: a Legend and its Topography', *Folklore*, 102 (1991), pp. 235-6.

32. Janet B.T. Christie, 'Reflections on the Legend of Wayland the Smith', *Folklore*, 80 (1969), pp. 286-94, esp. 289.

33. Alaric Hall, *Elves in Anglo-Saxon England: Matters of Belief, Health, Gender and Identity* (Woodbridge, Suffolk: Boydell, 2007), p. 41.

34. Charles R. Beard, *The Romance of Treasure Trove* (London: Sampson Low, 1933), p. 25.

35. William of Newburgh, *Historia Rerum Anglicarum*, Hans Claude Hamilton, ed., (English Historical Soc. 16, 1856), pp. 77-8. My translation.

36. See the references under these names in the county volumes of the English Place-Name Survey: Oxfordshire, 23-4 (1953), Derbyshire, 27-9 (1959), Norfolk, 61, 72, 79 (1989-2002), Cumberland. 20-2 (1950-2), North Riding, 5 (1928), West Riding, 30-7 (1961-3). The reference to Folkton is from Leslie V. Grinsell, *Folklore of Prehistoric Sites in Britain* (Newton Abbot: David and Charles, 1976), p. 173.

37. Hilda R. Ellis, *The Road to Hel: A Study of the Conception of the Dead in Old Norse Literature* (Cambridge: University Press, 1943), pp. 87-8.

38. Peter Alderson Smith, *W.B. Yeats and the Tribe of Danu: Three Views of Ireland's Fairies* (Buckingham: Colin Smythe, 1987), p. 85.

39. Walter Scott, *Letters on Demonology and Witchcraft* (London: John Murray, 1830), p. 165.

40. John Stuart, ed., *The Miscellany of the Spalding Club* (Spalding Club, 3, 6, 16, 20, 24, 1841-52), pp. 1-119.

41. Lizanne Henderson and Edward J. Cowan, *Scottish Fairy Belief: A History* (East Linton: Tuckwell, 2001), p. 41.

42. Richard Bovet, *Pandaemonium: Or, the Devil's Cloister*, Montague Summers, ed., (Aldington: Hand and Flower, 1951), pp. 104-5.

43. Robert Pitcairn, *Criminal Trials in Scotland* (Bannatyne Club, 1833), pp. 3, 602-16.

44. Wilfrid Bonser, 'Magical Practices against Elves', *Folk-Lore*, 37 (1926), pp. 350-63, esp. 355-6.

45. Robert Kirk, *The Secret Common-Wealth*, Stewart Sanderson, ed., (Folklore Society, 1976), pp. 58-9.

46. Stuart Piggott, *Ancient Britons and the Antiquarian Imagination: Ideas from the Renaissance to the Regency* (London: Thames and Hudson, 1989), pp. 86, 92.

Chapter 2: Recycling the Past: Ancient Monuments and Changing Meanings in Early Medieval Britain

1. In the past twenty years, this literature has included prehistorians, historians, folklorists, place-name scholars, landscape historians and historical geographers. See, for example: John Blair, 'Anglo-Saxon Minsters: a Topographical Review', in John Blair and Richard Sharp, eds, *Pastoral Care before the Parish* (Leicester: University Press, 1992), pp. 226-66; John Blair, 'Anglo-Saxon Pagan Shrines and their Prototypes', *Anglo-Saxon Studies in Archaeology and History*, 8 (1995), pp. 1-28; Richard Bradley, 'Time Regained: the Creation of Continuity', *Journal of the British Archaeological Association*, 140 (1987), pp. 1-17; *Altering the Earth* (Society of Antiquaries of Scotland Monograph Series 8, Stroud: Sutton, 1993); Margaret Gelling, *Signposts to the Past*, 2nd ed. (Chichester: Phillimore, 1988); Leslie Grinsell, *The Ancient Burial Mounds of England*, 2nd ed. (London: Methuen, 1953); *The Folklore of*

Prehistoric Sites in Britain (Newton Abbot: David and Charles, 1976); Della Hooke, *The Landscape of Anglo-Saxon England* (Leicester University Press, 1988); Richard Morris, *Churches in the Landscape* (London: Dent, 1989).

2. Sarah Semple, 'A Fear of the Past: the Place of the Prehistoric Burial Mound in the Ideology of Middle and Later Anglo-Saxon England', *World Archaeology,* 30:1 (1998), pp. 109-26.

3. See, for example: Bede, *Historia Ecclesia,* 4, 19, in Leo Sherley-Price, trans. *Bede: Ecclesiastical History of the English People* (London: Penguin, 1955), p. 237; Peter Carelli, 'Thunder and Lightning, Magical Miracles: On the Popular Myth of Thunderbolts and the Presence of Stone Age Artefacts in Medieval Deposits', in Hans Andersson, Peter Carelli and Lars Ersgard, eds, *Visions of the Past: Trends and Traditions in Swedish Medieval Archaeology* (Lund: Central Board of Antiquities, 1997), pp. 393-417; Helen Geake, *The Use of Grave-goods in Conversion-Period England, c. 600-850* (British Archaeological Reports British Series, 261, Oxford: BAR, 1997); Michael Hunter, 'German and Roman Antiquity and the Sense of the Past in Anglo-Saxon England', *Anglo-Saxon England,* 3 (1974), pp. 29-50; Michael Greenhalgh, *The Survival of Roman Antiquities in the Middle Ages* (London: Duckworth, 1989); George Speake, *A Saxon Bed Burial on Swallowcliffe Down* (London: Historic Buildings Commission for England, 1989).

4. See R. Adkins and M.R. Petchey, 'Secklow Hundred Mound and other Meeting-place Mounds in England', *Archaeological Journal,* 141 (1984), pp. 243-51; Nicholas Griffiths, 'An Unusual Medieval Strap-end from Market Lavington', *Wiltshire Archaeological and Natural History Magazine,* 91 (1998), p. 149.

5. See also Howard Williams, 'Remembering and Forgetting the Medieval Dead', in Howard Williams, ed., *Archaeologies of Remembrance: Death and Memory in Past Societies* (New York: Kluwer/Plenum, 2003), pp. 227-54.

6. See, for example, Richard Bradley and Howard Williams, *The Past in the Past, World Archaeology,* 30:1 (1998); Richard Bradley, *The Significance of Monuments* (London: Routledge, 1998); *The Past in Prehistoric Societies* (London: Routledge, 2002); Ruth Van Dyke and Susan Alcock, *Archaeologies of Memory* (Oxford: Blackwell, 2003).

7. See, for example, Cornelius Holtorf and Howard Williams, 'Landscapes and Memories', in Dan Hicks and M. Beaudray, eds, *Cambridge Companion to Historical Archaeology* (Cambridge: University Press, 2006), pp. 235-54.

8. See, for example, Blair, *Anglo-Saxon Minsters;* 'Churches in the early English Landscape: Social and Cultural Contexts', in John Blair and Carole Pyrah, eds, *Church Archaeology Research Directions for the Future* (Council for British Archaeology Research Report, 104, York: CBA, 1996), pp. 6-18; Sam Lucy, 'The Significance of Mortuary Ritual in the Political Manipulation of Landscape', *Archaeological Review from Cambridge,* 11:1 (1992), pp. 93-105; Morris, *Churches in the Landscape;* Howard Williams, 'Ancient Landscapes and the Dead: the Reuse of Prehistoric and Roman Monuments as Early Anglo-Saxon Burial Sites', *Medieval Archaeology,* 41 (1997), pp. 1-32.

9. See, for example, Aliki Pantos and Sarah Semple, *Assembly Places and Practices in Medieval Europe* (Dublin: Four Courts Press, 2004); Alexandra Sanmark and Sarah Semple, 'Archaeologies of Assembly: New Discoveries in Sweden and England', *Fornvännen,* 4 (2008), pp. 245-59.

10. See: Richard Bradley, 'Time Regained: the Creation of Continuity', *Journal of the British Archaeological Association,* 140, pp. 1-17; Lucy 'Significance of Mortuary Ritual'; John Moreland, *Archaeology and Text* (London: Duckworth); Morris, *Churches in the Landscape;* Sarah Semple, 'Burials and Political Boundaries in the Avebury Region, North Wiltshire', *Anglo-Saxon Studies in Archaeology and History,* 12 (2003), pp. 71-91; Sarah Semple, 'Polities and Princes, AD 400-800: New Perspectives on the Funerary Landscape of the South Saxon Kingdom', *Oxford Archaeological Journal,* 27: 4 (2008), pp. 407-29; Howard Williams 'Ancient Landscapes and the Dead', pp. 1-32; Chris Humphrey and W.M. Ormrod, eds, *Death, Memory and Time: A Consideration*

of the Mortuary Practices at Sutton Hoo (Woodbridge: York Medieval Press, 2001), pp. 35-72.

11. Howard Williams, 'Monuments and the Past in Early Anglo-Saxon England, *World Archaeology,* 30:1 (1998), pp. 96-7; 'Burial Practice in Early Medieval Eastern England: Constructing Local Identities, Deconstructing Ethnicity', in Sam Lucy and Andrew Reynolds, eds, *Burial in Early Medieval England and Wales* (London: Society for Medieval Archaeology Monograph, 17, 2002), pp. 72-87; 'Early Medieval Burial at Yeavering: a Retrospective', in Paul Frodsham and Colm O'Brien, eds, *Yeavering: People, Power, Place* (Stroud: Tempus, 2005), pp. 127-44.

12. Building on Howard Williams' seminal paper, 'Ancient Landscapes and the Dead', in which the author recognised the ubiquity of 'funerary reuse' in Anglo-Saxon England and the diversity of monument types adopted as places for burial.

13. See, however, Sam Lucy, *The Early Anglo-Saxon Cemeteries of East Yorkshire* (BAR British Series, 272, Oxford: BAR, 1998); Semple, 'Burials and Political Boundaries'; Williams, 'Monuments and the Past'; Lucy, 'Constructing Local Identities'; 'Early Medieval Burial at Yeavering'; Stuart Brookes, 'Walking with Anglo-Saxons: Landscapes of the Dead in Early Anglo-Saxon Kent', *Anglo-Saxon Studies in Archaeology and History,* 14 (2007), pp 154-62.

14. Semple, 'Burial and Political Boundaries', pp. 72-91.

15. See: Semple, 'Burial and Political Boundaries'; Sarah Semple and Howard Williams, 'Excavations on Roundway Down', *Wiltshire Archaeological and Natural History Magazine,* 94 (2001), pp. 236-9.

16. I. F. Smith and D.D. Simpson, 'Excavation of Three Roman Tombs and a Prehistoric Pit on Overton Down', *Wiltshire Archaeological and Natural History Society Magazine,* 59 (1964), pp. 68-85; Bruce Eagles, 'Pagan Anglo-Saxon Burials at West Overton', *Wiltshire Archaeological and Natural History Magazine,* 80 (1986), pp. 103-20; A.C. Smith, 'Sketch of the Parish of Yatesbury', *Wiltshire Archaeological and Natural History Magazine,* 18 (1879), pp. 331-33; Semple, 'Burial and Political Boundaries'.

17. See Semple, 'Burial and Political Boundaries', pp. 82-4; Semple and Williams, 'Excavations on Roundway Down'.

18. See Mark Gardiner, 'An Anglo-Saxon and Medieval Settlement at Botolphs, Bramber, West Sussex', *Archaeological Journal,* 147 (1990), pp. 216-75; 'Economy and Landscape Change in Post-Roman and Early Medieval Sussex, 450-1175', in David Rudling, ed., *The Archaeology of Sussex to AD 2000* (Norfolk; Heritage Marketing Publications, 2003), pp. 151-60; Martin Welch, 'Early Anglo-Saxon Sussex: from Civitas to Shire', in P. Brandon, ed., *The South Saxons* (London: Phillimore, 1978), pp. 13-35.

19. See Andrew Fitzpatrick, *Archaeological Excavations on the Westhampnett Bypass, West Sussex* (1992), Vol. 2, *The Late Iron Age, Romano-British and Anglo-Saxon Cemeteries* (Salisbury: Trust for Wessex Archaeology, 1997); Gardiner, 'Economy and Landscape', pp. 158-9.

20. See J.H. Pull, 'The Blackpatch Excavations', *South Eastern Naturalist,* 34, (1929), pp. 29-30; *The Flint Miners of Blackpatch* (London: Williams and Norgate, 1932); Welch, *Early Anglo-Saxon Sussex,* vol. 2, pp. 459-60; Semple, 'Princes and Polities'.

21. See Christopher Arnold, *The Anglo-Saxon Cemeteries of the Isle of Wight,* (London: Batsford, 1982); G. Hillier, 'Excavations on Brightstone and Bowcombe Downs, Isle of Wight', *Journal of the British Archaeological Association,* 11 (1855), pp. 34-40; Semple, 'Princes and Polities', pp. 9-10.

22. Semple, 'Princes and Polities'.

23. See Lucy, *Cemeteries of East Yorkshire,* p. 85; Caroline Stoertz, *Ancient Landscapes of the Yorkshire Wolds* (Swindon: RCHME, 1997).

24. Lucy, *Cemeteries of East Yorkshire,* pp. 85-9.

25. Sarah Semple, 'Anglo-Saxon Attitudes to the Past: A Landscape Perspective', DPhil. thesis, Oxford University, pp. 106-27.

26. See W. Greenwell and G. Rolleston, *British Barrows* (Oxford: Clarendon,

1877), pp. 135–6; J. R. Mortimer, *Forty Year's Researches in British and Saxon Burial Mounds of East Yorkshire* (London: A. Brown, 1905), fig. 731.

27. Semple, 'Anglo-Saxon Attitudes', p. 110; Lucy, *Cemeteries of East Yorkshire*, pp. 88–9.

28. See Catherine Hills, *The Origin of the English* (London: Duckworth, 2003); Sam Lucy, *The Anglo-Saxon Way of Death* (Stroud: Tempus, 2000); 'Burial Practice in Early Medieval Eastern England: Constructing Local Identities, Deconstructing Ethnicity', in Sam Lucy and Andrew Reynolds, eds, *Burial in Early Medieval England and Wales* (London: Society for Medieval Archaeology Monograph, 17, 2002), pp. 72–87; 'Early Medieval Burial at Yeavering: a Retrospective', in Paul Frodsham and Colm O'Brien, eds, *Yeavering: People, Power, Place*, (Stroud: Tempus, 2005), pp. 127–44.

29. See Rosemary Cramp, 'Anglo-Saxon Settlement', in John Chapman and Harold Mytum, eds, *Settlement and Burial in Britain, 1000 BC–AD 1000*, (BAR British Series, 119, Oxford: BAR, 1983), pp. 263–97; also Lucy, 'Changing Burial Rites'.

30. D. Coggins, 'Durham: Binchester (NZ 210313)', *Medieval Archaeology*, 23 (1979), p. 236, fig. 1; Cramp, 'Anglo-Saxon Settlement', p. 268.

31. See, for example, arguments for continuity put forward in Martin Biddle, 'The Archaeology of the Church; a Widening Horizon', in Peter Addyman and Richard Morris, eds, *The Archaeological Study of Churches* (Council for British Archaeology Research Report, 13, London: CBA, 1976), pp. 65–71; Richard Morris, *Churches in the Landscape*; Warwick Rodwell, 'Churches in the Landscape: Aspects of Topography and Planning', in Margaret Faull, ed., *Studies in Late Anglo-Saxon Settlement* (Oxford: University Press, 1984), pp. 1–23.

32. John Blair, *Anglo-Saxon Oxfordshire* (Stroud: Alan Sutton, 1994), pp. 31–4.

33. Williams, 'Ancient Landscapes of the Dead', pp. 22–3.

34. See, for example, Helen Geake, *The Use of Grave-goods in Conversion-Period England, c. 600-850* (British Archaeological Reports British Series, 261, Oxford: John and Erica Hedges, 1997), p. 127; Geake, 'Persistent Problems in the Study of Conversion-Period Burials in England', in S. Lucy and A. Reynolds, eds, *Burial in Early Medieval England and Wales* (London: Society of Medieval Archaeology, 2002), pp. 144–55.

35. Martin Carver, *Sutton Hoo: Burial Ground of Kings?* (Philadelphia: University of Pennsylvania, 1998), p. 107; Williams, 'Placing the Dead'.

36. Williams, 'Death, Memory and Time'.

37. See Brian Hope Taylor, *Yeavering: An Anglo-British Centre of Early Northumbria* (Department of the Environment Archaeological Reports, 7, London: HMSO, 1977); also, Frodsham and O'Brien, *Power, People and Place*.

38. N.B. Clayton, 'New Wintles, Eynsham, Oxon', *Oxoniensia*, 38 (1973), pp. 382–4, fig. 2; Martin Millet and Simon James, 'Excavations at Cowdery's Down, Basingstoke, Hampshire, 1978-81', *Archaeological Journal*, 140 (1983), p. 163, fig. 5; H. Hamerow, *Excavations at Mucking 2: The Anglo-Saxon Settlement* (English Heritage Research Report, 21, London: English Heritage in association with the British Museum Press 1993).

39. Hope Taylor, *Yeavering*; Anthony Harding, 'Excavations in the Prehistoric Ritual Complex near Milfield, Northumberland', *Proceedings of the Prehistoric Society*, 47 (1981), pp. 87–135.

40. Stephen Driscoll, 'Picts and Prehistory: Cultural Resource Management in Early Medieval Scotland', *World Archaeology*, 30:1 (1998), p. 143; 'Ad Gefrin and Scotland: the Implications of the Yeavering Excavations for the North', in Frodsham and O'Brien, *Yeavering, People, Power, Place*.

41. Ryan Lavelle, *Royal Estates in Anglo-Saxon Wessex: Land, Politics and Family Strategies* (Oxford: Archaeopress, 2007).

42. Blair, 'Minster Churches in the Landscape'; 'Anglo-Saxon Minsters: a Topographic Review'; Morris, *Churches in the Landscape*.

43. See, for example, Tyler Bell, *The Religious Reuse of Roman Structures in Early Medieval England* (BAR British Series, 390, Oxford: Archaeopress, 2005).

44. A. Hadrian Allcroft, *The Circle and the Cross: a Study in Continuity*, 2 vols, (London: Macmillan, 1927-30); Morris, *Churches in the Landscape*.

45. Morris, *Churches in the Landscape*, pp. 81-4.

46. Blair, 'Anglo-Saxon Minsters a Topographic Review', p. 233; 'Minster Churches in the Landscape', pp. 41-4; 'Anglo-Saxon Minsters: a Topographic Review', p. 234; 'Churches in the Early English Landscape', p. 9.

47. Ibid.

48. Morris, *Churches in the Landscape*, pp. 46-76.

49. John Blair, 'Bampton: an Anglo-Saxon Minster', *Current Archaeology*, 160 (1998), pp. 124-30; *The Bronze Age Barrows and Churchyard*, Bampton Research Paper, 5 (1999), p. 27.

50. See, for example, John Blair, *Anglo-Saxon Oxfordshire* (Stroud: Alan Sutton, 1994), pp. 63-4, fig. 44.

51. Blair, 'Minster Churches in the Landscape'.

52. See, for example, Audrey Meaney, 'Hundred Meeting Places in the Cambridge Region', in A.R. Rumble, A.D. Mills, eds, *Names, Places and People: an Onomastic Miscellany in Memory of John McNeal Dodgson* (Stamford, 1997).

53. Aliki Pantos, 'Assembly Places in the Anglo-Saxon Period: Aspects of Form and Location', D.Phil thesis, University of Oxford (2002); Pantos and Semple, 'Assembly Places and Practices'.

54. Audrey Meaney, 'Pagan English Sanctuaries, Place-names and Hundred Meeting-Places', *Anglo-Saxon Studies in Archaeology and History*, 8 (1995), p. 36.

55. See Sarah Semple, 'Locations of Assembly in Early Anglo-Saxon England', in Pantos and Semple, eds, *Assembly Places and Practices in Early Medieval Europe*; Howard Williams, 'Assembling the Dead', in ibid.

56. Adkins and Petchey, 'Secklow Hundred Mound', pp. 243-51.

57. See papers in Pantos and Semple, eds, *Assembly Places and Practices in Early Medieval Europe*; see also H. Christiansson and E. Nordahl, 'Tingshögen and Kungsgårdsplatåerna in Gamla Uppsala: a Preliminary Report of Trial Excavations', *Tor*, 22 (1989); Sanmark and Semple, 'Places of Assembly'.

58. Richard Warner, 'The Archaeology of Early Historic Irish Kingship', in S. Driscoll and M. Nieke, eds, *Power and Politics in Early Medieval Britain and Ireland* (Edinburgh: University Press, 1988), pp. 47-68; Conor Newman, *Tara: An Archaeological Survey* (Dublin: Royal Irish Academy 1997); 'Reflections on the Making of a "Royal Site" in Early Ireland', *World Archaeology*, 30:1 (1998), pp. 127-41.

59. See, for example, Bradley, 'Time Regained', pp. 1-17; also, papers in Pantos and Semple, *Assembly Places and Practices*; and Sanmark and Semple, 'Archaeologies of Assembly'.

60. Hope Taylor, *Yeavering*; Frodsham and O'Brien, *Power, People, Place*.

61. Jeremy Haslam, *Anglo-Saxon Towns in Southern England* (Chichester: Phillimore, 1984).

63. See Andrew Reynolds, *Later Anglo-Saxon England: Life and Landscape* (Stroud: Tempus, 1999).

64. Andrew Reynolds, 'Anglo-Saxon Law in the Landscape: An Archaeological Study of the Old English Judicial System', Ph.D. thesis, University of London (1998); Reynolds, *Later Anglo-Saxon England*.

65. The burial, excavated in 1923, was interred in a roughly cut grave, too small to accommodate the body. A male, approximately 28-32 years old, had been decapitated, the head removed by a single blow from the rear-right side. The victim is suggested to have been kneeling with the head raised, with the assailant standing behind. See, Mike Pitts, et al, 'An Anglo-Saxon Decapitation and Burial at Stonehenge', *Wiltshire Archaeological and Natural History Magazine*, 95 (2002), pp. 131-46.

66. Ibid.

67. Semple, *A Fear of the Past*; 'Illustrations of Damnation in Late Anglo-Saxon Manuscripts', *Anglo-Saxon England*, 32 (2004), pp. 231-45.

68. See Andrew Reynolds, 'The Definition and Ideology of Anglo-Saxon Execution Sites and Cemeteries', in G. de Boe and F. Verhaeghe, eds, *Death and Burial in Medieval Europe*, 2 (Zelik: Instituut voor het Archeologisch Patrimonium, 1997), pp. 33-41; 'Anglo-Saxon Law in the Landscape'; *Life and Landscape*; 'Burials, Boundaries and Charters in Anglo-Saxon England: a Reassessment', in Sam Lucy and Andrew Reynolds, eds, *Burial in Early Medieval England and Wales* (Society for Medieval Archaeological Monograph, 17, London: SMA, 2002), pp. 171-194.

69. Reynolds, 'Definition and Ideology'; *Life and Landscape*; 'Burials, Boundaries and Charters'.

70. Semple, 'A Fear of the Past'; 'Illustrations of Damnation'.

Chapter 3: 'A Small Journey into the Country': William Stukeley and the Formal Landscapes of Avebury and Stonehenge

1. For full biographies of Stukeley, see Stuart Piggott, *William Stukeley: An Eighteenth-Century Antiquary*, 2nd ed. (London: Thames and Hudson, 1985), and David Boyd Haycock, *William Stukeley: Science, Religion and Archaeology in Eighteenth-century England* (Woodbridge: Boydell and Brewer, 2002). I first addressed this theme in *Producing the Past: Aspects of Antiquarian Culture and Practice, 1700-1850*, in Martin Myrone and Lucy Pelz, eds (Aldershot: Ashgate, 1999), pp. 67-79.

2. William Stukeley, notes for 'Iter Cantabrigiense' (1754), MS 494 fol. i, Society of Antiquaries, London.

3. See Christopher Tilley, *A Phenomenology of Landscape: Places, Paths and Monuments* (Oxford: Berg, 1994).

4. Rosamund Cleal, K.E. Walker, R. Montague et al., *Stonehenge in its Landscape: Twentieth-century Excavations* (London: English Heritage, 1995), p. 18.

5. William Stukeley, *Abury: A Temple of the British Druids* (London: for the author, sold by W. Innys, R. Manby, B. Dodd, et al., 1743), p. 18.

6. William Stukeley, *The Commentarys, Diary, and Common-Place Book of William Stukeley* (London: Doppler, 1980), p. 3.

7. See Stukeley's diary, 15 September 1747, at Boughton with the Duke of Montagu: 'his Grace & I rode alone round the Serpentin walks in his chase woods, wh[ich] I persuaded him to make in contrast to the strait ones.' Bodleian Library, Oxford, MS Eng. misc. e.667/5.

8. John Dixon Hunt and Peter Willis, *The Genius of the Place: the English Landscape Garden, 1620-1820* (London: MIT Press, 1988), p. 25.

9. See Stephen Daniels, 'Goodly Prospects: English Estate Portraiture, 1670-1730', in Nicholas Alfrey and Stephen Daniels, eds, *Mapping the Landscape: Essays on Art and Cartography* (Nottingham University Art Gallery, 1990).

10. William Stukeley, *Itinerarium Curiosum, or, an Account of the Antiquitys and Remarkable Curiositys in Nature or Art, observ'd in Travels thro' Great Brittan. Illustrated with Copper Prints. Centuria I* (London: for the author, 1724), p. 44.

11. Ibid., 'Preface' (unpaginated).

12. Ibid., p.3.

13. William Stukeley, *Stonehenge: a Temple Restor'd to the British Druids* (London: W. Innys and R. Manby, 1740), p. 9.

14. Ibid.

15. William Stukeley, 'Celtic Temples', Bodleian Library, Oxford, MS Eng. misc. c.323, ff.120-9.

16. Stukeley, *Abury*, p. 28.

17. Ibid., pp. 27-33.

18. John Smith, *Choir Gaur; The Grand Orrery of the Ancient Druids, Commonly called Stonehenge, on Salisbury Plain, Astronomically explained, and Mathematically proved to be a Temple erected in the earliest Ages, for Observing the Motions of the Heavenly Bodies* (London: for the author and sold by E. Easton, R. Horsfield, and J. White, 1771), p. 29.

19. See, for example, George Bickham the Younger's *The Beauties of Stowe, or*

a Description of the Most Noble House, Gardens and Magnificent Buildings therein (London: G. Bickham, 1753) or William Fordyce Mavor's *New Description of Blenheim* (London: printed for T. Cadell, E. Newbery, and Jackson, Fletcher and Cooke, 1793).

20. There is interesting research to be done on the relationships between these antiquaries and the representation of the past.

21. Catherine Levesque, *Journey Through Landscape in Seventeenth-century Holland: the Haarlem Print Series and Dutch Identity* (University Park, PA: Pennsylvania State University Press, 1994), p. 13.

22. Ibid., pp. 13-14.

23. For reproductions, as well as an excellent discussion of these plans, see Peter Ucko, Michael Hunter, Allan Clark and Andrew David, *Avebury Reconsidered: from the 1660s to the 1990s* (London: Unwin Hyman, 1991), pp. 132-56.

24. Sarah Bridgeman, *A General Plan of the Woods, Park and Gardens of Stowe* (London: for the author, 1739).

25. Stukeley, *Stonehenge*, p. 35.

26. See Cleal et al., *Stonehenge in its Landscape*, pp. 291–329.

27. Stukeley, *Stonehenge*, p. 35.

28. John Dixon Hunt, *Gardens and the Picturesque: Studies in the History of Landscape Architecture* (Cambridge, Mass: MIT Press, 1992), p. 114.

29. Stukeley, 'Celtic Temples', f. 119.

30. Ibid., f. 109.

31. John Dixon Hunt, *The Figure in the Landscape: Poetry, Painting, and Gardening during the Eighteenth Century* (London: The MIT Press, 1976), p. 143.

32. Hunt, *Gardens and the Picturesque*, pp. 115-17.

33. Max F. Schulz, 'The Circuit Walk of the Eighteenth-century Landscape Garden and the Pilgrim's Circuitous Progress', *Eighteenth-century Studies*, 15:1 (1981), p. 18.

34. Ibid., p. 3.

35. Stukeley, *Abury*, p. 50.

36. John Fothergill to Dr Robert Key, London, 6 August 1744, in Christopher C. Booth and Betsy C. Corner, eds, *Chain of Friendship: Selected Letters of Dr John Fothergill of London, 1735-1780* (London: Oxford University Press, 1971), pp. 94-5. For a full analysis of the reception of Stukeley's books, see Haycock (2002), chapter 10, '"These Learned Lives": The Influence of Dr Stukeley'.

37. Hunt and Willis, *Genius of the Place*, p. 196.

38. Ibid., p. 198.

39. See Edward Harwood, 'Personal Identity and the Eighteenth-century English Landscape Garden', *Journal of Garden History*, 13:1-2 (1993), pp. 36-48.

40. Quoted in Michael Charlesworth, 'Sacred Landscape: Signs of Religion in the Eighteenth-century Garden', *Journal of Garden History*, 13:1-2 (1993), pp. 56-68, quoted from 58-9.

41. Quoted in Hunt and Willis, *Genius of the Place*, pp. 198-9.

42. Stukeley, 'Celtic temples', f. 175.

43. Stukeley, *Stonehenge*, p. 30.

44. William Stukeley, 'The Creation, Music of the Spheres, K[ing] S[olomon's] Temple. Micro & Macrocosm Compared &c. &c.' (1718—1734), MS 1130 Stu (1), Freemason's Library, Grand Lodge, London.

45. William Stukeley, *William Stukeley: the Family Memoirs*, W.C. Lukis, ed., Surtees Society, 76 (1883), 2.159.

46. Letter from Stukeley to Samuel Gale, Oct. 1728, quoted in *William Stukeley: the Family Memoirs*, W.C. Lukis, ed., Surtees Society, 73 (1881), 1.209.

47. Stukeley, *Abury*, 'Dedication'.

48. See John Webb, ed., *The Most Notable Antiquity of Great Britain, Vulgarly Called Stone-Heng, on Salisbury Plain, Restored by Inigo Jones, Architect Generall to*

the Late King (London: printed by J. Flesher for D. Pakeman and L. Chapman, 1655).

49. William Stukeley, 'Catalogue of Druids', MS 4720, fol. 2, Wellcome Institute for the History of Medicine Library, London.

50. Stukeley, *Itinerarium*, p. 64.

51. Stukeley, 'The Creation', p. 32.

52. Quoted in Charlesworth, 'Sacred Landscape', p. 59.

53. Stukeley, *William Stukeley: The Family Memoirs*, 1.363-4i.

54. William Stukeley, *The Medallic History of Marcus Aurelius Valerius Carausius, Emperor in Brittain*, 2 vols (London: Charles Corbet, 1759), 2.v.

55. Stukeley, MS Eng. misc. e.390, fol. 10, Bodleian Library, Oxford.

56. Stuart Piggott, *The Druids*, 2nd ed. (London: Thames and Hudson, 1975), pp. 143-4.

57. Anon. *A Description of Stonehenge, Abiry &c. in Wiltshire. With an Account of the Learning and Discipline of the Druids* (London: Collins and Johnson, 1776), p. 17. In this text, the author writes 'Mr. Jones' in the square bracket where I have substituted 'Wood': this was clearly an error, as Wood was, of course, the architect of the Circus at Bath.

58. For a discussion of the many representations of Druids and their monuments in this period, see Sam Smiles, *The Image of Antiquity: Ancient Britain and the Romantic Imagination* (New Haven and London: Yale University Press, 1994).

59. David R. Coffin, *The English Garden: Meditation and Memorial* (Princeton, NJ: Princeton University Press, 1994), pp. 121-2.

Chapter 4: Thomas Rickman's Handbook of Gothic Architecture and the Taxonomic Classification of the Past

1. The early career of Thomas Rickman, seen within the context of his extended Quaker family, is detailed in the doctoral dissertation by John Baily: 'Thomas Rickman, Architect and Quaker: the Early Years to 1818', PhD dissertation, Department of Fine Art, University of Leeds, 1977; a copy is on deposit at the library of the Religious Society of Friends, Euston Road, London. Baily published a brief account of Rickman in Jane Turner, ed., *The Dictionary of Art* (London: Macmillan, 1996), pp. 361-2.

2. The scientific fervour of the age is brilliantly captured by Jenny Uglow in *The Lunar Men: the Friends who Made the Future, 1730-1810* (London: Faber and Faber, 2002).

3. Nikolaus Pevsner has traced the evolution of Rickman's terminology in *Some Architectural Writers of the Nineteenth Century* (Oxford: Clarendon, 1972), p. 29, and has compared Rickman's *Attempt* to other early nineteenth-century publications on Gothic architecture. The term 'Perpendicular' has been widely accepted as Rickman's own invention.

4. There is, even today, debate on this interesting subject. For a discussion of early attempts at histories of Gothic architecture, see Michael McCarthy, *The Origins of the Gothic Revival* (New Haven and London: Yale University Press, 1987), particularly pp. 17-25. Roman remains were seen to offer 'hard evidence' for antiquarian study, as opposed to the world of 'myth and legend' which is discussed in Chapter 1 of this volume. See Sam Smiles, *The Image of Antiquity: Ancient Britain and the Romantic Imagination* (New Haven and London: Yale University Press, 1994), pp. 9-14; Borlase is quoted on p. 14.

5. On James Hall, see Megan Aldrich, *Gothic Revival* (London: Phaidon, 1994), p. 109, and pp. 112-3 for illustrations. The watercolour of the wicker cathedral by Alexander Carse is in the collection of the Royal Institute of British Architects, London. For Stukeley and the Druids, see the chapters by David Haycock and Robert J. Wallis in this volume.

6. The education of Quakers is discussed in Arthur Raistrick, *Quakers in Science and Industry*, rev. ed. (Newton Abbot: David and Charles, 1968), pp. 32-43. Latin schools for Quakers of both sexes were established by the end of the seventeenth century, and many schools offered some Latin, Greek

and Hebrew. However, the emphasis of a typical Quaker education was on practical subjects like science and engineering, as many Quakers were industrialists or merchants.

7. See 'Thomas Rickman's personal diaries', Royal Institute of British Architects, London; Drawings Collection, vol. 4, esp. entries for 4–6 Jul. 1808.

8. Ibid., endpapers, vol. 8; and Pevsner, note 3, above.

9. Thomas Rickman, 'On the Architectural History of Chester Cathedral', *Architectural, Archaeological and Historical Society for the County of Chester*, vol. 2 (1864), p. 277.

10. Ibid., pp. 277-8.

11. Rickman's personal diaries, vol. 6, entry for 10 Jul. 1810.

12. See the 'Encyclopedia Britannica Online' at www.britannica.com.

13. Richard Kirwan (1733-1812) was involved in the battle between the British and French chemists, represented by Joseph Priestly and Antoine Lavoisier, respectively. See chapter 30, 'Fire', in Uglow, *Lunar Men*.

14. According to the diary entries for 18-21 Dec. 1811, for example, the principal conflict seemed to lie with the schoolteacher, Joseph Bradley, a founder member, whose strong views regarding the rules of the new society clashed with Rickman's own. Noting the rules of the Derby Society, Rickman commented, 'they admit discussion' (15 Jan. 1812).

15. See St George's, Everton (1812-14), and St Michael's, Toxteth (1814-15); a third church in this group by Rickman and Cragg, St Philip's, Hardman Street (1815-16), was demolished in 1882. See Quentin Hughes, *Liverpool: City of Architecture* (Liverpool: Bluecoat Press, 1999), pp. 38-40; and Howard Colvin, A *Biographical Dictionary of British Architects, 1600-1840*, 3rd ed. (New Haven and London: Yale University Press, 1995), p. 814.

16. St Luke's, Berry Place (1811-31), is now a burnt out shell, having been nearly destroyed in the Blitz during the Second World War. It was the work of John Foster the Elder and his son, John Foster, Junior, with Rickman as a 'consultant' on the Gothic window tracery. See ibid., p. 23. For information on the Fosters, see Colvin, *Biographical Dictionary*, pp. 373-5.

17. Diary entry for 9 Oct. 1811.

18. *The Lunar Men*, p. 267. See chapter 23, 'Plants & Passions', for more on the importance of Linnaeus to British intellectual endeavour during this period. The most recent biography of Linnaeus is by Gunner Broberg: *Carl Linnaeus*, trans. Roger Tanner, (Stockholm: Swedish Institute, 2006).

19. See the website of the Linnaean Society, London, at www.linnean.org. Rickman, or one of his contacts, may have been aware of the biography: Dietrich Heinrich Stoever, *The Life of Sir C. Linnaeus*, trans. J. Trapp (London: B. and J. White, 1794).

20. Howard's beautiful watercolours of the clouds are preserved in his sketchbook which is owned by the Royal Meteorological Society in Reading but on permanent loan to the Science Museum in London as of 2008.

21. See John E. Thomas, *John Constable's Skies* (Birmingham: University of Birmingham Press, 1999), p. 52.

22. For further information, see the website of the Royal Meteorological Society at www.rmets.org/weather/observing/luke-howard; and for fuller biographical information on Howard, see the BBC website at www.bbc.co.uk/dna/h2g2.

23. Thomas Rickman, *An Attempt*, Preface to the First Edition, as cited in the second (1819) edition, pp. iii-iv.

24. The church of St Martin at Horsley was built in 1838-9 under the supervision of Rickman's second partner, Richard Charles Hussey (1802-87). Rickman had already begun to hand over the day-to-day running of the office to Hussey after 1835, owing to his poor health. However, the church at Horsley still shows the unmistakeable characteristics of Rickman's architectural style. See David Verey and Alan Brooks, *The Buildings of England: Gloucestershire 1, The Cotswolds*, 3rd ed. (London: Penguin, 1999), pp. 100, 415-6.

25. On pages 54 and 46, respectively, of the 4th edition: *An Attempt*

to Discriminate the Styles of Architecture in England, from the Conquest to the Reformation (London: Longmans, 1835). This volume preserves the text of the first edition of 1817, augmented by the next three editions.

26. Ibid. p. 66.

27. Ibid. p. 90.

28. See Megan Aldrich, 'Gothic Architecture Illustrated: the Drawings of Thomas Rickman in New York', *The Antiquaries Journal,* 65 (1985), pp. 427-33.

29. Edmund Sharpe, *A Treatise on the Rise and Progress of Decorated Window-Tracery in England* (London: Van Voorst, 1849), Introduction, pp. 1-2.

30. In *A Glossary of Terms Used in English Architecture* (London: Methuen, 1906); and *The Cathedrals of England* (London: Thames and Hudson, 1967), p.121.

31. *A Dictionary of Architecture* (Oxford: University Press, 1999), p. 550.

32. 'C'est en Angleterre qu'on s'est d'abord livré avec le plus de zèle et de succés a l'étude des monuments du moyen âge.' *Histoire Sommaire de l'Architecture Religieuse, Militaire, et Civile au Moyen Age* (Caen, Paris, Rouen, Poitiers, Rennes, 1836), p. 8.

33. The exact quotation reads: 'Il ne faut pas oublier l'essai de M. Rickman qui renferme des renseignemens fort étendus sur la statistique monumentale de l'Angleterre et l'énumeration des caractères qui distinguent les principaux genres d'architecture qui se sont succédé dans ce pays; l'ouvrage forme un volume de 400 pages orné de 14 planches: la dernière édition a paru en 1825.' (Ibid., p. 12.) I am grateful to my colleague, Dr Catherine Morel, for checking my translation and suggesting refinements.

34. Henry Van Brunt, 'Synopsis of Rickman's Gothic Architecture', MS. *c.* 1890; Avery Architectural Library, Columbia University, New York; reference number AA/737/V27/V278.

Chapter 5: Antiquarianism and the Creation of Place: the Birth of Japanese Archaeology

1. See, for example, V. Harris and K. Goto, *William Gowland: the Father of Japanese Archaeology* (London and Tokyo: British Museum and Asahi Newspapers, 2003).

2. For example, M. Diaz-Andreu, *A World History of Nineteenth-century Archaeology: Nationalism, Colonialism and the Past* (Oxford: University Press, 2007).

3. H.I. Pai, *Constructing 'Korean' Origins: a Critical Review of Archaeology, Historiography, and Racial Myth in Korean State Formation Theories* (Cambridge, Mass: Harvard University Asia Centre, 2000).

4. F. Ikawa-Smith, 'Co-traditions in Japanese Archaeology', *World Archaeology,* 13 (1982), pp. 296-309. See also Diaz-Andreu, *A World History of Nineteenth-century Archaeology.*

5. See Harris and Goto, *William Gowland;* and Simon Kaner, 'William Gowland: a Biographical Portrait' in H. Cortazzi, ed., *Biographical Portraits,* 9 (2007).

6. P. Bleed, 'Almost Archaeology', in R. Pearson, et al., eds, *Windows on the Japanese Past* (Ann Arbor: University of Michigan Press, 1986), p. 58.

7. Ibid. See also J. Nakaya, *Nihon Senshigaku Joshi [The Early History of Japanese Prehistory]* (Tokyo: Iwanami Shoten, 1935), pp. 43-4; and T. Saito, *Nihon Kokogakushi [History of Japanese Archaeology]* (Tokyo: Yoshikawa Kobunkan, 1974), pp. 2-3.

8. Bleed, 'Almost Archaeology', p. 60.

9. Ibid.

10. Ibid., p. 61. See also Saito, *Nihon Kokogakushi,* pp. 47-53.

11. Bleed, 'Almost Archaeology', p. 61.

12. Ibid., p. 62; and Nakaya, *Nihon Senshigaku.*

13. Bleed, 'Almost Archaeology', pp. 62-3; see also T. Saito, *Kiuchi Sekitei* (Tokyo: Yoshikawa Kobunkan, 1962).

14. Bleed, 'Almost Archaeology', p. 63.

15. Ibid., p. 62.

16. W. Edwards, 'Monuments to an Unbroken Line: the Imperial Tombs and the Emergence of Modern Japanese Nationalism', in Susan Kane, ed., *The Politics of Archaeology and Identity in a Global Context* (Boston, Massachusetts: Archaeological Institute of America, 2005), p. 11–30. See, also, W. Edwards, 'Japanese Archaeology and Cultural Properties Management: Prewar Ideologies and Postwar Legacies', in J. Robinson, ed., *A Companion to the Anthropology of Japan* (Oxford: Blackwell, 2006) pp. 34–49.

17. Ibid.

18. Bleed, 'Almost Archaeology', p. 64; see also Saito, *Kiuchi Sekitei*, p. 81.

19. See Edwards, 'Monuments to an Unbroken Line', p.18.

20. Bleed, 'Almost Archaeology', pp. 66–7.

21. Regarding Gowland's career, see C. Chippendale, *Stonehenge Complete*, 4th ed. (London: Thames and Hudson, 2004).

22. See Pai, *Constructing 'Korean' Origins*, p. 23.

23. Ibid., pp. 24–5.

24. Ibid., p. 26.

25. J. Wilkinson, 'Gordon Munro: Ventures in Japanese Archaeology and Anthropology' in I. Nish, ed., *Britain and Japan: Biographical Portraits* (Folkestone: Japan Library, 1994), p. 219.

26. Neil Gordon Munro, *Coins of Japan* (Yokohama, 1904).

27. See Wilkinson, 'Gordon Munro', p. 225. Munro was writing in *Prehistoric Japan*, published in Yokohama in 1911.

28. M. Hoffman, 'The Rise of Antiquarianism in Japan and Western Europe', *Arctic Anthropology*, 11 (1974), p. 187.

29. See J. Habu and C. Fawcett, 'Jomon Archaeology and the Representation of Japanese Origins', *Antiquity*, 281 (1999), pp. 587–93.

30. See K. Mizoguchi, *Archaeology, Society and Identity in Modern Japan*. (Cambridge: University Press, 2006).

Chapter 6: Recording the Past: the Origins and Aims of the Church Monuments Society

1. David Starkey, 'Making History', in David Gaimster, Sarah McCarthy and Bernard Nurse, eds, *Making History: Antiquaries in Britain, 1707-2007* (London: Royal Academy of Arts, 2007), pp. 11–5.

2. Andrew Sargent, 'RCHME, 1908–1998: a History of the Royal Commission on the Historical Monuments of England', *Transactions of the Ancient Monuments Society*, 45 (2001), pp. 57–81.

3. Editorial, *ISSCM Bulletin*, 1 (1979), p. 1.

4. John Physick, 'The Society for Preserving the Memorials of the Dead', *Church Monuments Society Newsletter*, 5:1 (1989), p. 22.

5. Anne Norman, 'A.V. Norman (1930–98) and the Church Monuments Society', *Church Monuments*, 19 (2004), pp. 5–19.

6. Claude Blair and Richard Knowles, 'Obituary: A.V.B. (Nick) Norman, 1930-1998', *Church Monuments*, 13 (1998), p. 110.

7. Philip J. Lankester, personal communication.

8. Claude Blair, personal communication.

9. Ibid.

10. John K. Bromilow, personal communication.

11. John Physick and Nigel Ramsay, 'Mrs Katharine Ada Esdaile, 1881–1950', *Church Monuments*, 1:2 (1986), p. 115.

12. See, for example, K.A. Esdaile, *English Monumental Sculpture since the Renaissance* (London: Society for the Promotion of Christian Knowledge, 1927); and K.A. Esdaile, *English Church Monuments, 1510-1840* (London: Batsford, 1946). To gauge the extent of her campaigning, see John Physick and Nigel Ramsay, 'Katharine Ada Esdaile: a Bibliography', *Church Monuments*, 1:2 (1986), pp. 117–36.

13. See, for example, Margaret Whinney, *Sculpture in Britain, 1530-1830*

(Harmondsworth: Penguin Books, 1964).

14. Matthew Craske, *The Silent Rhetoric of the Body: a History of Monumental Sculpture and Commemorative Art in England, 1720-1770* (New Haven and London:Yale University Press, 2007), p. 1.

15. John Stow, *A Survey of London, Written in the Year 1598*, rev. 1603; reprint (Stroud: Alan Sutton, 1994).

16. Peter Burman, *Church Restoration in the Nineteenth Century with Reference to Norfolk Churches*, Booklet 4 (Wymondham: Friends of Wymondhyam Abbey, 1997). See also Peter Burman, ed., *Treasures on Earth: a Good Housekpeeing Guide to Churches and their Contents* (London: Donhead, 1994).

17. Ruth Gledhill, 'Vandalism and Theft Cost Insurer £5 Million a Year', *The Times* (30 Sept. 1997), n.p.

18. Phillip Lindley, '"Disrespect for the Dead?": the Destruction of Tomb Monuments in Mid-sixteenth-century England', *Church Monuments*, 19 (2004), pp. 53–80.

19. John Weever, *Ancient Funerall Monuments* (London: 1631), p. 38.

20. Clive Easter, personal communication.

21. Richard Bradley, *Altering the Earth: the 1992 Rhind Lectures*, Monograph Series, 8 (Edinburgh: Society of Antiquaries of Scotland, 1993).

22. Nadezdha Mandelstam, *Hope Abandoned: a Memoir* (Harmondsworth: Penguin Books, 1974), p. 191.

23. Simon Watney, 'The Pleasure of Monuments', *The Churches Conservation Trust Review and Report, 2002-2003* (2003), pp. 32-7.

24. Bertolt Brecht, *The Life of Galileo*, Howard Brenton, trans. (London: Methuen, 1980), p. 115. In scene 12: 'Unhappy the land that is in need of heroes'.

Chapter 7: Modern Antiquarians? Pagans, 'Sacred Sites', Respect and Reburial

1. Orthographically, I capitalise the various pagan paths and their practitioners (e.g. Druidry and Druid) because this is nomenclature that pagans use to identify themselves (as a Christian or Muslim would tend to do). In lower case, 'pagan', 'druid', and so on delineate generic if contested terms, past and present, and I am clear in the text when it is the ancient or modern form at issue since, while there are interfaces, the contemporary and ancient forms are evidently not the same.

2. Julian Richards, *Stonehenge: a History in Photographs* (London: English Heritage, 2004), p. 32.

3. The Stonehenge Free Festival originated in the 'Peoples Free Festival' in Windsor, 1972-4. For discussion of the history of the festival at Stonehenge and its demise, see, for example: NCCL (National Council for Civil Liberties), *Stonehenge: a Report into the Civil Liberties Implications of the Events relating to the Convoys of Summer 1985 and 1986* (New Haven and London: Yale University Press, 1986); Christopher Chippindale, Paul Devereux, Peter Fowler, Rhys Jones and Tim Sebastion, *Who Owns Stonehenge?* (London: Batsford, 1990); Kevin Hetherington, 'Place, Space and Power: Stonehenge and the Travellers', *Here and Now*, 12 (1992), pp. 25-8; *New Age Travellers: Vanloads of Uproarious Humanity* (London: Cassell, 2000); Barbara Bender, *Stonehenge: Making Space*, (Oxford: Berg, 1998); Tim Sebastion, 'Alternative Archaeology: Has it Happened?', in Robert J.Wallis and Kenneth J. Lymer, eds, *A Permeability of Boundaries: New Approaches to the Archaeology of Art, Religion and Folklore* (Oxford: British Archaeological Reports, 2001), pp. 125–35; Andy Worthington, *Stonehenge: Celebration and Subversion* (Loughborough: Heart of Albion, 2004); and ed., *The Battle of the Beanfield* (Teignmouth: Enabler, 2005); Jenny Blain and Robert J.Wallis, *Sacred Sites, Contested Rites/Rights: Contemporary Pagan Engagements with the Past* (Brighton: Sussex Academic Press, 2007). The most recent summary of events is offered in an overview of Stonehenge in the 'Wonders of the World' series: Rosemary Hill, *Stonehenge* (London: Profile, 2008).

4. See, for example, Robert J. Wallis, 'Queer Shamans: Autoarchaeology and Neo-shamanism', *World Archaeology*, 32:2 (2000), pp. 251-61; 'Waking the Ancestors: Neo-shamanism and Archaeology', in Neil Price, ed., *The Archaeology of Shamanism* (London: Routledge, 2001), pp. 213-330; *Shamans/neo-Shamans: Ecstasy, Alternative Archaeologies and Contemporary Pagans* (London: Routledge, 2003); 'Between the Worlds: Autoarchaeology and Neo-Shamans' in Jenny Blain, Doug Ezzy and Graham Harvey, eds, *Researching Paganisms* (Walnut Creek, CA: Altamira, 2004), pp. 191-215.

5. See, for example, Robert J. Wallis, and Kenneth J. Lymer, eds, *A Permeability of Boundaries: New Approaches to the Archaeology of Art, Religion and Folklore* (Oxford: British Archaeological Reports, 2001).

6. See the Sacred Sites project website at www.sacredsites.org.uk.

7. See, for example, Jenny Blain and Robert J. Wallis, 'A Living Landscape? Pagans and Archaeological Discourse', *3rd Stone: Archaeology, Folklore and Myth – the Magazine for the New Antiquarian*, 43 (Summer 2002), pp. 20-7; 'Sacred Sites, Contested Rites/Rights: Contemporary Pagan Engagements with the Past', *Journal of Material Culture*, 9:3 (2004), pp. 237-61; 'Sites, Texts, Contexts and Inscriptions of Meaning: Investigating Pagan "Authenticities" in a Text-based Society', *The Pomegranate: The International Journal of Pagan Studies*, 6:2 (2004), pp. 231-52; 'Pasts and Pagan Practices: Moving beyond Stonehenge', *Public Archaeology*, 5:4 (2006), pp. 3-16; 'Re-presenting Spirit: Heathenry, New-indigenes, and the Imaged Past', in Ian A. Russell, ed., *Images, Representations and Heritage: Moving beyond Modern Approaches to Archaeology* (London and New York: Springer, 2006), pp. 89-108; 'Sacred, Secular, or Sacrilegious? Prehistoric Sites, Pagans and the Sacred Sites Project in Britain', in Judith Schachter and Stephen Brockman, eds, *(Im)permanence: Cultures In/Out of Time* (Pittsburgh: Carnegie Mellon Center for the Arts in Society, 2008), pp. 212-23; 'Heathenry and its Development', in Jim Lewis and Murph Pizza, eds, *Handbook of Contemporary Paganism* (Leiden and Boston: Brill, 2008), 413-31; 'Sites, Sacredness, and Stories: Interactions of Archaeology and Contemporary Paganism', *Folklore*, 114:3 (2003), pp. 307-21; 'Sacred Sites in England', in Bron Taylor and Jeffrey Kaplan, eds, *Encyclopedia of Religion and Nature* (New York and London: Continuum, 2005), pp. 1460-2; '"Sacred" Sites, Artefacts and Museum Collections: Pagan Engagements with Archaeology in Britain', in Lewis and Pizza, *Handbook of Contemporary Paganism*.

8. See, for example, Wallis, 'Queer Shamans', pp. 251-61.

9. See, for example, Blain and Wallis, *Sacred Sites, Contested Rites/Rights: Contemporary Pagan Engagements with the Past* (Brighton: Sussex Academic Press, 2007)

10. Friedrich Nietzsche, *Untimely Meditations*, 2nd ed. (Cambridge: University Press, 1997).

11. Julian Cope, *The Modern Antiquarian: a Pre-Millennial Odyssey through Megalithic Britain* (London: Thorsons, 1998); see also *The Megalithic European: the Twenty-first Century Traveller in Prehistoric Europe* (London: Thorsons, 2004).

12. Cope, *The Modern Antiquarian*, p. ix.

13. Ibid., p. 28.

14. Julian Cope, speaking in an interview with B. Thompson, 'Cliff Richard is a Pagan', *The Independent Weekend Review* (24 Oct. 1998), p. 12.

15. Ibid.

16. Neil Mortimer, personal communication.

17. Michael Dames, *The Silbury Treasure* (London: Thames and Hudson, 1976); *The Avebury Cycle* (London: Thames and Hudson, 1977).

18. For early academic archaeological comment on goddesses, see O.G.S. Crawford, *The Eye Goddess* (London: Phoenix House, 1957); Vere Gordon Childe, *The Prehistory of European Society* (Harmondsworth: Penguin, 1958); Glyn Daniel, *The Megalith Builders of Western Europe* (London: Hutchison, 1958). Gimbutas' theories are outlined in Marija Gimbutas, *The Goddesses and Gods of Old Europe: Myths and Cult Images* (London: Thames and

Hudson, 1974). Archaeologists have pointed out that Gimbutas' idea of patriarchal, violent kurgan Indo-Europeans of the steppes invading a peaceful, matriarchal pre–Indo-European culture of 'Old Europe' simplifies the archaeological evidence – see, for example, Lynn Meskell, 'Goddesses, Gimbutas and "New Age" Archaeology', *Antiquity*, 69 (1995), pp. 74–86. Nonetheless, many goddess worshippers, particularly women, have utilised Gimbutas' reclaiming of 'the goddess' as greatly empowering in their daily lives – see, for example, Kathryn Rountree, *Embracing the Witch and the Goddess: Feminist Ritual-makers in New Zealand* (London: Routledge, 2003).

19. This idea has been rendered sculpturally in a small goddess figurine, available for sale in the Avebury 'Henge Shop'.

20. Terence Meaden, *The Secrets of the Avebury Stones* (London: Souvenir, 1999).

21. See the Amazon website review of the book: www.amazon.co.uk/ Secrets-Avebury-Stones-Britains-Megalithic/dp/0285635018.

22. See, for example, Graham Harvey, and Charlotte Hardman, eds, *Paganism Today: Wiccans, Druids, the Goddess and Ancient Earth Traditions for the Twenty-first Century* (London: Thorsons, 1995); Graham Harvey, *Listening People, Speaking Earth: Contemporary Paganism* (London: Hurst, 1997); 'Pagan Studies or the Study of Paganisms? A Case Study in the Study of Religions', in Jenny Blain, Graham Harvey and Doug Ezzy, eds, *Researching Paganisms* (Walnut Creek, CA: AltaMira, 2004), pp. 241–68; Joanne Pearson, *Wicca: Magic, Spirituality and 'the Mystic Other'* (London: Routledge, 2003); Jenny Blain, *Nine Worlds of Seid-Magic: Ecstasy and Neo-shamanism in North European Paganism* (London: Routledge, 2002); Wallis, *Shamans/neo-Shamans*; Jenny Blain, Doug Ezzy and Graham Harvey, eds, *Researching Paganisms* (Walnut Creek, CA: AltaMira, 2004).

23. See, for example, Ronald Hutton, *The Triumph of the Moon: a History of Modern Pagan Witchcraft* (Oxford: University Press, 1999); also Pearson, ibid.; Rountree, ibid.

24. See: Ronald Hutton, *The Druids* (London: Hambledon Continuum, 2007); also *The Origins of Modern Druidry*, The Order of Bards Ovates & Druids Mount Haemus Lecture for the Year 2000, available online: http:// druidry.org/pdfs/first_mt_haemus_lecture.pdf.

25. See Blain, *Nine Worlds*; Wallis, *Shamans/neo-Shamans*.

26. See, for example, Kathryn Rountree, 'Is there Hope for a Straw Goddess? The Challenges of Multivocality at Çatalhöyük', paper presented in the 'Archaeology and the Goddess: Creating Dialogue' session in the 'Archaeology of Spirituality' theme, 6th World Archaeological Congress, University College, Dublin (29 Jun.–4 Jul. 2008).

27. Margaret Murray, *The Witch-cult in Western Europe* (Oxford: Clarendon, 1921); *God of the Witches* (Oxford: University Press, 1933).

28. Hutton, *The Origins*, p. 16.

29. Ibid.

30. Ibid.

31. C. Oakley, 'National Trust Guardianship Scheme', *Pagan Dawn*, 126 (Lammas 1997), p. 9.

32. BBC News (21 Jun. 2008), 'Thousands Mark Summer Solstice', available online: http://news.bbc.co.uk/1/hi/england/wiltshire/7465235.stm.

33. Tristan Cork, 'Stone Circle Village Goes to War over Pagans in the Car Park', *Western Daily Press* (12 Oct. 2006), available online: www.westpress. co.uk.

34. Paul Davies, 'Respect and Reburial', *The Druid's Voice: the Magazine of Contemporary Druidry*, 8 (Summer 1997), pp. 12-13; see also 'Speaking for the Ancestors: the Reburial Issue in Britain and Ireland', *The Druid's Voice: The Magazine of Contemporary Druidry*, 9 (Winter 1998-9), pp. 10-12.

35. Philip Shallcrass, personal communication.

36. See also press coverage of pagan calls for reburial, such as James Randerson, 'Give Us Back Our Bones, Pagans Tell Museums', *The Guardian*

(5 Feb. 2007), available online: www.guardian.ac.uk/science/2007/feb/05/religion.artnews.

37. See, for example, *The Stonehenge Project*, available online: www.thestonehengeproject.org/.

38. Mike Pitts, 'Stonehenge: Now What?', *British Archaeology*, 99 (Mar./Apr. 2008), available online: http://www.britarch.ac.uk/BA/ba99/feat1.shtml.

39. Active pagan interest in the management of Stonehenge remains undiminished, however. Most visibly, following the government's withdrawal of the proposed management plan, King Arthur Pendragon attacked English Heritage as 'grossly incompetent' and stated:

> 'I therefore give "NOTICE TO QUIT" to English Heretics & H.M. Government
> "Pick up thy fence & Walk"
> And return [Stonehenge] to its rightful owner
> The peoples of this Once Green & Pleasant Land'

(Press Release [17 Jul. 2008]; see also 'Authorities must fix Mess: King Arthur', *Western Daily Press* [3 Jul. 2008], available online: www.westpress.co.uk/new/util/content.jsp?id=21005555; also http://www.facebook.com/home.php?ref=home#/pages/Arthur-Pendragon/18894188726?ref=share and http://honour-thy-spoken-word.kk5.org/). Arthur is a long-standing campaigner for free and open access at Stonehenge: see, for example, Arthur Pendragon, 'Sacred Sites', *Druid Lore*, 3 (2000-1), pp. 20-1; Arthur Pendragon, and C.J. Stone, *The Trials of Arthur: the Life and Times of a Modern-Day King* (London: Element, 2003).

40. A good example of the complexities of Druid politics is how a second COBDO group based in London claims that it is the 'real' COBDO, not the group in the west of England to which Davies belongs; furthermore, the London COBDO does not support calls for reburial in the same way. See http://www.gazetteandherald.co.uk/mostpopular.var.1164290.mostviewed.druids_call_for_burial.php.

41. See the COBDO West website: www.cobdowest.org/reburial1.html.

42. See Nigel Kerton, 'Druids Call for Reburial', *Wiltshire Gazette & Herald* (2 Feb. 2007), available online: www.gazetteandherald.co.uk/mostpopular.var.1164290.mostviewed.druids_call_for_burial.php.

43. DCMS (Department of Culture, Media and Sport), *Report of the Working Group on Human Remains, 2003*, available online: www.culture.gov.uk/Reference_library/Publications/archive_2003/wgur_report2003.htm. See also: DCMS. *Guidance for the Care of Human Remains in Museums 2005*, available online: www.culture.gov.uk/NR/rdonlyres/0017476B-3B86–46F3–BAB3–11E5A5F7F0A1/0/GuidanceHumanRemains11Oct.pdf.

44. See the COBDO West website: http://www.cobdowest.org/reburial.html.

45. Paul Davies, personal communication.

46. See: BBC News (22 Feb. 2007): 'Druids Request Re-burial of Bones', available online: http://news.bbc.co.uk/1/hi/england/wiltshire/6385675.stm.

47. See the HAD website: www.honour.org.uk/index.html.

48. Emma Restall Orr, personal communication.

49. See the HAD website: www.honour.org.uk/articles/reburial_rite.html.

50. Historically, reburial is not necessarily contrary to the interests of archaeologists, however. The case of the reburial of human remains from the Gokstad and Oseberg ship burials in Norway, in the first half of the twentieth century, and recent reburial of an early Saxon woman in the Woodford Valley near Stonehenge by Wessex Archaeology, mark instances of archaeologically legitimated reburial in north-west Europe. For discussion of the Norwegian examples, see: Elisabeth Arwill-Nordbladh, 'Re-arranging History: The Contested Bones of the Oseberg Grave', in Yannis Hamilakis, Mark Pluciennik and Sarah Tarlow, eds, *Thinking through the Body: Archaeologies of Corporeality* (New York: Kluwer Academic / Plenum Publishers, 2002), pp.

201-15. For discussion of the Wessex example, see Jacqueline McKinley, 'A Wiltshire Bog Body?: Discussion of a Fifth/Sixth Century AD Burial in the Woodford Valley', *Wiltshire Studies*, 96 (2003), pp. 7-18.

51. James Steele, British Association for Biological Anthropology and Osteoarchaeology (BABAO): Response to the DCMS Consultation Document 'Care of Historic Human Remains'. Prepared on behalf of the Association by James Steele (BABAO Chair), University of Southampton, available online (undated): http://www.babaotemp.bham.ac.uk/BABAOFinalVersionDCMSConsultationResponse.pdf.

52. Emma Restall Orr, personal communication.

53. See Aburrow's Wiki at http://pagantheologies.pbwiki.com/Finding+a+compromise; also *Finding a Compromise – Keeping Places*, paper presented at the 'Respect for Ancient British Human Remains: Philosophy and Practice' Conference, Manchester Museum, November 2006, available online: http://www.honour.org.uk/articles/Aburrow.pdf.

54. See 'Pagans for Archaeology' on Facebook: http://www.facebook.com/group.php?gid=16336348284; also the Pagans for Archaeology Blog at http://archaeopagans.blogspot.com/ and Pagans for Archaeology Yahoo group discussion list at http://groups.yahoo.com/group/archaeopagans/.

55. For further information, see the websites of the 'Save Tara' campaign http://www.savetara.com and 'Sacred Ireland' http://www.sacredireland.org/.

56. Officially known as the 'M3 Clonee to North of Kells road scheme'.

57. Specifically, the Dunshaughlin-Navan section of the M3 affects Tara.

58. Maggie Ronayne, 'The State We're In on the Eve of World Archaeological Congress (WAC) 6: Archaeology in Ireland vs Corporate Takeover', *Public Archaeology*, 7:2 (2008), pp. 114–29, available online: http://www.nuigalway.ie/faculties_departments/archaeology/documents/ronayne_wac.pdf

59. For discussion of this view, see the following letters in the Irish press: Maggie Ronayne, 'Archaeology Needs to Recover its Core Principles and Ethics', *Irish Times* (15 Jul. 2008), available online: http://www.irishtimes.com/newspaper/opinion/2008/0715/1215940930850.html; Margaret Gowan, 'Archaeology in Ireland can be Proud of its Standards', *Irish Times* (22 Jul. 2008), available online: http://www.irishtimes.com/newspaper/opinion/2008/0722/1216627319721.html; Ronayne, Maggie (and various signatories), 'Archaeology in Ireland', *Irish Times* (5 Aug. 2008), available online: http://www.irishtimes.com/newspaper/letters/2008/0805/1217628550381.html.

60. The press release is available at: http://www.savetara.com/statements/072108_bodies.html.

61. See the WAC website: http://www.worldarchaeologicalcongress.org/site/wacpress_19.php.

62. Ibid.

63. See the 'Tara Pixie' website: http://www.tarapixie.net/.

64. See the discussion in Blain and Wallis, *Sacred Sites, Contested Rites/Rights: Contemporary Pagan Engagements with the Past.*

65. Bryan Sitch, *Lindow Man Consultation, Saturday 10th February 2007: Report,* available online: http://www.museum.manchester.ac.uk/aboutus/ourpractice/lindowman/fileuploadmax10mb,120485,en.pdf.

66. See the 'Lindow Man blog' at: http://lindowmanchester.wordpress.com/2007/12/14/hello-world/#comments.

67. Eilean Hooper-Greenhill, *Museums and the Interpretation of Visual Culture* (London, Routledge, 2003).

68. See the HAD website: http://www.honour.org.uk/projects/care-museums.html.

69. Wallis and Blain, 'No One Voice'.

70. Frank Olding, 'Letter', *British Archaeology*, 79 (Nov. 2004), available online: http://www.britarch.ac.uk/ba/ba79/letters.shtml.

Chapter 8: Continuity and Revival in Modern Chinese Culture: the Woodblock Prints of Wang Chao

1. The author is very grateful to David Barker for his assistance and advice during the writing of this article. Part of this article was delivered at a research meeting at Sotheby's Institute of Art London, which took place on 22-3 Feb. 2007. The author would like to thank Tony Godfrey for the time he spent in considering the draft of an article on Wang Chao that was subsequently absorbed into the present essay. For current scholarship on conceptual art in contemporary China, see Li Xianting, 'Major Trends in the Development of Contemporary Chinese Art,' in *China's New Art, post-1989*, ex. cat. (Hong Kong: Hanart T Z Gallery, 1993), pp. x-xxii; Gao Minglu, ed., *Inside Out: New Chinese Art* (Berkeley, Los Angeles and London: University of California Press, 1998); Jiang Jiehong, ed., *Burden or Legacy: from the Chinese Cultural Revolution to Contemporary Art* (Hong Kong: University Press, 2007); the publication of six papers delivered at the symposium 'The Visual Legacy of the Chinese Cultural Revolution in Contemporary Art,' held at the Birmingham Institute of Art and Design, University of Central England, in May 2004; and Iain Robertson's section on 'China' in Iain Robertson, Victoria L. Tseng and Sonal Singh, '"Chindia" as Art Market Opportunity,' in Iain Robertson and Derrick Chong, eds, *The Art Business* (London and New York: Routledge, 2008), pp. 83-7.

2. See *China's New Art, post-1989*; and Karen Smith, *Nine Lives: the Birth of Avant-Garde Art in New China*, rev. ed. (Timezone 8, n.d.).

3. Julia F. Andrews and Kuiyi Shen, 'Transformations of Tradition, 1980 to the Present: Chinese Painting in the Post-Mao Era,' in Julia F. Andrews and Kuiyi Shen, eds, *A Century in Crisis* (New York: Guggenheim Museum, 1989), pp. 277-323.

4. Chinese intellectuals have regarded the major arts of pre-modern times in the hierarchical order of poetry, prose, calligraphy and painting, but foreign scholars have often regarded painting as being foremost. See F. W. Mote, 'The Arts and the "Theorizing Mode" of Civilization', in Christian F. Murck, ed., *Artists and Traditions: Uses of the Past in Chinese Culture* (New Jersey: Princeton University Press, 1976), p. 3.

5. Michael Sullivan, *Art and Artists of Twentieth-century China* (Berkeley, Los Angeles and London: University of California Press, 1996), pp. 36-41, 255-81.

6. Known as the Five Classics of Poetry, History, Ritual, Changes and the Spring and Autumn Annals. A sixth classic, the Classic of Music, was destroyed during the Burning of the Books in the early third century BC. See Michael Dillon, ed., *China: a Cultural and Historical Dictionary* (Richmond, Surrey: Curzon Press, 1998), pp. 35, 103.

7. Culturally important documents were engraved into stone from as early as the third century BC. The classics were first engraved in stone in the Xiping reign period of the Emperor Lingdi of the Eastern Han dynasty, in a project begun in 175 AD and completed in 183 AD; they were known as the Xiping Stone Classics. See Kenneth Starr, *Black Tigers: A Grammar of Chinese Rubbings* (Seattle and London: University of Washington Press, 2008), p. 6.

8. Dillon, *China*, pp. 94-6.

9. The Xia dynasty has been regarded as a legendary period of Chinese history. However, the recent excavation of an early Bronze-age site at Erlitou in Henan has led archaeologists to speculate whether this site might give historical evidence for its existence. See Dillon, *China*, p. 351.

10. Wu Hung, *The Wu Liang Shrine: the Ideology of Early Chinese Pictorial Art* (Stanford, California: Stanford University Press, 1989), pp. 92-6; Jeannette Shambaugh Elliott and David Shambaugh, *The Odyssey of China's Imperial Art Treasures* (Seattle and London: University of Washington Press, 2007), pp. 5-8.

11. Elliott and Shambaugh, *The Odyssey of China's Imperial Art Treasures*, p. 9 ff.

12. Ibid., pp. 13, 25-8.

13. A detailed examination of the seals and inscriptions on a painting of major historical importance is given in Wang Yao-t'ing, 'Beyond the *Admonitions* Scroll: a Study of its Mounting, Seals and Inscriptions', and Nixi Cura, 'A "Cultural Biography" of the *Admonitions* Scroll: The Qianlong Reign (1736-1795)', both in Shane McCauseland, ed., *Gu Kaizhi and the Admonitions Scroll*, pp. 192-218 and 260-76, respectively. The Qianlong emperor (1736-95) added inscriptions to the base of rare, twelfth-century ceramics in his collection. See Wen C. Fong and James C.Y. Watt, eds, *Possessing the Past: Treasures from the National Palace Museum, Taipei* (New York and Taipei: Metropolitan Museum of Art and the National Palace Museum, 1996), pp. 238-9, figs. 93-4.

14. In, for example, the collection, inscriptions and theoretical writings of the scholar-official, calligrapher and painter Dong Qichang (1555-1636). See Fong and Watt, *Possessing the Past*, pp. 419-25.

15. Laurence Sickman and Alexander Soper, *The Art and Architecture of China* (Harmondsworth: Penguin Books, 1971), pp. 132-4; Susan Bush and Hsio-yen Shih, eds, *Early Chinese Texts on Painting* (Cambridge, Mass., and London: Harvard University Press, 1985), pp. 10-7.

16. Mayching Kao, 'Art Training: Traditional', in 'China' pt. 15, 1, in vol. 7, *The Dictionary of Art* (London and New York: Macmillan and Grove, 1996), pp. 147-8.

For example, the well-known painting, *Travellers amid Streams and Mountains* by the Northern Song painter Fan Kuan (d. after 1023), recurs in copies by seventeenth-century artists. See Fong and Watt, *Possessing the Past*, pls. 59, 274b and 278.

17. James C.Y. Watt, 'Antiquarianism and Naturalism', in Fong and Watt, *Possessing the Past*, pp. 219-28.

18. Chu-tsing Li, 'The Uses of the Past in Yüan Landscape Painting', in Murck, *Artists and Traditions*, pp. 73-88.

19. Wai-kam Ho, 'Tung Ch'i-ch'ang's New Orthodoxy and the Southern School Theory', op. cit. pp. 113-29.

20. Wen C. Fong, 'Archaism as a "Primitive" Style', op. cit. pp. 89-109.

21. Referred to as *jinshixue* (literally 'bronze and stone studies'). See Stephen Little, 'New Songs on Ancient Tunes: 19th-20th Century Chinese Painting and Calligraphy from the Richard Fabian Collection,' and Qianshen Bai, 'Chinese Calligraphy in the Mid to Late Qing and Republican Periods (1850-1950)', both in Stephen Little, ed., *New Songs on Ancient Tunes: 19th-20th Century Chinese Paintings and Calligraphy from the Richard Fabian Collection* (Honolulu: Honolulu Academy of Arts, 2007), pp. 33-5 and 66-79, respectively.

22. Inscriptions in archaic scripts were applied as overglaze decoration on ceramics of the late Qing (1644-1911) and Republican (1911-49) periods. See Liu Yang, *Qianjiang Ceramics (Qianjiang Caici Pinjian)* (Nanchang: Jiangxi Education Publishers, 2005), pp. 64-5, cat. no. 35, p. 163 cat. no. 140.

23. Xiaoneng Yang, ed., *The Golden Age of Chinese Archaeology: Celebrated Discoveries from the People's Republic of China* (New Haven and London: Yale University Press, 1999), p. 28.

24. Cheng-hua Wang, 'Luo Zhenyu, his Collection, and the Categorical Formation of *Qiwu* in the 1910s', and Shih-ming Pai, 'Luo Zhenyu's Knowledge of Antiquity and his Theory of "Returning to the Classics, Trusting the Ancient', two unpublished papers delivered at the workshop entitled, 'Lost Generation: Luo Zhenyu, Qing Loyalists and the Formation of Modern Chinese Culture', organised by the School of Oriental and African Studies (SOAS), London, and Christie's Education, London, held at SOAS on 28-9 Aug. 2008.

25. Chu-tsing Li, *Trends in Modern Chinese Painting: the C.A. Drenowatz Collection*, Artibus Asiae Supplementum, 36 (Ascona, Switzerland: Artibus Asiae Publishers, 1979), p. 62.

26. Yang, *The Golden Age of Chinese Archaeology*, pp. 33-45.

27. Mayching Kao, 'The Beginning of the Western-style Painting Movement

in Relationship to Reforms in Education in Early Twentieth-century China', in *New Asia Academic Bulletin*, 4 (1983), pp. 373-400; Mayching Kao, 'Art Training: 20th Century,' in 'China' pt. 15, 2, in vol. 7, *The Dictionary of Art* (London and New York: Macmillan and Grove, 1996), pp. 148-9.

28. Shirley Hsiao-ling Sun, 'Lu Hsun and the Chinese Woodcut Movement: 1929-1935', PhD dissertation, Stanford University (1974); Xiaobing Tang, *Origins of the Chinese Avant-garde: the Modern Woodcut Movement* (Berkeley: University of California Press, 2008); Andrews and Shen, 'The Modern Woodcut Movement', in Andrews and Shen, *A Century in Crisis*, pp. 196-225.

29. Tang, *Origins of the Chinese Avant-garde*, pp. 135-6.

30. Frances Wood, 'A History of Chinese Printing till 1900', in *The Art of Contemporary Chinese Woodcuts* (London: Muban Foundation, 2003), pp. 13-31.

31. Tang, *Origins of the Chinese Avant-garde*, pp. 108-10.

32. The academy, opened in October 1938 for the instruction of artists in propaganda techniques, was the first in China to teach printmaking. See Anne Farrer, ed., *Chinese Printmaking Today: Woodblock Printing in China, 1980-2000* (London: The British Library, 2003), p. 191. Reproductions of prints made by Yan'an artists are included in a publication of personal narratives in Israel Epstein, *I Visited Yenan: Eye Witness Account of the Communist-led Liberated Areas in North-West China* (Bombay: People's Publishing House, 1945).

33. The 'Yan'an Forum on Literature and Art' was a two-week workshop held in 1942 in which Mao set out the Marxist stance for contemporary writers, and the place of art in society. He pointed out that art must serve the workers, peasants and soldiers. These talks led to a renaissance of highly colourful folk prints (*nianhua*, or 'new year picture') as a means of connecting to the wider audience in China. See Ellen Johnston Laing, *The Winking Owl: Art in the People's Republic of China* (Berkeley, Los Angeles and London: University of California Press, 1988), pp. 3-4, 36-7.

34. Iris Wachs and Chang Tsong-zung, *Half a Century of Chinese Woodblock Prints: from the Communist Revolution to the Open Door Policy and Beyond, 1945-1998* (Israel: Museum of Art Ein Harod, 1999), pp. 96-107; Iris Wachs and Haim Finkelstein, *Poetry, Painting and Politics: Chinese Urban Woodblock Printing Studios in an Age of Revolution, 1949-2000* (Israel: Avraham Baron Art Gallery and Ben-Gurion University of the Negev, 2003), pp. 112-4, 82, 74; Weimin He and Shelagh Vainker, *Chinese Prints, 1950-2006, in the Ashmolean Museum* (Oxford: Ashmolean Museum, 2007), p. 8.

35. Julia F. Andrews, *Painters and Politics in the People's Republic of China* (Berkeley: University of California Press, 1994), pp. 34-109.

36. Wachs and Finkelstein, *Poetry, Painting and Politics*, pp. 106-7. For printing techniques, see Diana Yu, 'The Printer Emulates the Painter – the Unique Chinese Water-and-ink Woodblock Print', *Renditions*, 6 (spring 1976), pp. 95-101; David Barker, *Traditional Techniques in Contemporary Chinese Printmaking* (London: A and C Black, 2005), pp. 19-73.

37. The history of Rongbaozhai is available online: 'Rongbaozhai': www.chinaculture.org/gb/en_artqa/2004-10/19/content_62454.htm, pp. 1-9; accessed 24 Oct. 2008.

38. A history of the academy is available in Farrer, *Chinese Printmaking Today*, p.191.

39. Wachs and Finkelstein, *Poetry, Painting and Politics*, p.107.

40. Andrews, *Painters and Politics*, pp. 71, 129-30; Farrer, *Chinese Printmaking Today*, p. 190.

41. Andrews, *Painters and Politics*, pp. 277-83.

42. Anne Farrer, 'The Growth of Woodblock Art in Contemporary China', in Farrer, *Chinese Printmaking Today*, pp. 29-30.

43. Britta Erickson, *Words Without Meaning, Meaning Without Words: the Art of Xu Bing* (Washington, D.C.: Sackler Gallery, Smithsonian Institution and University of Washington Press, 2001); Farrer, *Chinese Printmaking Today*, pp.

77, 161-3, 182-3; Smith, *Nine Lives: the Birth of the Avant-Garde in New China*, pp. 322-69; Anne Farrer, 'The Print and Contemporary Art', in *China Macht Druck (China Presses on)*, (Heidelburg: Kehrer Verlag, 2008), pp. 47-53.

44. Tsong-zung Chang, 'Beyond the Middle Kingdom: An Insider's View', in Gao Minglu, ed., *Inside Out: New Chinese Art* (Berkeley: University of California Press: 1998), pp. 67-9.

45. Andrews and Shen, *A Century in Crisis*, pp. 277-323.

46. These include the calligraphers Wang Dongling (b. 1945) and Sa Benjie (b. 1948), and the painters Shu Chuanxi (b. 1932), Zeng Mi (b. 1935), Lu Fusheng (b. 1949) and Chen Ping (b. 1960).

47. The remainder of this paper offers sustained visual analysis of Wang Chao's work. Wang Chao's work is itself published in Wachs and Chang, *Half a Century of Chinese Woodblock Prints*, pp. 174-5; *The Art of Contemporary Chinese Woodcuts*, pp. 178-9; David Barker, *Wang Chao: Recent Woodcut Printed Books and Single Sheet Prints* (Belfast: Belfast Print Workshop and University of Ulster, n.d.); (a) Farrer, 'The Growth of Woodblock Art in Contemporary China,' (b) Frances Wood, cat. nos. 8-9, (c) Farrer, cat. no. 101, in *Chinese Printmaking Today*, pp. 33-4, 62-5, 101; He and Vainker, *Chinese Prints, 1950-2006, in the Ashmolean Museum*, p. 137.

48. Maria Galikowski, *Art and Politics in China, 1949-1984* (Hong Kong: the Chinese University Press, 1998), pp. 175-249.

49. The Jiuli Studio is 'Jiulifang', in Chinese. Wang Chao uses another studio name, the 'Golden Bowl Studio' (Chinese: *Jinpenzhai)* in the album *Images of Heavenly Phenomena* (1997). The 'Golden Bowl' refers to the enamelled wash-basin, the subject of the album.

50. This is an accurate self-portrait. See Wang Chao's photograph in David Barker, *Traditional Techniques in Contemporary Chinese Printmaking* (London: A and C Black, 2005), p. 31.

51. Hsio-yen Shih, 'On Ming Dynasty Book Illustration', MA dissertation, University of Chicago (1958); Michela Bussotti, *Gravures de Hui: Étude du Livre Illustré Chinois de la Fin du XVIe Siècle à la Première Moitié du XVIIe Siècle*, Mémoires Archéologiques, 26 (Paris: École Française d'Extrême-Orient, 2001).

52. Duoyunxuan, Shanghai, in collaboration with the Shanghai Museum produced a facsimile of the *Trumpetvine Pavilion Catalogue of Variations on Stationery Paper Designs (Luoxuan biangu jianpu)* (1627). The date of publication of the facsimile is not recorded but was probably in the early 1980s. Duoyunxuan produced a facsimile of another exceptionally important work in the history of late Ming colour printing, the illustrations of *The Romance of the West Chamber (Xixiangji)* (1640), which exists in a single original copy in the Museum für Ostasiatische Kunst in Cologne. In 1985, Roger Goepper, curator of the Museum für Ostasiatische Kunst, donated a photo-offset reproduction of the illustrations published in Germany in 1977 to Duoyunxuan, who completed their own woodblock facsimile in 1990. Rongbaozhai, Beijing, produced a facsimile of the compilation *Ten Bamboo Studio Letter Papers (Shizhuzhai jianpu)* (1644), in several facsimile editions in 1934, the early 1950s and in the intervening period up to 1996. For references to these works, see Edith Dittrich, *Hsi-hsiang Chi Chinesische Farbholzschnitte von Min Ch'i-chi 1640*, Monographien des Museums für Ostasiatische Kunst, I, Museen der Stadt Köln (Cologne: Museum für Ostasiatische Kunst der Stadt Köln, 1977); Wachs and Finkelstein, *Poetry, Painting and Politics*, pp. 115, 92-5; Suzanne E. Wright, '*Luoxuan Biangu jianpu* and *Shizhuzhai jianpu*: two late-Ming catalogues of letter paper designs', *Artibus Asiae* 63:1 (2003), p. 70 n. 5.

53. For details of the late Ming publication, see Sören Edgren, *Chinese Rare Books in American Collections* (New York: China Institute in America, 1984), pp. 114-5, and Frances Wood, catalogue entry for *Images of Heavenly Phenomena*, in Farrer, *Chinese Printmaking Today*, pp. 64-5.

54. *Luoxuan biangu jianpu* (1627) and *Shizhuzhai jianpu* (1644). Wright, 'Two

late-Ming Catalogues'.

55. Wright, 'Two late-Ming Catalogues', pp. 88, 105-10.

56. See also Wang Chao's prints, *Printed Traces of Faded Colours* (2000) and *Dreaming of Earlier Generations in the Thatched Cottage in Spring* (2002), published in: Barker, *Wang Chao: Recent Woodcut Printed Books and Single Sheet Prints*, cat. nos. 30-31.

57. The Chinese title of this print is *Zoujin mouri*, which can be translated as 'Looking back to a day in the past', with the meaning that the imagery in the print is close to the past, but does not fully achieve its representation. (Personal communication with the Artist on 8 April 2007).

58. The principal room is *zhongtang*, or *zhengtang*, in Chinese.

59. Although the *zhongtang* is still part of traditional Chinese architecture in rural areas, pictures and objects have changed considerably, reflecting the political and cultural changes of the last fifty years. See Ronald G. Knapp, *China's Vernacular Architecture: House Form and Culture* (Honolulu: University of Hawaii Press, 1989), pp. 51-3.

60 Terese Tse Bartholomew, *Hidden Meanings in Chinese Art* (San Francisco: Asian Art Museum, 2006), p. 218.

61. This print has not been published. A copy of the print was given to the author in March 1993 by Han Likun, then head of the printmaking department.

62. Bartholomew, *Hidden Meanings in Chinese Art*, pp. 47-9, 251.

63. Ronald G. Knapp, *China's Living Houses: Folk Beliefs, Symbols, and Household Ornamentation* (Honolulu: University of Hawaii Press, 1999), p.157, fig. 8.39.

64. James Cahill, *The Distant Mountains: Chinese Painting of the Late Ming Dynasty, 1570-1644* (New York: Weatherhill, 1982), 26 col. pl. 18, p. 248; Wen C. Fong, 'The Expanding *Literati* Culture', in Fong and Watt, *Possessing the Past*, pp. 412-5.

65. Scholars' desk objects included the 'four treasures' of the scholar's studio (ink, inkstone, brush and paper), together with seals, table-screens, wrist-rests, brush-rests, water-droppers, scroll weights and other objects. In the late Ming period, these were made from fine materials and were highly decorated, becoming collectors' items carrying important social status for their owners. See Chu-tsing Li and James C.Y. Watt, eds, *The Chinese Scholar's Studio: Artistic Life in the Late Ming Period* (New York: Thames and Hudson and the Asia Society Galleries, 1987), pp. 123-41, 180-93.

66. See, for example, the interplay of visual imagery in the illustrations in the 1640 edition of the *Romance of the Western Chamber* (see n. 56).

67. This portfolio contains prints by sixty print-artists from the People's Republic of China. It was commissioned in 1997 by the Muban Foundation, Putney, as a means of benefiting the artists and publicising contemporary Chinese printmaking. A detail of Wang Chao's print was used for the cover illustration of the publication that accompanied the portfolio, *Art of Contemporary Chinese Woodcuts* (*Dangdai Zhongguo Muban yishu*), (London: Muban Foundation, 2003).

68. In, for example, illustration 5, 'Shocked by a Nightmare', in Zhang Shenzhi's edition of the *Romance of the Western Chamber*, illustrated by Chen Hongshou and produced in 1640. See: Wan-go Weng, *Chen Hongshou: His Life and Art*, 3 (Shanghai: Shanghai People's Fine Arts Publishing House, 1997), pp. 128-9.

69. Cahill, *The Distant Mountains*, p. 246.

70. For a discussion of this painting genre, see Nancy Berliner, 'The "Eight Brokens": Chinese *Trompe-l'oeil* Painting,' in *Orientations* (Feb. 1992), pp. 61-70. Wang Chao borrowed the term 'dust pile of brocades' (*jinhuidui*) from the title of a series of publications containing a miscellany of writings on Chinese art by the twentieth-century scholar Wang Shixiang. Wang , in turn, borrowed the term from the title of a painting by the artist Qian Xuan (*c.* 1235-after 1301) depicting leftovers from a meal that included a shrimp tail, a chicken bone, etc. (Communication with the artist on 7 Nov. 2008).

71. Andrews and Shen, *A Century in Crisis*, pp. 277-323.

72. Peter Sturman, 'In the Realm of Naturalness: Problems of Self-Imaging by the Northern Sung *Literati*', in Maxwell K. Hearn and Judith G. Smith, eds, *Arts of the Sung and Yüan* (New York: Metropolitan Museum of Art, 1997), pp. 165-85.

73. For example, the prints of Wang Jieyin, Yang Chunhua, Han Likun, Zhou Baoping, Zhang Fang, et al., in Farrer, *Chinese Printmaking Today*, pp. 147, 149-51, 154.

74. For a discussion of the technical aspects of colour printing with water-based inks, see David Barker, 'Woodblock Printing in China, 1980-2000: Tools and Techniques', in Farrer, *Chinese Printmaking Today*, pp. 36-42; and Barker, *Traditional Techniques in Contemporary Chinese Printmaking*, pp. 50, 70, 122.

75. Barker, *Traditional Techniques in Contemporary Chinese Printmaking*, pp. 48-9.
The techniques of colour printing are used in a variety of different ways by contemporary artists to achieve different effects and to simulate the appearance of other pictorial media: Yu Qihui incorporates stone rubbing techniques into the water-soluble colour-printing process; Shen Roujian and Shao Keping use oil-based coloured inks which are sometimes thinned to build up colour to simulate pictorial effects from painting; and Zhang Fang simulates the monochrome brushwork of traditional painting. See: Farrer, *Chinese Printmaking Today*, cat. nos 25, 76, 77 and 85.

Afterword:

1. Michael Clark, *The Politics of Pop Festivals* (London: Junction, 1982).

2. Joseph Ward Swain, trans., *The Elementary Forms of Religious Life* (New York: Free Press, 1965), p. 483.

About the authors

Megan Aldrich is Academic Director of Sotheby's Institute of Art in London and a Fellow of the Society of Antiquaries of London. She has written a number of articles and books on historicist design, including *Gothic Revival*, (1994), and contributed to the catalogues of the Pugin (1995) and William Beckford (2001) exhibitions. Her most recent publication is 'Thomas Rickman in Ireland' in *Studies in the Gothic Revival* (2008), edited by Michael McCarthy and Karina O'Neil. She is currently writing a monograph on Rickman, the subject of chapter 4.

Anne Farrer is Programme Director of the MA in East Asian Art at Sotheby's Institute of Art, and was formerly Assistant Keeper in charge of the Chinese Painting and Chinese Central Asian collections at the British Museum. She specialises in the history of Chinese printmaking and has curated a number of exhibitions on this subject, as well as contributing to the accompanying catalogues, most recently in *Chinese Printmaking Today: Woodblock Printing in China, 1980-2000* (2003) to accompany an exhibition held at the British Library; in chapter 8 of this volume she discusses the work of the contemporary Chinese printmaker Wang Chao.

Jeremy Harte is Curator of The Bourne Hall Museum in Surrey. His research interests encompass a broad spectrum across the fields of folklore and archaeology, with a particular interest in sacred spaces and tales of encounters with the supernatural. His books include *Cuckoo Pounds and Singing Barrows: Folklore of Ancient Sites in Dorset* (1986), *The Green Man* (2003), *Explore Fairy Traditions* (2004) and *English Holy Wells* (2008). Dragons and other guardians of barrows are the theme of chapter 1.

David Boyd Haycock is Curator of Seventeenth-Century Imperial and Maritime History at the National Maritime Museum, Greenwich. He read modern history at St John's College, Oxford, art history at the University of Sussex, and was Wellcome Research Fellow in the history of medicine at The London School of Economics. His PhD, undertaken at Birkbeck College, London, was an intellectual biography of the eighteenth-century antiquary, Dr William Stukeley, published as *William Stukeley: Science, Religion and Archaeology in Eighteenth-century England* (2002), the subject of chapter 3.

Simon Kaner is Assistant Director of the Sainsbury Institute for the Study of Japanese Arts and Cultures and formerly Senior Archaeologist at Cambridgeshire County Council. He specialises in the prehistory of Japan, and has taught and published on many aspects of East Asian and European archaeology. He has recently translated and adapted, with the assistance of Oki Nakamura, *Jomon Reflections: Forager Life and Culture in the Prehistoric Japanese Archipelago* by Kobayashi Tatsuo (2004), and in chapter 5 of this book he explores the development of archaeology in Japan.

Alex Seago is Professor of Cultural Studies at Richmond the American International University in London where he chairs the Department of Humanities, Social Sciences and Communications. With an interdisciplinary academic background in American studies, cultural history, sociology and cultural studies, his research interests focus upon the area of cultural globalisation, with particular reference to music, art and design. His book, *Burning the Box of Beautiful Things* (1995), examines the relationship between art and design education and the rise of contemporary pop culture in the UK during the 1950s and 1960s. His recent work explores cultural globalisation and popular music.

Sarah Semple is a lecturer in the Department of Archaeology at the University of Durham, specialising in the early medieval archaeology of Britain and north-west Europe. She has taught previously at the universities of Oxford and Chester, and worked in field archaeology with a number of professional units. Her research and publications currently focus on the archaeology of assembly, governance and administration in medieval north-west Europe, cult-sites and cult-practices in pre-Christian England and Europe, and death and burial in early medieval Britain, themes she explores in chapter 2.

Robert J. Wallis is Associate Professor of Visual Culture and Director of the MA in Art History at Richmond the American International University in London, and a research fellow in archaeology at the University of Southampton. His research interests include shamans and animism in indigenous and prehistoric art, and the re-presentation of the past in the present, especially by contemporary pagans, and the implications of such engagements for heritage management – themes he addresses in chapter 7. His most recent book is *Sacred Sites, Contested Rites/Rights: Contemporary Pagan Engagements with Archaeological Monuments* (2007), with Jenny Blain. He is currently working on a monograph critically examining the construction of shamanism and art.

Simon Watney is a leading authority on contemporary art and photography. For many years he worked in the independent HIV/AIDS sector. A prolific writer, he is the author of numerous books, and also reviews regularly for *The Burlington Magazine* and *The Art Newspaper*. Here, he demonstrates another side to his interests, as the Conservation Cases Recorder for the Church Monuments Society. He published 'The Pleasure of Monuments' in *The Churches Conservation Trust Review and Report* for 2003, and explores the important but often neglected role of learned societies in the antiquarian tradition in chapter 6 of this book.